FIRST STEPS IN THE
CLINICAL PRACTICE OF
PSYCHOTHERAPY

FIRST STEPS IN THE CLINICAL PRACTICE OF PSYCHOTHERAPY

A Practice-Oriented Psychodynamic Approach

by
Maxa Ott

Jason Aronson

This book was set in 12 pt. New Baskerville by Pageworks of Old Saybrook and Lyme, CT, and printed and bound by Book-mart Press, Inc. of North Bergen, NJ.

Library of Congress Cataloging-in-Publication Data

Ott, Maxa.
    First steps in the clinical practice of psychotherapy : a practice-oriented psychodynamic approach / by Maxa Ott.
       p. cm.
    Includes bibliographical references and index.
    ISBN 0-7657-0320-3
    1. Psychodynamic psychotherapy. 2. Psychotherapy—Practice. I. Title.
RC489.P72 O88 2001
 616. 89'14—dc21   2001022556

Printed in the United States of America on acid-free paper. For information and catalog write to Jason Aronson Inc., 230 Livingston Street, Northvale, NJ 07647-1726, or visit our website: www.aronson.com

To M.S.
Thank you for bearing with me through it all.

CONTENTS

PART II
PRACTICAL CONSIDERATIONS: FIRST STEPS INTO CLINICAL PRACTICE

PREFACE

Although this book addresses itself specifically to the psychotherapist in the first few years of practice, it is also meant to be used as a tool in supervision and teaching. Seasoned therapists who do not work with a psychodynamic approach but are interested in learning more about it will also find much practical information here.

Beginning to see clients in treatment is a milestone in your training and education as a therapist, an event that is often accompanied by much anxiety. After all, it is one thing to study in a classroom, read books, and write papers. It is quite another thing to see real people in therapy.

You are probably wondering: What will you actually say to your clients? What do they expect from you? How should you present yourself? What will be helpful to say, and when? What is better left unsaid, and why? What if your client expresses doubt regarding your qualifications? What if you make a mistake? What if your client gets angry? What if you do?

This book is designed to help you navigate the entry into the world of the practicing therapist by addressing questions like the ones raised here. It is meant to facilitate your first steps into clinical practice by offering you scenarios that are likely to occur and suggestions on how to deal with them, basic issues that will arise, and actual words to say. Here is a *practical* guide to use as you begin clinical work, as you embark on the process of deciding on a particular theoretical approach, and until you have mastered that theory and learned to work with the technique of your specific approach.

This book is presented in three parts. "Part I: Preliminary Considerations" will provide a framework that is meant to assist you in developing a professional self-understanding and in translating that into practice. Issues addressed include a discussion of what it means to be a therapist and what the expected behavior of a therapist is, what it takes to develop and enhance your clinical skills, as well as a brief theoretical framework that will help you orient yourself as you begin practical work.

The bulk of this book is dedicated to "Part II: Practical Considerations." Here you will find a hands-on presentation of practical issues, from making an initial contact on the phone; how to conduct a consultation and assessment; how to diagnose; what to do when you are asked to be directive, as in the case when a client is suicidal; to how to work with a variety of situations that arise in any clinical practice. All of these interventions are firmly anchored in a psychodynamic understanding of clinical issues.

In "Part III: Theoretical Considerations," I will address theoretical presuppositions and concepts underlying the preceding portion of this book. Here you will find a discussion of psychodynamic theory and some of its concepts.

Throughout this book I use ample clinical examples to facilitate the application of the concepts I present.

Appendix I offers a sample list of referrals meant as a beginning guide for you to build your own referral base. Finally, Appendix II is devoted to a compilation of suggested further readings on topics of interest. For example, should you find yourself wanting to know more about a particular theoretical orientation, about a theoretical concept, or about a practical treatment issue, I have endeavored to present a minimum of three bibliographical references per topic.

When I made my own first steps into clinical practice—those steps from academia to practical work—I looked for a book such as this to point the way and help me with basic questions I had. Alas, there was no such book. It is my hope that this book will indeed become your survival manual as you venture into the world of clinical practice, that you will find in this writing now what I was looking for then: clarification, practical tips, and helpful suggestions.

A WORD OF CAUTION

Psychotherapeutic work carries great responsibilities: never forget the impact you have on your clients and the weight that your words and actions as their therapist carries. You must always keep the clients' best interests at heart. Therefore, being a therapist in training, you should *never* see clients without receiving supervision from a qualified, licensed clinician. This book is explicitly *not* designed to be used alone but as an adjunct to ongoing education and training, clinical supervision, and, it is hoped, your own personal therapy. All of these will be invaluable in your endeavor to become a skillful therapist.

Don't be too alarmed if it seems like a daunting task: it is. Keep in mind that all therapists who ever practiced their profession have been where you now find yourself, and that includes your teachers, your supervisors, your mentors, your own therapist, as well as the authors of the professional literature, including myself. With this fact in mind, let us begin.

A WORD OF CAUTION

PART I

PRELIMINARY CONSIDERATIONS:
FRAMEWORK FOR BECOMING A THERAPIST

INTRODUCTION

In Part I, I will discuss some practical considerations relevant to your becoming a skillful psychotherapist. These considerations are termed preliminary because they should be considered *before* you actually begin seeing clients in clinical practice. Such issues include thoughts on what it means to be a psychotherapist and to conduct psychotherapy; what a psychotherapist's professional conduct entails; the role of clinical supervision, your own therapy, as well as academic training; and finally, a brief introduction to a theoretical issue that is of high relevance for your practical work.

In a manner of speaking, what is being discussed in this part will help you consider whether becoming a psychotherapist is for you, since you will gain a preliminary idea of what this profession requires. This will help you to decide whether you really want to embark on this road.

1

HOW TO CONDUCT YOURSELF

In this chapter we will take a first look at what it means to be a therapist and what general conduct is expected of a therapist.

PSYCHOTHERAPIST DEFINED

Perhaps one of the most difficult things to understand is what it actually means to be a therapist. This is a question that cannot be answered without an understanding of what *therapy* is. How you understand what therapy is in turn depends greatly on your theoretical orientation and can only partially be answered in so many words; many of the components of that answer derive from well-supervised practice, your own therapy, and ongoing study and training. A useful way of looking at this question is to attend to it in the negative: Let us therefore look at what a therapist is *not*, and what therapy is *not*.

Most beginning therapists have an idea that they want to "help others." However, many beginning therapists (and some seasoned ones as well) have not defined to themselves what they mean when they say "help": A therapist does *not* direct a client's life; does not "know" whether a client should or should not stay in a relationship, take a job, move, and so forth. It is not a therapist's responsibility to arrange the client's life to either the

client's or the therapist's liking. In fact, it would be irrespon-
sible, unprofessional, and unethical to do any of those things.

Many clients come to their therapist with exactly this idea: to
talk to someone who will tell them what to do. Many beginning
therapists believe that this is what is expected of them. I hope
you are relieved to hear that this is not so.

If we look at how the media portray therapist–client relationships, we get the idea that therapists routinely transgress boundaries, befriend clients, and even have sex with them. None of
that is therapy. If it happens under the guise of therapy, it is
unprofessional, unethical, and at times (as in the case of a therapist having sex with his or her client) illegal.

We can say, then, that the therapeutic relationship (that is,
the relationship between a therapist and a client) is a special
kind of relationship. It is *not* an everyday social relationship. As
a therapist, you are not your client's friend. The therapeutic
relationship is not symmetrical, insofar as you do not usually
disclose information about yourself: you don't share good or
bad news pertaining to yourself. You don't reveal casually how
your client impacts you: when he makes you angry, when she
moves you. You don't criticize. You do conduct therapy in a well-
defined setting. You don't meet with your client casually or outside the therapy sessions. You don't do favors for your client
(even if you could), and you will not allow your client to do
favors for you (even if he or she attempts to do so). You rarely
give gifts. You rarely accept gifts. And when you do, never without exploring the meaning of the giving and the receiving. I
will address these scenarios later in more detail. Suffice it here
to keep in mind: you are not your client's friend. And she or
he is not yours.

Being a therapist does not mean that you give advice: it is
not your job to answer your client's every question and to direct her in her actions. It *is* your job to facilitate her exploration of who she is, of what she wants to do, and of what stands
in her way, and to help find alternatives and make choices possible. But you do not *make* the choices for your client.

You are not your client's spiritual adviser or priest; it is not your job to direct your client as to what he or she must or must not do. You do not purport to know what is best for your client, and you do not give absolution. Also, unlike a priest, you are mandated to break confidentiality in some instances. Your clients cannot tell you about everything in their lives without some real, at times drastic, consequences. Never forget that there are limits to your client's right to confidentiality.[1]

Does all this mean that you are not engaging in a real relationship with your client? That your client doesn't mean anything to you? That you have no feelings in regard to your clients? Does it mean, then, that you never make suggestions and that you do not ever give advice? No, it doesn't mean that either. The therapeutic relationship is real, but it is not an ordinary relationship: here you have two—indeed real—people meeting for the purpose of engaging in a relationship (the therapeutic relationship) in order to address issues one of them (the client) has.

The other—that is, you, the therapist—is using her or his own self as the tool with which these issues are being addressed. In the process of doing so, you come to know the client and you develop feelings for your client. However, what you do with these feelings and this knowledge—that is, how you conduct yourself in this relationship—is much different from any other relationship, in that it is all geared toward maximum clinical benefit for your client.

As for advice and suggestions, the less supportive and the more expressive the therapy is, the less advice and suggestions you will give. However, that does not mean that you won't tell your client that you recommend he or she see a psychiatrist if you deem it necessary or that you recommend that this person not skip a session. It *does* mean that you will explore underlying

---

[1]For a discussion of this topic, see Bollas and Sundelson (1995), *The New Informants,* as well as Chapter 6.

issues with the client, such as what led to your making this suggestion as well as what this suggestion means to him or her, to
name just two. When you have finished reading this book, you
will have a better understanding of what it means to be a therapist, what a therapist does, and what therapy is.

A perusal of the legal and ethical standards pertaining to your
field in your state will give you some idea regarding the expected
and accepted therapist behavior toward your clients. For example, the standards in California state clearly that you do not
make decisions for your client, that you must respect your clients' autonomy, that you cannot engage in a sexual relationship with your clients, that bartering your services is not acceptable, and that you should not engage in dual relationships.

ON SELF-DISCLOSURE

When I talk about self-disclosure, I am referring to making verbal statements about yourself, your thoughts and feelings, and
your private life to your client, either in response to the client's
direct question or of your own accord. Of course, we constantly
disclose information about ourselves in many ways: by the
clothes we wear, what we choose to attend to in session, our
choice of words, an accent we might have, the way we furnish
our office,[2] and the like. This is not about trying to become a
blank screen for your client, which is neither desirable nor
possible. However, this *is* about understanding that what we say
and how we say it matters.

At this point in your training I recommend the general stance
of *do not self-disclose*. Although you may later, as you become

---

[2]This would be a reason not to put up pictures of your family in your office. Even if
you do decide to disclose information about your family at some point, it should
not be information that you routinely make available to your clients.

more skilled, decide that it is clinically feasible to make self-disclosures in certain instances, and while you may actually adopt a theoretical standpoint that not only permits but maybe even requires self-disclosure, at this point in your development as a therapist you will most likely not know why you make a self-disclosure, whether you should, and what impact it might have on the treatment. You will not know how to look for the impact it does have and will not be able to address it. Consequently, your self-disclosures will burden the client and can ultimately be detrimental to the therapy, if not the client.

Let me give an illustration of how self-disclosure might burden your client:

Imagine that you had to cancel a session because your mother was ill. You say as much to your client. Your client, perhaps assuming that you are worried about your mother, now may feel protective of you, may feel that he has to spare you additional difficult feelings. Thus, although your canceling has made the client angry and he would have liked to express that to you, he now feels that he cannot do so because you had a "good reason" for canceling and it would be cruel of him to express anger in the face of your mother's illness. Thus, your client may have been deprived of expressing his true feelings regarding your cancellation.

Another scenario:

Your client is telling you about difficulties with her spouse and then asks you, "Are you married?" Let's say you are and you tell her so. The client may then go on expounding on her difficulties and you may never address what prompted this question, nor will you know what the answer means to the client. Did she fear not being understood? Did she hope you would or would not be married? Is she imagining that your marriage is better than hers, perhaps feeling envy? Or is she perhaps jealous of your spouse, who gets to have so much more of you than she does?

These two scenarios suffice to illustrate that all you say in the session has meaning. Moreover, it has meaning that is not readily obvious or often readily available even upon exploration. It takes time, training, good supervision, and your own therapy for you to learn to explore how you impact the client (working with the transference) and how the client impacts you (working with the countertransference).[3]

Until then, if you do disclose information about yourself, it is often not in the service of the therapy—that is, in the service of the client—but in the service of making yourself feel better, perhaps by reducing your anxiety, expressing your anger, or boosting your self-esteem.

In my experience, there are four main reasons why beginning therapists tend to make self-disclosures:

1. Beginning therapists often simply are not aware that it is advisable *not* to make self-disclosures.
2. If they are aware that it is generally best not to do so, beginning therapists often do not know *how to keep from making self-disclosures.*
3. Beginning therapists often make one self-disclosure and then find that this one statement leads to a whole string of self-disclosures that they had not planned on making. With each additional self-disclosure, it appears to become harder to stop it.
4. Beginning therapists as a group are naturally more prone to act on countertransference issues since they have not had the opportunity yet to conceptualize and address them in a sustained way (in training, supervision, and their own therapy). These countertransference issues might include

---

[3]See more on the concepts of transference and countertransference in Part III.

the therapist's own difficulties in saying "no"; the therapist's wish to appear knowledgeable and without fault; the therapist's insecurity in the face of the knowledge that as a beginner, he or she has much to learn; and the therapist's fear of engendering anger, among other things.

There is no need for your clients to know that you are or are not married; that you have or do not have children; that you are going hiking on the weekend; that your child is sick; that you, too, had a hard time as a teenager; that you understand what it means to wake up with a hangover; that your cat ran away; and so forth. In keeping this information from your client, you in fact allow your client to fantasize about these issues and thus open them up to be addressed in depth. For example:

A client who may have ambivalent feelings regarding his sexual orientation may not be able to explore this matter so easily with you if he knows that you are a married father with children, as when he does not know this fact and thus can more readily fantasize that you are gay and living in a way that he might wish for himself. In addition, he can, under these latter circumstances, more easily direct his feelings toward you and fantasize about your reciprocating them. In the long run, the two of you will be better able to explore this whole complex of his sexuality; of his feelings toward other men, toward men in authority, or toward you in particular; and so forth.

And let us not forget the propensity of many people, including your clients, to comply with what they feel is expected of them. Once your client knows that you are married, she may feel it is expected of her to be in a committed relationship as well, and so she might keep from you her promiscuous lifestyle, fearing that you would disapprove.

Of course, *not* making any self-disclosing statements about your private life is not enough. In order to explore these issues fruitfully and appropriately, you will need ongoing clinical supervision, an orientation to working with the transference, and an ability to monitor and utilize your countertransference reactions.

Overall, then, it is advisable at this stage of your training *not to make self-disclosures*. If you feel that a client might benefit from a self-disclosure, discuss this first with your clinical supervisor. When you do make a self-disclosure, whether planned or inadvertently—and there will be more inadvertent self-disclosures during your career as a therapist than you might currently imagine—pay attention to the client's reaction to it. Explore what it means to the client to know this piece of information about you. Be aware that your client is not necessarily conscious of this meaning but might express it in the way he or she acts in the rest of this or the following hour. For example:

> Does a cancellation follow the self-disclosure of the fact that you went hiking with friends last weekend and had a lot of fun? This might indicate that your client has strong feelings about this fact—perhaps envy or jealousy—and that he is acting those feelings out by "punishing" you with his absence. It would then be important to address his behavior, namely, the cancellation as well as the preceding self-disclosure.[4]

If you find that you are making self-disclosures often, take this, too, to your supervisor to determine the meaning and effects of it: Does it happen only with a certain client or clients? Or is this your usual way of relating to your clients? Have you tried not to make self-disclosures and found it impossible? Should you do something about it, and if so, what? This is an issue well worth exploring and monitoring, so as to provide your clients with the best possible therapy.

---

[4]See Chapter 16 on how to address cancellations.

I will discuss this issue at greater length further along in the text and give you ways of handling your clients' direct questions, which are aimed at learning more about the facts of your life. That is, I will address in more detail *how* to go about not making self-disclosures.

DRESS CODE

Another way in which we always let our clients know about ourselves is in the way we dress. Therefore, let me just say a few words regarding appropriate dress when seeing clients. A rule of thumb is not to wear anything too extreme: no very short, sheer, or overly seductive dresses; no plunging necklines; no shorts; no muscle-shirts; and so forth. I have seen beginning therapists appear at work in ill-fitting, much too small shorts; with shrunken T-shirts exposing their naked bellies; with belly-button piercings visible; with dresses so sheer you could see their underwear; and in clothes so dirty that it was insulting, to name just a few. None of that is acceptable or professional.

Just keep in mind what I have discussed previously—namely, that you want to refrain from making casual statements about your personal life to your client—and apply this understanding to the way you dress. That means that you definitely don't want to appear in session fresh from the beach in bathing trunks (which would also be very seductive), you would not want to come into sessions loaded down with gold chains and diamonds, and you would be well advised to dress relatively unpretentiously. This dress code sounds like a true paragon of mediocrity and in fact *is* designed not to disclose much about your personal preferences. You would not appear in a ball gown to work as a receptionist; you would not appear in your weekend sweatsuit to a sales job in a bookstore. Some professions have a rigid dress code (think of nurses or doctors in the hospital, who wear a uniform), and in this way we have a lot more freedom as therapists. This leaves you plenty of room to dress in your personal

style. Just remember to dress in a way that is generally acceptable, that won't direct your client's attention to the way your
person is adorned, and use your common sense to do so.

This means, too, that you should not appear at a session with
visible tattoos, body-piercings, blue hair, or the like—not because anything is inherently wrong with any of that (it isn't),
but because, being a therapist, you want to facilitate your clients' concentrating on *their* issues and not on you. Removing
what draws attention is somewhat like the surgeon disinfecting
her hands before surgery. Nothing is wrong with those bacteria
under ordinary circumstances, but there is no place for them
in surgery. Just so, wear your more colorful and outrageous
clothes, your flashy jewelry, and your brow-rings in your free
time, not in the therapy room. If you have strong feelings about
these issues and find it difficult to dress professionally, address
this issue with your supervisor. Most likely, countertransference
issues are at work here that need to be addressed.

2

WHAT A BEGINNING THERAPIST CANNOT DO WITHOUT:
CLINICAL SUPERVISION, PERSONAL THERAPY, CONTINUING EDUCATION

In order to become a skillful therapist, you cannot do without supervised clinical work, your own therapy, and continuing education. In fact, you can look upon these three elements as the three legs that your development as a clinician rests on. All three are essential. Therefore, I will say a few words about each of these topics to illustrate their usefulness and necessity for your development as a therapist.

SUPERVISED CLINICAL WORK

Supervised clinical work, as mentioned earlier, is one of the three legs of your education. It consists of practical work and clinical supervision. Thus, as a beginning therapist you will always work with a licensed clinician who will provide supervision for the cases you work with. You cannot underestimate the influence your supervisors will have on the way you learn to practice your craft. Therefore, let us look for a moment at some issues that may arise around your clinical supervision, particularly at your choice of group supervision or individual supervision, issues of confidentiality pertaining to supervision, your supervisor's theoretical orientation, receiving supervision from more than one supervisor, and how to choose a supervisor and evaluate the ongoing supervision you receive.

Most beginning therapists do not have much choice in the supervision made available by the place where they practice. Usually, you will receive group supervision by the clinical supervisor on staff and will thus not be able to choose either the modality of the supervision or the theoretical orientation of your supervisor.

Let us assume that this is the case and you are receiving group supervision offered through your place of work. You will find yourself with a supervisor and a number of colleagues whom you have not personally chosen. Although the content of supervisory sessions is confidential, always keep in mind your mandate to protect your client's confidentiality as much as possible. In order to do so, it is wise to withhold your clients' names and any identifying information, as you address the work you are doing. For example, when discussing one of your clients, you may say something like this: "This is a young man in his early twenties. I'll call him Joe," instead of disclosing his real name in full and giving a detailed description of him.

You might consider raising the issue of confidentiality with your fellow supervisees and the supervisor *before* supervision begins, if the supervisor does not raise it. Ask for clarification of how information about other clients and their treatment will be handled. Be aware of the fact that, legally, whatever you hear discussed in supervision is confidential—that is, that you cannot disclose information to others that you received in supervision. That means, if you work in an agency and receive supervision with four other therapists in training, you will hear treatment discussed of clients with whom you may be in frequent contact, although not as their therapist. Even if those clients are not identified by name, you may often know exactly who is being talked about. You may *not* allude to the information you have received, either in regard to that client or to other colleagues. This will, in fact, amount to an additional demand on your capacity to contain information, your thoughts, and your feelings. It is not unusual, especially for beginning therapists, to experience difficulties with this issue. If this is the case, bring it up in supervision and bring it to your own therapist so that you can start addressing underlying issues that might contribute to your difficulties.

Another issue regarding group supervision is the following: You will be one of between two to eight supervisees, and your opportunity to present cases and receive feedback will be proportionally less, depending on the number of participants in the group. Also, you might find yourself reluctant to openly address difficulties you may encounter in your work, mistakes you may have made, anxieties you may experience, questions you may have, and just generally personal issues that might be stirred up by your work with your clients. It is not easy to lay open these issues in front of others. In addition, you might not trust some of your colleagues to be as conscientious regarding issues of confidentiality as others might be and might find yourself inhibited about speaking freely of your clients for that reason.

Finally, since you did not get to choose your clinical supervisor, his or her theoretical orientation might not be the only orientation that is of interest to you, or it might even be an orientation that does not particularly appeal to you.

All of the issues mentioned here might cause a greater reluctance to discuss treatment in all its facets in group supervision than you would perhaps experience in individual supervision.

In individual supervision, on the other hand, while issues of confidentiality are between you and your supervisor, while you have ample opportunity to address treatment of your clients, and while it may be easier to bring up difficulties you may experience in treating your clients (countertransference issues), you will miss out on the varied viewpoints your fellow supervisees can offer in group supervision, as well as on the support they can give you. It is therefore advisable to have the experience of both group and individual supervision during your training years.

If you have more than one supervisor at any given time, an area of potential difficulty for you could be the integration of two (or more) different theoretical approaches you might encounter. Your supervisor shares with you the legal liability for the work you do, and you are expected to follow his or her suggestions regarding treatment. Therefore, you should not receive supervision on the same cases from different supervisors at the same time. Rather, split the cases between supervisors, or, if you don't have enough cases to do so but would like to receive a different kind of supervision than your place of work offers, discuss this with your clinical director. It is often possible to receive supervision outside the facility you work for, when your private supervisor (and this could be group or individual supervision) has signed a form of agreement with your place of work that he or she will provide supervision for the clients you treat. Check with both your facility and your state's licensing agency regarding the requirements for such arrangements. If your place of work does not allow for outside supervision of your cases, you may nonetheless consider working with an outside clinician of your choice as a consultant. This would mean that you would meet with another clinician for the purpose of professional development and enhancement of knowledge. It will be encumbent upon you to follow the directions of the clinical supervisor who is signing off on your hours and thus is legally responsible for the treatment you give.

For all of the reasons discussed here, I recommend that you begin early on to think about which theoretical orientation is of interest to you and what you would like to learn in more depth. Start looking around for a clinician who might be willing to take you on for individual or group supervision, either in addition to or instead of that which your place of work makes available. Many qualified clinicians are quite willing to work something out with prospective supervisees, so don't be too shy. Don't wait for a supervisor to present herself to you; present yourself to her.

Be aware that, just as between therapist and client, there is the matter of "fit" between supervisor and supervisee, a matter quite apart from theoretical orientation. With some, you will personally get along better than with others; some will speak "your language," while others won't you will experience some as encouraging and trustworthy, while with others you might find it hard to candidly report on your cases. Do keep an eye on these issues, and *discuss them with your supervisor as they arise.* Only when you have tried and it seems that these issues cannot be addressed fruitfully and satisfactorily do I recommend that you consider looking for a different supervisor because of lack of fit.

In the course of your training you should aim at having several supervisors, preferably of differing orientations, until you have selected which orientation works for you. This is one of the best ways to find out what *will* work for you, since you will thoroughly and intensely be exposed to the theories and applications of different approaches.

With good supervision, you will feel stimulated and intellectually and emotionally challenged. You will be able to address difficult cases, mistakes you have made, your own feelings regarding your work, as well as questions you have. If you find yourself avoiding to mention where you blundered (and blunder you will), where you feel insecure (which you will feel often), what you don't know (and there will be much), take this as a warning sign. The first step here is to address your reluctance explicitly with your supervisor. You might say: "I find it difficult to tell you when I make mistakes. Can we talk about this?" or "It is really hard for me to let you see how insecure I feel as a therapist" or something to that effect.

If your supervisor is not able to address these issues, you need to look for someone else, because you will not be able to learn much if you cannot be open. If you cannot establish a relationship of trust with your supervisor, that person's supervision will not be of much value to you. However, give this development of trust time before you decide that a particular supervisory situation is not working for you. Also, if you find yourself switching supervisors often because of "lack of fit," you should consider that perhaps you don't *want* to be open with your supervisor for reasons that you might not be aware of. This would be an issue to address in your own therapy.

Here, then, is a list of issues to keep in mind when you select a supervisor and as you receive supervision.

Selection of a Supervisor

- **Gender/Race/Age:** Ask yourself whether you would work equally well with someone of the same or of a different gender, ethnicity, age, and so forth. Some of us have issues trusting members of a group similar to or different from our own and it is important that you are aware of these. I do not necessarily recommend that you avoid a supervisor of a group that you usually have difficulties with, since you might actually work out some of these issues in supervision. However, I do recommend keeping in mind whether you have such reservations and addressing them with your supervisor.
- **Theoretical Orientation:** Ask your prospective supervisor what her theoretical orientation is. As I mentioned previously, you cannot underestimate the influence this person will have on your professional development. Therefore, choose a supervisor whose theoretical orientation you want to learn more about.

- **Transference/Countertransference:** Since I assume that you have not yet studied the different theoretical approaches in depth, let me emphasize that a supervisor who works with issues pertaining to transference and countertransference will attend to issues pertaining to the relationship between your client and you, issues that get stirred up in the client and that manifest in the relationship to you, as well as issues that get stirred up in you. Especially for a beginning therapist, it is helpful to work with a supervisor who regularly addresses these issues. This will teach you to get into the habit of observing yourself and will hone your awareness of the fact that all you do (and do not do) in therapy has an effect on your client. It is my bias that working with transference and countertransference issues not only is essential for therapeutic work but also instills the proper awareness in therapists as to their impact on their clients, as well as their clients' impact on them.

- **Pay Attention to How You Feel:** Pay careful attention to how you feel when you interact with the prospective supervisor. As with selecting a therapist, you are looking for a good "fit"; you are looking for someone with whom you can work constructively and with whom you can be as open and unguarded as possible. This does not mean that you will always feel comfortable. However, it is important that you can address how you feel, particularly when it is uncomfortable, and that you can engage in dialogue about this issue with your supervisor.

- **Money Issues:** Attend to the matter of the prospective supervisor's fee. Ask how much he or she charges, and if it is too much, say so. Come to the meeting with an idea of what you can spend. Consider taking part in supervision less frequently (perhaps every two weeks) or sharing the hour with one or more of your colleagues. In this way, it will be more affordable and you still get the supervision of your choice.

PERSONAL THERAPY

Your own therapy is the next leg that your education as a therapist stands on. Once you start practical work with clients, you will realize that doing such work will stir up "your own stuff." Some of this "stuff" can be addressed in supervision. However, even with this being the case, supervision can only do so much: you *cannot* address in depth what certain issues mean to you and you cannot work issues through in supervision. In addition, your own therapy will help you address issues that you are not even conscious of, so that they don't become "stumbling blocks" when you practice therapy.

Here is an example: Let us say that your parents divorced when you were 10 years old and that prior to that divorce, they had serious difficulties in their marriage: your father had an affair and left your mother and you. All this affected you in more ways than you are conscious of. Let us now say that you begin to work with a married man who tells you that he is having an affair. This situation is bound to give rise to powerful countertransference feelings. That means: feelings connected to your own experiences in the past might be activated. You might feel angry with your client, you might find yourself blaming him (either outright or subtly), you might find yourself unwilling or unable to explore what the affair means to your client because of what it means to you. In short, you might find yourself unable to appropriately and usefully explore his issues because your own issues obscure your vision and you begin to act (unconsciously) according to that experience and not in your client's best interest.

On a more general level, it can be said that each one of us developed from an infant to an adult. The experiences of this development (and that means the experiences of our life, really) shape who we are, largely unconsciously. However, these experiences will be and are being reactivated in our relationships to others, including our clients. In order not to blindly react to these reactivations, it is necessary that we first be conscious of them. And we become conscious of them in our own therapy where we can also work through some of our difficulties. Thus, our own therapy helps us "clean our glasses," so to speak, so that we can see our clients and their issues as unobstructed by personal issues as possible. Of course, there are limits to this "cleaning of glasses," and in the end we will always see our clients through the glasses of our personal reality. Nonetheless, personal therapy helps us monitor our own issues as they are being stirred up by our clients, which is why such therapy *prior to and accompanying* our training as therapists is highly recommended. Many therapists continue their own therapy or analysis into their career as licensed professionals. In short, your own therapy will help you work with countertransference issues as they arise. As an added benefit, it will provide you with an experience of what it is like to "be a client" and thus will increase your empathy for your clients as they come to see you.

I will now list some points to keep in mind when selecting a personal therapist. This is a very important choice to make, so take your time with this selection.

Selecting a Personal Therapist

- **Gender/Race/Age**: As in selecting a supervisor, ask yourself how you feel about working with a therapist of the same or of a different gender; someone who is your same age, younger, or older; and so forth. I do not necessarily recommend that you avoid the gender, age, race, and so on, that you feel you might have some difficulties with, since it might be fruitful and helpful to explore this in therapy. However, address these issues with a prospective therapist and see how you feel about the interaction.
- **Training**: Think about what level of training your therapist should have. Do you want to work with an intern or a licensed professional? Of course, this issue will often be

related to the amount of money you can spend on the fee for therapy: a licensed clincan's fee will be higher than that of an intern. Contrary to what I advised regarding supervision, do *not* settle for seeing a licensed clinician less frequently in order to afford seeing her or him at all. Even though the clinician may be more highly trained, if you cannot see your therapist at least once weekly, treatment will suffer. In fact, many interns are very knowledgeable and well able to provide good therapy. Make your choice accordingly.

- **Theoretical Orientation**: For your own therapy as a preparation for, and accompaniment of, your training as a therapist, I recommend that you select a therapist who works in depth and long term in a psychoanalytically or psychodynamically oriented psychotherapy or psychoanalysis. This is because you are embarking on the process of learning about yourself, about what is so far unconscious and how it impacts your current life and your current relationships, including the relationships to your clients. Psychodynamically oriented psychotherapy and psychoanalysis are tailored to accomplish just that. In addition, this model is very helpful in addressing issues like competition, competence, envy, insecurity, and related topics that get notoriously stirred up for the beginning therapist.

  If you consider working with an intern who receives clinical supervision, ask for this person's clinical supervisor's theoretical orientation, since the supervisor will have much influence on the intern's work with you.

- **Fee:** Ask your prospective therapist what her or his fee is. Come to the initial consultation with an idea of how much money you can realistically spend in order to see your therapist at least once a week, preferably more often. Think about how important this part of your education is to you; prioritizing may be in order, so that you can allow yourself to get the full benefit of an ongoing, depth-oriented therapy. If you cannot afford this therapist's fee, ask her or him to refer you to a respected colleague who will accept a lower fee.

- **Frequency of Meetings:** The frequency of sessions is something to be decided between your therapist and you. However, I recommend that you do not see a therapist less often than once a week, preferably more often. Increased frequency will make for increased depth and intensity of the therapeutic work. Do not sacrifice that if you can help it.

CONTINUING EDUCATION

This topic refers to the third leg in your training as a therapist—namely, the academic part. Whatever the requirements to complete this part of the training, they only comprise a currently agreed-upon minimum that keeps changing with the particular license that you are working toward—be it Clinical Psychology, Marriage and Family Therapy, or Clinical Social Work—over time. Most licensing boards now require a certain amount of formal "continuing education credits" for you to renew your license once you have received it.

I encourage you to look upon this issue of academic training not only as a part of your initial training as a therapist but as a lifelong process that will enrich your work as a therapist as well as your life. "Becoming a therapist" is not something that you definitively achieve at one point—say, when you receive your degree or your license—but is a living process that you are continuously engaged in. Continue to explore theoretical topics of interest to you, continue to engage in inquiry, continue to participate in study groups, and so forth—that is, continue to expand your horizons, your interests, and your knowledge. In tandem with engaging in your own therapy or analysis and engaging in ongoing supervision or consultation, you will see how *being* a therapist really is, in many respects, the process of *evolving* as a therapist.

However, on a more concrete level the academic "leg" of your training is a necessary (if not sufficient) part of this process of becoming a therapist. It is not enough to do practical work under clinical supervision; it is not enough to receive your own therapy. It is necessary that you develop an understanding of the theoretical approaches underlying the practical work as well, because, as you will see, much of your practical work will be determined by your understanding of the theory.

3

THE THERAPEUTIC FRAME:
SETTING AND MAINTAINING BOUNDARIES

Although the concept of the frame is highly theoretical, it has a direct impact on the practical work that you will provide. In fact, I consider the theoretical concept of the frame to be exceedingly helpful, enabling beginning clinicians to understand what kind of behaviors are and are not acceptable for a therapist and why this is so. Therefore, I will include the concept in this chapter, which otherwise contains more practically oriented preliminary considerations.

The concept of the frame gives the theoretical background for a code of conduct that might otherwise appear rather arbitrary. In a nutshell, the concept of the frame defines a code of conduct and a basic attitude for the therapist that is aimed at creating a space in which the therapeutic process between therapist and client can safely and fruitfully unfold.

This concept was advanced by Robert Langs in the context of his discussion of the bipersonal field in the analytic (or therapeutic) situation.[1] Langs understands the frame as being made

---

[1] See Langs (1994), *The Therapeutic Interaction.*

up of "the implicit and explicit ground rules and boundaries, including certain basic attitudes of the analyst, that distinguish a given analytic [or therapeutic] situation from the rest of the world" (Langs 1994, p. 28). Langs distinguishes components of the frame that are fixed, relatively constant, and nonhuman from such components that he terms human and sees as stemming basically from the analyst/therapist. The concept of the frame thus pertains to the "framework" of therapy, the construction of the "space" in which therapy takes place. Another way of looking at the frame is understanding it in the sense of Winnicott's "holding environment," like a mother's arms that hold a baby securely. Underlying it is the basic understanding that something takes place between the therapist and the client (the therapeutic or analytic process) in a relatively stable environment (the frame), the latter of which actually facilitates the former. Langs (1994) states:

> It [the frame] defines the optimal distance for both participants in the relationship and creates the conditions for the development of an interface of communication between them. . . . It is the behavioral and institutional guide that gears the relationship toward verbalization, analyzable interactions, cognitive insight and constructive introjective identifications for the patient, and, to a lesser extent, for the analyst. In essence, it creates the therapeutic qualities of the field and renders it safe for the communication of pathological needs and derivatives, and serves as the guarantor of their analyzability and use towards therapeutic ends. (p. 34)

Even if you do not practice a dynamically (or psychoanalytically) oriented psychotherapy, the value of the concept of the frame, which renders the therapeutic situation safe, maximally predictable, consistent, and coherent by including certain kinds of behavior as therapeutic while excluding others as untherapeutic and damaging, should be immediately obvious.

Langs (1994) conceptualizes the frame as constituted by two components: the relatively constant components and the human components.

The *relatively constant components* of the frame include:

- *Place:* Physical location of the office. Sessions are only conducted in the office.
- *Time:* Set time for sessions, as well as set frequency of sessions.
- *Fee:* Set fee for sessions, and agreed-upon way of collecting the fee.
- *Availability outside sessions:* Restriction of phone contact between sessions.
- *Physical contact:* Therapy entails solely verbal exchanges, no physical contact.
- *Responsibilities:* Clear role responsibilities for both client and therapist, in which the client agrees to tell the therapist freely all that is on his mind, as well as all important developments in his life, while the therapist agrees to attend to all the client's communications and respond in role.

The *human components* of the frame pertain to:

- The therapist's offer and capacity to provide a basic hold for the client and a container for his pathology.
- The therapist's relative anonymity.
- The therapist's "neutrality," that is, her being nonjudgmental, nonpunitive, and not invested in particular communications or actions from the client.[2]

---

[2]The analytic term *technical neutrality* denotes analyst equidistance from all psychic structures (Id, Ego, Superego) and reality. I have rendered that concept in terms relating to actual therapist behavior and feelings.

- The therapist's use of neutral interventions (this relates directly to technical neutrality, since it implies that all communications and behaviors will be equally explored).
- The therapist's capacity to offer appropriate gratifications (through management of the frame and interpretations) and exclusion of extratherapeutic, inappropriate gratifications.

Violations of these issues will directly impact the work you do with your client. You are thus asked, on the one hand, to monitor your own behavior and, on the other hand, to monitor and address your client's behavior. A frame violation may result, in fact, not so much from your active behavior but rather from your failure to attend to your client's frame violation by neglecting to direct attention to it, discuss it, and reestablish the frame.

Here is a list of a few common frame (or boundary) violations to be alert to:

- You are often late.
- Client is often late or often misses a session.
- You habitually run over at the end of the session.
- You meet your client outside the therapy hour.
- You are overly invested in your client not getting angry at you.
- You tell your client about your personal life.
- You regularly hug your client hello or goodbye.
- You let large debts accumulate.
- You are available to your client at all hours.
- You are inconsistent about charging for missed sessions.

I will discuss these issues and how to deal with them in depth in Chapter 16. Suffice it here to direct your attention to making efforts to maintain the frame securely. When you find yourself or your client engaging in any of the previously mentioned behaviors, be aware that you are dealing with frame violations that need to be addressed. You will learn how to do this in your clinical supervision and personal therapy.

I hope that you get a sense of how the concept of the frame safeguards the therapy you conduct in that it directs your attention to issues that might endanger the work you engage in. It tells you what kind of behavior is and is not acceptable for a therapist and why, and it helps you monitor yourself and your behavior, as well as your client's behavior, and thus provides you with material to work with in the therapy itself.

PART II

PRACTICAL CONSIDERATIONS:
FIRST STEPS INTO CLINICAL PRACTICE

INTRODUCTION

This section is oriented toward your clinical practice of psychotherapy with clients. Here, I will address how to deal with practical issues that arise: what to say, as well as when and how to say it.

The actual interventions and rationales for interventions are based on a psychodynamic approach. This approach and its theoretical underpinnings are described in more depth in Part III. Reading Part III is not necessary in order to be able to utilize the information presented to you here in Part II, which is concerned with the what, when, and how. However, if you want to get an idea about the why, make sure to peruse Part III as well.

Keep in mind that what is presented in the following are *suggestions* that should never be followed mindlessly. If you don't understand something, talk to your teachers and supervisors. If you disagree with something, do likewise. Ultimately, it is you as the clinician who will have to make the decision as to how you will proceed. Nevertheless, my suggestions have grown out of years of working with clients and years of conversing with beginning therapists about working with clients. It is my attempt at responding to the question that most beginning therapists ask time and again: "But how do I do that? When do I say this? And what do I actually say?"

4

FIRST CONTACT:
ON THE PHONE

Your first contact with a client is most often on the phone. You are probably calling back a prospective client who has requested to see a therapist. Two issues are of particular importance here: confidentiality and the frame.

TRYING TO MAKE CONTACT

This is where the confidentiality issue is prominent. Although this prospective client, whom I will in the following passages call Ms. Green,[1] is not yet an actual client, treat with utmost discretion the fact that she is considering to enter into a client–therapist relationship (with you).

Try to reach her directly, so that you need not leave a message on a machine that might be accessible to people other than Ms. Green herself, unless she has explicitly stated upon intake that you may leave a message. This might mean that you have to call several times before you actually reach her. If you

---

[1] I arbitrarily chose "Ms. Green" as the sample client for this text and will refer to "her" and "the client . . . she" throughout the text. Naturally, a client can be male and "Mr. Green . . . he" as well.

are in luck, Ms. Green has stated a time when she can be reached and is actually available when you try to make contact.

If someone other than Ms. Green picks up, just ask for her by name, ask when she will be back if she is not available, and state that you will call again. Alternatively, state your name (*not* your profession or affiliation, which might identify your profession and thus compromise Ms. Green, who might not want anyone else to know that she is considering therapy), a number you might be reached at (*not* your home phone number), and, when asked what this is regarding, state simply that you are returning Ms. Green's call. Sometimes, family members get suspicious and demanding, wanting to know your business with Ms. Green. Do not let yourself be pressured into giving more information than you had planned to give. Politely but firmly state (broken record–like) that you are returning Ms. Green's call and will talk to her. Take the intrusive attitude of the person on the phone as information about the circumstances of Ms. Green's life. Then wait for her call. This holds true for calls both at her home or at her workplace, if she left you both phone numbers.

If you cannot reach a real person with whom to leave a message, leave that same message with Ms. Green's machine. That is: your name, your work phone number, the fact that you are returning her call, and the request for her to call you back. However, it might not be clear to Ms. Green who you are (since she probably called the agency where you work and requested a therapist, without knowing who that would be).

Only if you do not get a response this way is it advisable to leave your agency's name: "Hello Ms. Green, this is MO[2] again with XYZ Mental Health Services. I am returning your call. Please give me a call back at the following number . . ."

---

[2]In the following examples, MO stands for my name, Maxa Ott. You, of course, will leave your own name.

Of course, if you are working for a private practitioner—let's say, Dr. Y—Dr. Y most likely told Ms. Green that you would be calling her back so that she is expecting a call from you and thus will know who you are when she hears your name. You might say something like: "My name is MO. Dr. Y asked me to call you back. Please give me a call at the following number . . ."

In summary: when trying to make initial contact with a prospective client, always be protective of the potential therapist–client relationship.

MAKING CONTACT

Now that you actually have Ms. Green on the phone, the issue of setting and maintaining the frame becomes important. With this first contact (including the phase of trying to make contact), you begin to set the frame.

A secure frame will include privacy and confidentiality, as well as the anonymity[3] of the therapist. Therefore, keep your telephone conversation to a minimum, try not to engage the client in a longer conversation, and guard against becoming thus engaged. Keep in mind that the prospective client already has a whole set of fantasies in place regarding you and therapy, when he or she makes first contact. Give as much information as necessary, but leave as much as possible to be addressed in person in the therapy room. This means that if Ms. Green begins to tell you all about her difficulties, gently interrupt her and let her know that you cannot address this with her on the phone but would like to hear more about it when you see her. Do not establish a first impression of unlimited telephone access to you.

---

[3] Refer back to the section on self-disclosure for thoughts on therapist anonymity.

Since we are not concerned with the actual telephone intake but with your follow-up to an intake, a call in order to make an appointment, the following points should be addressed on the phone:

Your Qualifications

If you are not asked about your credentials, you need not address this now. But, being pre-licensed, you legally have to address this issue in the first session (I will discuss this again further on).

If you are asked, be explicit about your training-status: Clearly state whether you are an MFT intern, an MSW, a psychiatric resident, a candidate in a program for clinical psychology, a registered trainee, and so forth.

When you are asked about your experience, again state it clearly. Thus, if Ms. Green asks you, "How many years have you been practicing?" and you are new to this, state truthfully that you are a beginning therapist who is being supervised by a licensed practitioner. Let us say she asks if you have experience working with issues of sexual abuse and you don't; state that you have no such experience. Ms. Green has a right to know what she is venturing into. If Ms. Green states she would prefer to engage in this therapeutic venture with a more experienced clinician, be respectful of this wish. Invite her to come in for an initial session to explore her concerns and get an impression of who you are and how you might work, but give the referral back to the referring source, detailing her wish, if she prefers you do so. If no experienced clinicians are available at your place of work, let her know this fact (maybe all the clinicians at your facility are in training), and make appropriate referrals to more highly experienced professionals if indicated. The fact that you are in training is not something to be ashamed of. All of us have to start somewhere. Maybe you are a paraprofessional with years of experience, supervised by a licensed clinician, and Ms. Green would prefer to work with a professional. Again, let her know of your experience, invite her in for an initial meeting to explore her concerns more in depth, but do not try to persuade her of your qualifications. In doing so, you would clearly break the frame, compelling Ms. Green to work with you because *you* would prefer it, not because she thinks it is best. It is not Ms. Green's responsibility to make you feel competent. But it *is* of utmost importance to be frank with your clients about your qualifications, your training, and your experience.

If the prospective client does not outright say, "I want to work with someone differently qualified," the following might be useful to express: "Why don't you come in for an initial meeting, so that you get an idea of who I am and what it might be like to work with me? We can address your concerns in more depth then. If you find that you would prefer to work with someone else, I can then better assist you with making the appropriate referral."

The Fee

You might or might not address the issue of the fee on the phone. If your agency sets the fee and you have no flexibility in setting it, address it now. You might say: "Have you been quoted a fee yet?" If she hasn't and she cannot afford the agency's fee, you will have to refer her elsewhere and spare her a trip to your office.

If you have flexibility in setting the fee, you might choose not to address this issue at this point but wait to do it in person with her. This means that you must be prepared for a low payment for the initial consultation in case she cannot afford what you would prefer her to pay. You might set a fee for the initial consultation meeting (the first session) now, but let her know that you will decide jointly on the set fee for the ongoing therapy should you find that you want to work together. You might say something like this: "Why don't you come in for an initial meeting? We will talk about payment then and work out a fee that we both can live with." Or "We have a sliding scale, based on your assets. According to your income your fee is $ . . . Oh, you can't afford that right now? Why don't you come in for an initial assessment, where we will work out a fee that we both can live with."

Initial Consultation versus Beginning of Treatment

Let her know that you are meeting her for an initial consultation. Ms. Green might not be appropriate for treatment with you. Since you don't know whether you will be able to work with any given client for a variety of reasons (e.g., you may lack the qualifications, you may have countertransference issues that you feel you cannot contain, the client might be actively abusing substances, the nature of the client's disturbance might not be best treated by the type of therapy you are practicing, the client might exhibit symptoms that are inappropriate for your agency, and so forth), and since you cannot know this until you have met the client and made an assessment, it is advisable to inform the client that you will be meeting for an initial consultation session.

This might go something like this: "Let's set a date for an initial consultation where we can get to know each other. You will get a sense of who I am and what it would be like to work with me, and I can collect some information that will help me see if I am the therapist who will be best able to help you, and then we can decide where we want to go from there."

In this way you leave it open for both yourself and your client whether you will actually end up working together, which should be anxiety-reducing for both of you. You may *not* be the therapist best suited to work with her, but you don't know that until you have made an assessment. She may find that she does not want to work with you, but she may not know this until she has actually met you.

If you prefer, you can address the fact that this is an initial consultation and assessment at the beginning of the first meeting. (Note: The assessment might need more than one session. We will address this in more depth further on.)

Appointment for Consultation

Set the date and time of your initial meeting. This is straightforward enough. Find a date and time that is mutually agreeable to both of you. If this particular time will not be the time slot you have available for ongoing therapy should the two of you decide to work together, it is advisable to let her know about it. In this way, she will not begin to form an attachment to this particular time and thus experience the shift to another time as a break of the frame. That is, your action is predictable and transparent, which is in the service of establishing a secure frame.

You might say: "I can meet you Wednesday at 4 p.m. for the initial consultation. This will not be our regular meeting time if we decide to work together. We will find a time and day that works for both of us for our regular meetings."

Finally, ask her to give you a call and let you know if for some reason she can't make it at the agreed-upon time. This might sound something like the following: "Give me a call if you can't make this appointment. We'll work something out to reschedule if necessary."

This conveys your flexibility as well as your expectation of her being responsible for her end of the encounter. You are setting the tone for the frame, which will include your cancellation policies.

5

MEETING THE CLIENT

Now the day and time have come to actually meet Ms. Green for the first time. Rest assured, as nervous as you might be, she is most likely far more nervous than you are. Consider this: Research has shown that the average time between a referral made to a potential client and that person actually picking up the phone and calling the therapist is six months to one year! This means that most clients have been thinking about seeing a therapist for a very long time before they actually found the courage to make that initial phone call. You can imagine how much anxiety might be attached to an actual meeting with a therapist. In my experience, a large percentage of prospective clients who make the initial phone call will then not show up for their first session. Many clients need several phone calls (sometimes separated by weeks, months, and even years) before they actually come into session. Consider that most clients do not know what to expect in therapy—and that the therapeutic experience can only be conveyed in words, to a certain extent, and has to be experienced to be "known"—and you will understand that Ms. Green, now waiting for you in the waiting room, is probably anxious and very ambivalent about being here and meeting you.

FROM THE WAITING ROOM TO THE CONSULTATION ROOM

You are now going out into the waiting room to meet Ms. Green in person for the first time. Ideally, you would have a private waiting room in which only Ms. Green would be waiting at this time. Should this be the case, just step into the waiting room, introduce yourself, and ask Ms. Green into your consultation room. Do not engage her in conversation outside the consultation room. In this way you begin to set the frame: Therapy takes place in the consultation room, not in the waiting room.

It is more likely that at this stage in your training, you work in a facility where other clients and perhaps also other therapists will be waiting in a common waiting room at the change of the hour. This means that you do not know which of the people waiting is Ms. Green.

Be protective of your client's right to privacy and do not ask for her by name in front of others. Instead, name yourself. State audibly to everyone in the waiting room something akin to the following examples:

"My name is MO; is anyone here waiting for me?"
"Does any one of you have an appointment with MO?"
"Does one of you have an appointment with me? My name is MO."

After announcing yourself, wait for Ms. Green to respond. You may have to come back to the waiting room more than once if she is not there yet. If a new person arrives, address her in the same way: "May name is MO; are you here to see me?"

The idea is *not to address Ms. Green by name in front of others to protect her confidentiality.*

This is a good rule to work with in the future as well. Greet your client when you see her on a regular basis with: "Hello" or "Are you ready?" or something similar that feels comfortable to you. Do *not* greet her by name in the presence of others.

In this way you protect your client's confidentiality as well as possible. Legally, the *fact* of the treatment relationship is confidential,[1] but in the case of your working in an agency where other clients and therapists see you meet your client, you may not be able to keep this fact confidential. You can and should, however, keep your client's *name* confidential.

In regard to beginning conversations with your clients in the waiting room or on your way to the consultation room: It is a matter of setting and protecting the frame not to do so. The therapeutic hour begins when the door to the consultation room closes. The therapeutic relationship is confined to what happens behind that door. Therapy takes place in the consultation room. In this way, you begin to define the boundaries of the therapeutic relationship and show yourself as a container, as well as capable of setting limits. Keep in mind: Whatever you do or do not do has meaning.

Do not begin the therapeutic interaction before you close the door of the consultation room. Since at this point of your training you most likely don't have the luxury of opening the door of the consultation room and asking the client in, or opening the door at the end of the hour and letting the client go—both helpful for keeping interaction outside the room to a minimum—stay as neutral as possible.

Of course, it is important not to simply ignore your client, since this would be rude. After all, you are two real people meeting. Therefore, if Ms. Green begins to talk to you in the hallway—maybe out of anxiety or maybe simply because she doesn't know that in this special relationship, you don't begin conversations before you close the door—you might say something like this: "Let's wait until we're in the consultation room. We have more privacy there."

If she continues to talk, do not let yourself be engaged. You have let her know that you are heading for the consultation

---

[1]Compare the legal and ethical standards ruling your profession.

room and that you will talk there. Most clients will take their cue from your behavior, so that if you don't talk, they eventually won't either. If Ms. Green tries to engage you in conversation every time you meet, it becomes something to be addressed with her in session.

IN THE CONSULTATION ROOM

Your main goal in the first session is to get to know Ms. Green, to give her a chance to get to know you, and to learn as much as possible about what brings her here—in short, to begin gathering information that will help you assess her appropriateness for treatment, as well as formulate a treatment plan. You will continue to set the frame, a process begun with the first contact over the phone, and you will begin educating Ms. Green regarding the process of therapy.

However, several topics *must* be addressed in the first session, which will limit the freedom you have in how to conduct this session. You might actually find it anxiety-reducing and thus helpful to have the structure of the topics that have to be addressed to help you navigate this first session. On the other hand, be alert to the fact that some clients might experience such a structure as an impingement, as an imposition, hindering them from telling you freely what is on their minds. Make note of such difficulties and leave room for your client to express her take on the situation.

In this first session you want to say only what is necessary and leave as much room as possible for Ms. Green to take the lead. You will never have another first meeting with this particular person again. You can learn much by leaving room for Ms. Green to address whatever comes to her mind and in whichever way she wants to address it. In the following chapter, we will discuss what must be said and what may be said when you first meet your client.

6

INITIAL
CONSULTATION

Once you are in the consultation room, there is one item that
you *best* address with Ms. Green *before* you start the intake/con-
sultation, and that is the issue of the limits of confidentiality.
After you have addressed this, several issues remain that must
be addressed in the first session, aside from the main issue of
what brings her and what she hopes to get out of therapy. This
fact will give you some structure as to how to proceed, even
though it will curb Ms. Green's spontaneity to some extent.

So now you are in the consultation room behind closed doors
for the first time. Ask Ms. Green to have a seat. Let her know
that you will have to attend to some paperwork and that you
have to inform her of a few items before you can start. Again,
keep in mind that however nervous you might be, Ms. Green is
probably more nervous, a fact that you might address in this
first hour—*her* anxiety, that is, not yours!

LIMITS OF CONFIDENTIALITY

Inform Ms. Green of the limits of confidentiality *before* she starts
telling you about herself and her issues. It is important that she
knows that if she makes disclosures of a certain kind—namely,

child abuse, elder and dependent adult abuse, as well as danger to self and others—you are mandated to take action. That means that her confidentiality will not be protected in these cases. You might address this issue as follows:

> "Before we begin, let me tell you that I am a mandated reporter of child abuse and elder and dependent adult abuse. That means that there are limits of confidentiality. Everything we say in here will be confidential *except* in the following cases: if you tell me about child abuse (you may want to elaborate on this: if you tell me that you are abusing a child, if you tell me about knowing that a child is being abused, if you tell me about you or another child having been abused in the past and the abuser might still be around children and a danger to them), or if you tell me about an elder or a dependent adult being abused (you may want to define what an elder and dependent adult is[1]). In those cases I am mandated to make a report to the appropriate agencies. There are two more instances where I am mandated to break confidentiality: if you tell me you are going to kill yourself and I believe that you are really going to do so, I must (and will) take reasonable steps to prevent you from doing so, and if you tell me you are going to hurt or kill someone else, I am mandated to report this to the intended victim and to the police."

To make sure that Ms. Green understands these limitations of confidentiality, ask her whether she understands and whether she may have any questions pertaining to this issue. *Don't be hesitant around this issue, but be direct and explicit.* It is your responsibility to make certain that Ms. Green knows what the consequences will be in case she does tell you anything falling

---

[1]For your own information, peruse a copy of the latest laws pertaining to your profession (MFT, LCSW, Clinical Psychologists, etc.) that relate to this issue. In California you can request a copy of these laws through the Board of Behavioral Sciences.

under the limits of confidentiality. If she does, you can assume that she wants you to know and that she wants you to take action, even if she states otherwise. We will explore this scenario in more depth later on.

You probably have an informed consent form or other paperwork detailing office policies and rights and responsibilities. Limits of confidentiality should be part of this form, which Ms. Green will sign when she enters into treatment with you (usually by the end of the first session).

FEE

Another issue that must legally be addressed by the end of the first session is the fee for your services. As I have stated earlier, you might not have any flexibility in this regard and in fact might have quoted her a fee already. In that case, the quoted fee will be what you will collect from Ms. Green, according to the policies of your agency: at the beginning or end of session, billing her monthly, billing her insurance, or whatever the agreed-upon method of payment is in your agency.

In the case of you having more freedom in setting the fee, you will have indicated to Ms. Green that you will discuss this issue in the first session. If she is not able to pay what you would like to receive, you are under no obligation to continue seeing her for a low fee, unless your contract with your employer states otherwise. However, if you have not set the fee on the phone, you are tacitly agreeing to accept whatever Ms. Green is able to afford for this initial assessment session. This might be less than what your usual fee would have been and might end up being the only session, in some cases. However, this is a relatively small price to pay for the chance to see Ms. Green in a first session with you and to be able to address this issue in person. Generally, it is much more likely that the two of you will be able to find a mutually agreeable fee when Ms. Green has met you and has been able to get a sense of what you have to offer. Keep in mind what I have said about the difficulties prospective clients experience with actually coming in for a first session; it is much easier for her to back out of even starting therapy on the phone and using the fee as a reason to do so.

Therefore, in the case of you having input on setting the fee, I recommend that you begin by stating your full fee. If your (or the agency's) full fee is $100 an hour, say so: "My fee is $100 an hour."

If you addressed the fact on the phone that Ms. Green can't afford the full fee, you should now refer back to that conversation and perhaps might add the following: "I know you said the full fee is too high for you at this time. What amount would be affordable to you?"

Let Ms. Green state the amount and negotiate a fee that you both can live with. This might take more than one meeting and might entail looking at her assets, her priorities, what she is willing to give up to afford therapy, whom she might ask for help with the fee, and so forth. When you settle on a fee per session that is lower than your full fee, you might make a statement such as this: "Let's settle on a fee of $ . . . for now. We will reassess your fee periodically and adjust it if indicated."

This lets Ms. Green know that the matter of the fee is not settled for good and gives you something to refer back to when you periodically bring up the fee for renegotiation. This might happen when Ms. Green finds a well-paying position, when she gets a raise, or just generally on a regular basis—perhaps every six months or every year.

Be aware that money issues and thus setting the fee, as well as paying the fee, are never neutral. As Horner (1991) aptly states: "It is not likely that we can separate payment for therapy from transference and countertransference input" (p. 182). You might see this in your own reactions to this issue: Setting a fee might not be as easy for you as you thought it would be. You might find yourself not wanting to address this issue; you might find yourself uncomfortable asking for a fee at all; you might, on the contrary, have strong feelings about working for a low fee. You might find that your client reacts strongly to the process of setting of the fee; you might find yourself quickly setting a very low fee, even while having the impression that your client can afford a higher fee; you might find yourself becoming irritated if you can't set the fee at a sum that you thought fair. You might find your client becoming angry with you for expecting her to pay at all; or you might find your client agreeing to a fee that, it soon turns out, he cannot afford. Suffice it here to say that the issue of the fee is a loaded issue indeed. It makes good sense for you to address this topic with your supervisor.[2]

STATUS OF EDUCATION

Since you are not yet licensed, you are legally mandated to inform your clients of this fact at the beginning of treatment. If you have not addressed this issue on the phone, now is the time to let Ms. Green know about your training. That means you will let her know that you are an MFT Trainee, a Ph.D. candidate, working toward your MSW, a paraprofessional, or whatever the case may be; that you are not licensed yet and are working under supervision of a licensed clinician. As I discussed previously, be direct when asked about years of training, where you went to school, and the like.

However, do not forget to inquire after the underlying concern in regard to the questions asked. Thus, when you have answered the question regarding your experience, you may want to add something like the following: "I wonder whether you might be a little apprehensive about whether I will be able to help you?"

In this way you give Ms. Green the opportunity to express

---

[2]You will find more information regarding fee issues in Chapter 16. For literature pertaining to money in treatment, see Appendix II.

her fears. Chances are that when she finds that you are able to address her concerns with her, that you are able to hear her out and not get defensive or angry with her, she might feel comfortable with staying with you.

If fee and training are issues, it is fair to let her know the reality of her being unlikely to receive therapy at a drastically reduced price from a licensed clinician, if this is what she is looking for. Therapy at greatly reduced fees is mostly offered by agencies that employ paraprofessionals and therapists in training.

If she wishes to work with a licensed clinician, honor her wish and proceed through the channels established at your place of work; either give the referral back to an intake clinician or clinical director, or make appropriate referrals yourself. Be certain to let her know that you cannot guarantee that she will find the service she is looking for at the fee she is stating, but that you will do what you can to assist. Make at least three appropriate referrals.

A word regarding self-disclosure: You might ask yourself what the difference is between disclosing your experience and training and disclosing your marital status and where you live? The answer is quite simply that one (your training and experience) is necessary for Ms. Green to make an informed decision as a consumer whether she wants to work with you or not, while the other (your marital status and other personal issues) is *not* necessary to make such a decision. As stated previously, once you do disclose information regarding your training and experience, it is important to follow up by exploring the implications of this information for your client. Remember, everything you say and do not say has meaning.

On the whole, you are asked to maintain a delicate balance between the client's rights as a consumer and her right to be informed of your qualifications and background, on the one hand, and the clinical issues pertaining to the asking for, the giving, and the receiving of such information, on the other hand.

The issue of your sexual orientation when working with gay and lesbian clients exemplifies this dilemma well. There are widely differing opinions as to whether this is a personal issue best kept to yourself, or whether a gay or lesbian consumer is entitled to a gay or lesbian therapist. And what about a prospective heterosexual client who wants to ascertain that you are also heterosexual? As always, explore the importance of this matter to the prospective client, the underlying fears and concerns, and educate regarding the therapeutic process, including issues of therapist anonymity and neutrality. However, if your client insists on this (or any other personal) information, it will be your clinical decision whether you want to give or withhold it. Whatever the case, be certain to explore the impact and, if necessary, refer the prospective client to another qualified clinician if she decides not to work with you. Don't forget to address this in your supervision as well.

INTAKE INFORMATION AND INFORMED CONSENT

Depending on your agency's policies, you might have to fill out paperwork with your client detailing her personal data, emergency contacts, and the like. In addition, it is imperative that Ms. Green has the pertinent information about your office policies, including collection of fees, cancellation policy, policies regarding substance abuse, and so forth, as well as crucial rules governing therapeutic treatment such as limits of confidentiality, as part of making an informed decision whether she wants to work with you or not.

I am distinguishing here between informed consent, including office policies, on the one hand, and treatment contract, on the other hand. The latter entails a contract-setting process consisting of an evaluation period, gathering of information, as well as a mutual decision to enter into treatment together. I will detail this process in the next chapter. Informed consent, on the other hand, acquaints your client with the basic ground rules of working with you and, as such, is information that will go into her side of deciding whether she wants to enter into a treatment contract with you or not.

While letting her know about the limits of confidentiality should be addressed *before* Ms. Green begins her conversation with you (as detailed earlier), all other issues mentioned in this chapter can be addressed throughout or at the end of the first session. Therefore, you might want to give Ms. Green a choice as to when she wants to attend to these issues. That means that you will need to let your client know that you have to do some paperwork with her. You might state this at the beginning, right after addressing the limits of confidentiality, perhaps in a way similar to this: "We have to do some paperwork today. Would you like to do this now or would you like to do it at the end of the hour?"

Perhaps she is in a lot of distress and really wants to tell you why she is there before you go over office policies and the intake information that your agency requires. If she does choose to do the paperwork at the end of the hour, make sure you reserve approximately ten minutes to do so.

Intake Information

The actual intake information will vary, according to your agency's requirements, but should include:

- Name of client
- Date of birth
- Address
- Phone number
- Emergency contact
- Presenting problem (what brings you here)
- Any illness/disorder the client is currently being treated for and by whom

- Current and/or former substance abuse
- Past suicide attempts (when? how?)
- Name and phone number of current psychiatrist (if any)
- Name and dosage of currently prescribed medications, as well as name of prescribing physician

Other additional information will vary according to your place of work.

This initial intake form covers only the most basic intake information and cannot serve as a substitute for a thorough evaluation and contract-setting period (addressed further on). However, it will render data that will help you formulate an initial impression of Ms. Green's problems and guide your further actions. Let me illustrate this statement with a couple of examples:

In the first scenario, Ms. Green tells you that she has difficulties sleeping and often feels tired and without energy. She also tells you that she is taking strong pain medications for arthritis. You might or might not be faced with her suffering from depression (depending on further investigation), but you will definitely look at the fact that her chronic arthritis pain, as well as her pain medication, might be related to her symptoms of low energy and difficulties in sleeping.

In the second scenario, Ms. Green tells you that she is taking a psychotropic medication prescribed by a psychiatrist. You will want to get a release of information and speak to that psychiatrist to help you coordinate your treatment planning.

Informed Consent Form

The informed consent form should address the issues listed in the following sections and should be signed and dated by Ms. Green by the end of the first hour. Let her know that it details your office policies and other information pertaining to therapeutic treatment and that with her signature, she acknowledges having been informed of the topics addressed in the form and agrees to working with you under the detailed conditions.

Topics that should be addressed in the informed consent form are as follows:

Emergency: How you, the therapist, can be reached in an emergency. Do you carry a pager? Are you reachable through a telephone service? How quickly do you usually respond? Do you charge for phone contacts longer than a particular time frame? How much do you charge? I tell my clients that I do not carry a pager and that I check my messages often (which I do). I usually will get back to them within one business day in a non-emergency. They need to state clearly when it *is* an emergency, and I will return their emergency calls as soon as I am able, which will in all likelihood not be immediately. I let them know clearly that they must call 911 if they have a 911 emergency. I let them know that short phone contacts are free of charge, but that I will charge a pro-rated fee (depending on the hourly rate with a particular client) for phone contacts over fifteen minutes. If there is repeated short- or longer-term phone contact with a client, I will usually see this as evidence that the frequency of sessions needs to be increased to contain this client.

Here I already am making a choice as to who I will accept into treatment on an outpatient, private practice basis. Clearly, my clients must be generally able to function well enough to be able to wait for my return calls. Consequently, when a prospective client states that he is chronically suicidal and needs to be able to reach me at all hours so that I can help dissuade him from committing suicide or help hospitalize him, or if a prospective client tells me about numerous suicide attempts resulting in hospitalizations, I will most likely not work with him in a private practice setting, since, clearly, he needs a more structured environment than I can offer.

Cancellation Policy: This details whether you charge for a missed session and whether you allow for a particular time frame for cancellation without incurring a fee.

Clinicians vary in the ways they handle this issue. Some require one day notice of cancellation, others require two days' notice of cancellation, and still others do not charge if they can fill the hour otherwise. In the case of billing monthly for your services, you might bill per agreed-upon frequency of hours, whether these hours are actually utilized by your client or not. In any case, the important part is that you explain and discuss this topic with Ms. Green in the first session so that she knows what to expect if a cancellation becomes necessary.

Having addressed this topic and having it in writing will assist you when your client calls you one day, stating that her car broke down, and then becomes indignant the next scheduled hour when you expect her to pay for her missed session. You then can refer back to your cancellation policy as a starting point for exploring her feelings and thoughts about having to pay for a missed session.

Fee Collection: When is the agreed-upon fee to be paid: at the end or the beginning of a session? Weekly? Monthly? Will Ms. Green pay you directly or will she be billed through the mail? Your agency will have its own policy regarding when and how the fee will be collected, and this is the place to make this policy explicit. This is also when to let her know that you might utilize a collection agency for collection of outstanding fees (if this is something that you or the agency you work for will do).

Clean and Sober: What is your policy regarding the client showing up intoxicated? Most clinicians agree that therapeutic work cannot be accomplished if your client is not clean and sober during the therapy hour, and they will not see a client who is intoxicated.

If you plan on conducting therapy with your client only when she is clean and sober—and I suggest that you do—it is necessary to state this fact in the first session, so that you can refer back to it, if and when this should become an issue. That is to say, if Ms. Green one day appears in your office inebriated, you can remind her of the fact that you will only see her when she is sober, as discussed in the first session. However, this would not exempt you from the necessity of ensuring your client's safety. In this case, you might have to call a cab for Ms. Green or perhaps even a family member, if you feel she would endanger herself by driving. It is generally accepted practice to regard such a session as canceled without notice and charge for it as such. I suggest that you let Ms. Green know about this in the first session.

Limits of Confidentiality: This issue should briefly be stated in writing on the informed consent form so that there can be no doubt about the client having been informed of it.

The actual statement might look something like this:

Your confidentiality is limited in the following cases: in instances of Child Abuse and/or Neglect, Elder and Dependent Adult Abuse and/or Neglect, as well as when you appear to be a danger to yourself and/or others. I am a mandated reporter and am legally obligated to take steps to ensure the safety of yourself and/or others in these cases.

As discussed earlier, it is necessary that you explain this issue in detail.

If You Have Any Questions, Please Ask Me: It is advisable to have a statement similar to this one on your informed consent form. Make sure that Ms. Green understands that she can approach you at *any time* with questions pertaining to the informed consent form.

I Have Read, Understood, and Agree to Treatment under the above Elaborated Terms: Your form should contain a sentence similar to this that explicitly states that Ms. Green has read the form, has understood what it contains, and agrees to see you under these circumstances.

A Line for Signature and Date: Make sure Ms. Green signs and dates this form by the end of the first session. Give her a copy of this form for her reference.

Of course, your agency's actual form might look quite different. However, the previously listed topics should be addressed in it in some manner.

The easiest way to go over this form will probably be to read the contract with the client and discuss each topic to assure that she does understand it. If Ms. Green declines to sign it, I suggest that you investigate with her what her reluctance might be, in an attempt to resolve her reluctance. If she persists in her refusal to sign the form, I suggest that you do *not* continue assessment and do *not* begin treatment. It is really necessary for your legal protection that the informed consent form be signed by the end of the first hour if the two of you decide to continue working with each other. Treatment without a signed informed consent form leaves you open to liability, which I advise you not to incur.

Some clients become anxious about the fact that they are signing a "contract," fearing that they are entering into a legal commitment to stay in therapy and not being able to freely discontinue treatment should they wish to do so. Address this possibility. Make explicit that *with their signature they are acknowledging having been informed of the issues contained in the contract,* but that they have *not* entered into a legally binding contract that can compel them to stay in therapy. In fact, treatment is voluntary and can be terminated at any time. If treatment is court-ordered, it is the court order that is compelling, not your contract.

This scenario is in fact taken from my practice. I was seeing a client in initial assessment who was highly concerned about signing the informed consent form because of these issues. Although he did sign the form after I explained its implications and we addressed his fears, his reluctance was indicative of a stance of guardedness and fear of being taken advantage of that was diagnostic and comprised a major issue that we had to address in ongoing therapy. Therefore, even as you are going over forms and addressing highly formalized issues, be aware of the way your client is interacting with you, since this will yield important data to be dealt with in treatment.

7

THE ASSESSMENT PROCESS

We have covered the issues that *must* be addressed in the first session with your client. Now it is time to focus on how to interview your client and collect information that will lead to an assessment of her appropriateness for treatment, as well as to a diagnostic impression that will lend itself to initial treatment planning. This assessment process includes taking a history, doing a mental status exam, making a diagnosis (DSM-IV, as well as structural), and making a recommendation for treatment.

In the following selections I give you a list of topics to inquire about. Please take note that this list is meant as a structure for you to have in mind, as a guide to raise issues if your client does not do so herself; that it is meant to give you direction when you would otherwise not know what to ask for. It is explicitly *not* meant to be a list that you go down mechanically with your client. You will see that some clients require a little more structure than others, but, generally, it is preferable to let your client raise issues that seem important to her at her own pace.

Before we go into detail, I want to encourage you to give Ms. Green a forum to express what it is like for her to be in this session with you. If you pay attention, you will probably pick up an expression of unease, of anxiety, of not being comfortable (it might be as subtle as her shifting in her chair a lot). In my experience most clients seize the opportunity to reduce some of their initial anxiety when you give them a chance. You might therefore at an appropriate moment say something like this: "I imagine it must be strange to be sitting here with me." Or "I wonder what it is like for you to be here."

It is a good idea to acknowledge that this "strangeness" or lack of comfort might persist for a while and that it is not unusual. It is your job as the therapist to educate Ms. Green regarding therapy. Anticipating a period of discomfort is part of doing that. In addition, it helps her return to you in the second session, despite discomfort experienced initially.

Another way to help her reduce some of her initial anxiety is to inquire after her expectations. Thus, you might say: "I wonder what your expectations were about what it would be like to see a therapist?" or "Is meeting me the way you expected it to be?"

Listen carefully to the answers. Most clients who have not been in therapy before have gross misperceptions as to what therapy is like. Most often, they assume that they are going to meet someone who will tell them what is wrong with them and who will make it go away. Again, in the process of educating your client what therapy is about, you will want to let her know that it is a *collaborative* effort, that you and she will work together to explore what is going on for her and to find ways to alleviate her problems. While it is, of course, true that you have an expertise in this field—after all, you are the therapist—it is also true that therapy is not something to be administered by the therapist to the client but a process that therapist and client engage in together.

Don't expect to be able to collect the necessary information for making a recommendation regarding treatment and for entering into a treatment contract during the first hour. A thorough assessment process will take *several* hours. This is particularly true for beginning therapists who discuss their impressions with their supervisors. Most likely with increasing practice and skill you will become faster in your assessment.

As mentioned earlier, please be aware that some clients may experience your gathering of information as restrictive and intrusive. Be attentive and empathic to their needs. If a client has great difficulties allowing you to ask questions, this, too, will inform your assessment and initial treatment planning.

Let me emphasize again the importance of not asking the questions regarding the topics listed in the next sections as if you are rattling off a list. Remember that the topics listed are meant for you to keep in mind as you conduct your first several meetings with Ms. Green, *issues for you to be aware of and, if possible, to address as they come up.* Of course, sometimes you will have to raise a topic yourself, since it will otherwise not be mentioned. With increasing experience and skill, the initial assessment will become much easier and more natural for you: you will learn to weave your questions in as your client tells her story.

TAKING A HISTORY

The purpose of taking a detailed history is to gather as much information as possible to enable you to make a diagnosis, propose an initial treatment plan, and enter into a treatment contract. Some of the information you want to elicit in taking a history you already know about from your initial intake form, so you can use what you know to elicit more information.

Generally, a good starting point for information gathering is some form of the question "*What brings you here?*" This conveys your interest and creates a forum for your client to begin telling you about herself and her reasons for seeking therapy. Ms. Green might now launch into telling you about feeling sad and tearful, having difficulties sleeping, and having thoughts about death and dying, all related to the recent break-up with her spouse. This tells you several things: Ms. Green sounds depressed (and you might proceed along the lines of a Mental Status Exam to assess for severity of her depression, as well as to assess whether she is suicidal). Ms. Green has relationship difficulties (and you might ask her to tell you about the break-up and what led to it, in this way eliciting information regarding her marriage, possible children, and the dynamics of her relationship).

Here's how to go about taking a detailed history:

Chief Complaint

Purpose: To get a statement *in the client's own words* as to why she is seeking treatment now.

How to Go about It: Ask your client directly:

"Tell me what brings you here today?"
"What seems to be the problem?"
"What are your reasons for seeking therapy?" or the like.

This question regarding the chief complaint usually helps to overcome the difficulties some clients have with beginning to talk to you, since they do have a reason to seek you out and they probably expect you to ask for that reason. If a client has great difficulties articulating a reason for his or her seeking therapy now, this, too, is information for you. You will have to assess further whether a cognitive impairment exists, whether this client is intoxicated, whether perhaps English is not this person's first language, or whether this difficulty in talking about himself or herself is part of the problem.

History of Present Illness

Purpose: To collect information regarding the development of symptoms your client reported while elaborating on the chief complaint.

How to Go about It: Ask your client to tell you about the development of the symptoms she has described in response to the prior question. You want to get a sense of the life events that were going on during that time, whether there were any particular stressors, whether drug use was involved, and what the changes are from previous levels of functioning. If, for example, Ms. Green tells you that the problem is that she is feeling sad and lethargic, has difficulties sleeping, and cannot enjoy herself anymore, you will now ask questions like these:

"How long has this been going on?"
"When did it start?"
"What was happening in your life at that time?"
"What has changed since it first started?" (regarding personal
        life, work, recreational activities, illnesses)
"Has it been getting worse since it first started?"
"What have you done about it?"

The answers to these questions will assist you in making a provisional diagnosis, they will guide your further questioning (including the mental status exam), and they will inform your decisions regarding the treatment recommendation you will end up making.

Once you have an idea what brings Ms. Green to you and how long the problem has gone on, you can go into more details.

Chronological

Purpose: To get a sense of Ms. Green's chronological history, including major life events and the like. You will use this information (conjointly with the other information elicited in the anamnesis) to formulate an assessment of her current situation, of her difficulties, and for making a recommendation regarding treatment, as well as treatment planning.

How to Go about It: You may ask Ms. Green some version of the following: "Tell me about yourself, about the major events in your life, so that I can get a sense of who you are."

If Ms. Green seems unsure of what you want, you might specify a little further: "Tell me about your growing-up years, about going to school, work, important relationships . . . "

You are aiming to elicit information regarding major events in her life, including accidents, major illnesses, and other traumas.

Clients often experience it as helpful to have a concrete question to answer. Since they are new to therapy, they often do not know what is expected of them. Asking them to tell you about themselves opens up a topic that they know about. Listen carefully not only to *what* your client has to tell you but also to *how* she does so. Does she find it difficult to relate information to you? Is there an abundance of information? Does she register discomfort, or does it seem to come easy for her?

This request for a chronological history will give you some information that will pertain to the other topics. You can use this information as an opening to ask for more data regarding a particular topic.

Developmental

Purpose: To collect information regarding how Ms. Green mastered developmental tasks.[1] This will also give you information pertaining to the early relationships Ms. Green had to her primary caregivers, as well as about possible biological problems. This information will assist you in formulating a hypothesis regarding her current difficulties.

How to Go about It: Find out about Ms. Green's developmental milestones by gathering information about her development

---

[1]This section is based on Mahler's Developmental Model, as explicated in Part III.

during the first years of her life. You will want to know about the pregnancy of her mother, whether there were complications at birth, whether she was carried to term or born prematurely, any illnesses that she might have developed after birth, whether she was separated from her mother early on (as in a premature birth needing to be in an incubator), and whether mom breastfed her or not. This information is aimed at establishing what kind of disturbances might have influenced her early development. Whether there were biological abnormalities (as in complications in pregnancy, premature birth, early illnesses) and what her relationship to mother (or another primary caregiver) was like: Was Ms. Green separated from her mom early on or was she allowed to go home with her mother without complications? Was mom available? Was she depressed and therefore withdrawn and unable to care for her child? Difficulties in early development indicate a particular kind of derailment that can be of diagnostic value.[2]

Other developmental milestones pertain to learning to walk and talk, memories regarding early childhood that can indicate whether the individuation-separation phase was navigated well. You will want to know what role dad played: Was he rarely at home? Was *he* the primary caregiver? Was mom a single parent? and so forth. What about siblings? How many and how old are they? It makes a great difference if Ms. Green is the first-born of two, with her next sibling born when she was 3 years old, or whether she is the middle child of three, with her other two siblings one year apart each. In the first case, we can assume that Ms. Green had her parents' undivided attention for much of these first three years, which would indicate a relatively unimpaired development, including separation-individuation. Lack and deprivation might not be major themes for her, while competition, envy, and guilt might be. In the second case, Ms. Green's mother would probably have been very

---

[2]See Horner (1998), *Working with the Core Relationship Problem.*

busy with a 1-year-old when Ms. Green was born, thus not having as much time and energy to attend to her needs. With her third sibling being born when she was 1 year old, this state of affairs would have been compounded unless some other caregiver was present, substituting for mom. In this case, we can hypothesize that major themes in Ms. Green's life might revolve around want and deprivation, that adequate symbiosis was perhaps not provided for, and that therefore the following developmental milestones might have been compromised.

Familial/Social

Purpose: To collect information pertaining to Ms. Green's relationships, past and current, to assist with arriving at a hypothesis regarding developmental derailment and its expression in her current relationships.

How to Go about It: Part of this information will be elicited with the information regarding developmental milestones. Here you want to know more about Ms. Green's social background: about her mother, father, and siblings; about her friends, partner, and children; about her co-workers and boss. Did she grow up in a two-parent family, or a single-parent household? Did her parents divorce, remarry, die, leave and return? Perhaps her parents were gay or lesbian? Was there violence in the family? Whom was it directed against? Was there substance abuse? What were the parents' occupations? What was the socioeconomic background? Did she grow up in one place or did they move? If they moved, did they move often? Where there other family members nearby (grandparents, uncles, aunts)? How many siblings does she have and how did she get along with them over time?

Does Ms. Green have friends? Long-term friendships? How about her love relationships? Is she currently in a committed relationship? Is she married or divorced? Does she have children? How about work? Does she get along with co-workers? What is her relationship with her boss?

You want to get a flavor of what her relationships are like. Is Ms. Green capable of sustaining long-term relationships? How stormy are these relationships? Does she tend to idealize or denigrate people in her life? Is she gregarious and outgoing, with many friends and a string of lovers, or is she a loner, withdrawn, and isolative? Does she think her co-workers are conspiring against her and are out to get her, or does she like them and have some friends at work? You are gathering information that will, again, serve to indicate certain derailments in development and subsequent pathology,[3] which in turn will inform your treatment approach.

Sexual

Purpose: To determine any difficulties that may be related to Ms. Green's sexual development, her sexual practices, and her sexual orientation, general attitudes, or feelings.

How to Go about It: Ask Ms. Green whether there are any problems or concerns related to her sexual life. Part of learning about her sexual history may be asking questions such as these:

"How did you learn about sex?"
"Tell me about your first sexual experience."
"What is your sex life like?"

---

[3]Of course, further assessment is necessary to make a structural diagnosis regarding pathology resulting from developmental derailments. Refer to the chapter concerning itself with structural diagnosis, as well as Horner, 1998; Kernberg, 1984; and McWilliams, 1994.

It is here that you might find out about sexual abuse, issues regarding sexual orientation, or sexual dysfunctions. You might find that Ms. Green has never had a sexual relationship, or that she is compulsively engaging in sex with virtual strangers. You might find that she is uncertain regarding her sexual orientation, or that she is firmly hetero- or homosexually oriented. You might find that she first learned about sex when a neighbor exposed himself to her, that she used to "play doctor" with her siblings, or the like. You might find that Ms. Green finds the subject of sex "dirty" and inappropriate. She might get angry with you for having asked. You might find that she is very embarrassed and reluctant to address this issue. Or you might find that she does not seem to find it difficult at all to inform you of major sexual developmental milestones in her life. In any case, what she tells you and how she tells you about it are sources of information for you.

Educational and Vocational

Purpose: To collect information regarding Ms. Green's educational and vocational history.

How to Go about It: You want to know about Ms. Green's educational and work history. Pay attention to the affective flavor of what she is telling you: Is she proud of her achievements, is she ashamed of not making more money, does she feel entitled to a promotion? Does she want to go back to school or is she content with her current achievement? Does she derive pleasure from her work, or does she dread it and is only waiting for something else to come along? Note how long she has stayed with a particular profession, as well as with particular employers. Listening attentively to how Ms. Green speaks about her occupation will tell you much about her: how she approaches and solves problems, what she feels she deserves, her ambitions, her follow-through, her ability to deal with ambivalence and frustrations among others. Some of this information you might already have elicited when you inquired after her social relationships. Do not ask again about her relationships at work if you already have this information.

Recreational

Purpose: To get a sense of how Ms. Green spends her free time. What does Ms. Green do when she is not at work?

How to Go about It: Ask Ms. Green what interests she pursues, what her hobbies are, or what she likes to do outside work. Her answers will give you an indication whether she is a creative person, whether she is more oriented toward others, or whether she prefers to be on her own. Does she tend to be gregarious and outgoing, or is she more introverted, perhaps even isolative? If Ms. Green has told you that she works at home from her own desk, hardly meeting anyone during the day and preferring it this way, and now tells you that she doesn't like being with others in her free time either, but prefers to read at home or go for walks on her own, you will get a very different picture than if she had told you that she works in an office, enjoys chatting with her co-workers, and likes to go dancing with friends in her free time. Depending on the information you get, you will conceptualize what the current, manifest problem is, as well as what you hypothesize the underlying difficulties to be. This, in turn, will influence your recommendation, as well as treatment planning.

Cultural

Purpose: To collect information pertaining to Ms. Green's cultural background. This information will be invaluable in helping you understand Ms. Green's experiences and difficulties.

How to Go about It: Information that you are looking for includes: Ms. Green's race and/or ethnicity. Her country and language of origin. Her age and, consequently, which cultural climate she grew up in: it makes a difference whether she grew up in the '40s, the '50s, the '60s, the '70s, or the '80s. If she is not originally from the United States, where did she come from and what cultural norms applied there? When did she come to the United States? If she belongs to a minority group, what has her experience been with mainstream, majority America. If you yourself are from a different racial and/or ethnic background, you may want to ask her what this is like for her to sit here with you. For example, if you are a Caucasian therapist and Ms. Green is an African-American woman, you might say to her: "I wonder what this is like for you to be sitting with me, since I am white and you are black. Perhaps you have some concerns regarding this fact?"

Be straightforward with these issues. In my experience it is often met with relief when I bring up an obvious difference and invite the client to express his concerns. These obvious, clearly observable differences—including but not limited to age, gender, ethnicity, race, and country of origin, if there is a clearly discernable accent in one of you—usually do engender some feelings on both sides, your client's as well as yours. Be alert to any statements Ms. Green might make that refer to you directly or indirectly, and ask her to expand on them. Thus, Ms. Green might say, "I have always had difficulties talking to women," as she is telling you about her family. If you are a female therapist, you can assume that this statement refers on some level to you as well. It is a good idea to take her up on that and say something like the following: "You said you always found it difficult to speak to women. I am a woman. I imagine you must have some concerns whether you will be able to talk to me."

If she is much older than you and is making reference to how immature and self-centered today's young people are, make sure you address this: "As you talk about today's young people, I am wondering whether you might not have some concerns about my ability to help you, since I am one of those young people."

Or, if you have a clearly discernable accent: "As you talk about foreigners taking over the United States, I imagine that you must have some feelings about the fact that I have an accent and am clearly not originally from the United States."

The information that you can gather from such exchanges will be invaluable in helping you understand Ms. Green's experience of herself and the world.

Prior Suicide Attempts/Self-Mutilating Behavior

Purpose: To collect information that might be helpful in predicting future behavior, that will help assess current suicidality, and that is indicative of underlying pathology.

How to Go about It: Please refer to the section on suicide in Chapter 16 for an in-depth discussion regarding assessment and what to do in case you are dealing with a suicidal client. Suffice it here to say that this is a very important topic to address. Many beginning therapists are somewhat hesitant to ask their clients point-blank whether they have ever attempted to commit suicide, but it is necessary to do so. Ask Ms. Green directly. It will sound something like this:

"Have you ever tried to commit suicide?"
"Have you ever tried to kill yourself?"

Be blunt and to the point—this will make it easier for Ms. Green to answer you openly, as well as assist you in making an accurate assessment of the situation. If Ms. Green affirms that she has tried to kill herself in the past, ask for details: When was this? How often did she try it? How did she do it? Was she hospitalized for it? Did she see a psychiatrist? Has she been prescribed psychotropic medications?

You will also want to ask her whether she has engaged in other harmful behavior, regardless of whether she denies or confirms suicide attempts in the past. Behavior you are looking for includes: cutting herself; burning herself; scratching herself; other addictive behaviors, including compulsive sexual contacts, drinking, and using drugs. You might ask: "Have you hurt yourself in other ways? Like cutting yourself, or burning yourself, or the like?"

This information will be most helpful to you in planning her treatment, as well as in setting a treatment contract with her. If, for example, Ms. Green has a long history of suicide attempts, her treatment contract might include a statement to the effect that she will be hospitalized when suicidal, and that outpatient treatment with you can only be conducted if her suicidality is contained.[4]

If compulsive sexual acting out is an issue, you will have to address the topic of safer sex and sexually transmitted diseases, including HIV and AIDS, in addition to exploring what such self-endangering behavior means.

If Ms. Green uses drugs or alcohol on a regular basis, it will be necessary, in addition to exploring the reasons for her doing so, to set firm limits and clearly state in her treatment contract that she must be clean and sober when coming to sessions.

Prior Therapy

Purpose: To get a sense of the client's expectations of therapy and therapists as these relate to prior experience, as well as to collect information regarding the content of prior therapy, including the possibility of contacting the prior therapist(s) to obtain information that will help your treatment planning.

How to Go about It: Ask Ms. Green directly whether she has been in therapy before. If she answers in the affirmative, find

---

[4]See Kernberg et al., 1989.

out more: How many therapists? What kind of therapy? When and for how long? What had brought her to her prior therapist(s)? Was it helpful? Why did she discontinue therapy with the prior therapist? How come she's not going back to the prior therapist?

If you should find out that Ms. Green is currently seeing another therapist for the same modality of therapy that she wants to engage in with you, that is, if she comes for individual therapy and she already has an individual therapist or if she comes with her lover for couples therapy and they already have a couples therapist and the like, explore with her why she is seeking your services in addition to those she already is receiving. Let her know that it would be unethical and unprofessional for you to see her when she already has a therapist. Ms. Green might have a variety of reasons not to want to see her prior therapist anymore. Let her know that you cannot treat her *concurrently* with another therapist, but that, should she make the choice to end the treatment with her current therapist, you will consider working with her or making an appropriate referral to another clinician.

Note here that it is perfectly ethical for you to provide Ms. Green with a consultation session. However, unless there is a reason that would clearly indicate that it would be harmful for Ms. Green to return to her therapist—for example, when she tells you that her former therapist has attempted to have sex with her or the like, which is illegal—it is good practice to refer her back to her therapist to address whatever issues she might have with her or him.

More likely, you might find that Ms. Green has received therapy in the past. Try to get a sense of what this experience was like for her since it will color her expectations and initial experience of her therapy with you. You also might find yourself wanting to confer with her former therapist. In that case, you have to ask Ms. Green for a written release of information to be able to do so. However, I suggest that you wait until you have made your own assessment before contacting another clinician, since that person's input is liable to influence the way you experience Ms. Green. That is, information from a former therapist should be an *addition* to the impression you have received in your own assessment, not in lieu of it.

History of Violence and Trauma

Purpose: To collect information regarding the client's exposure to trauma, both as victim and/or as perpetrator.

How to Go about It: Please refer to the section on abuse issues regarding how to practically deal with violence and trauma.

There are many ways in which someone can be exposed to violence: in her family of origin; in her other relationships; as the victim or the perpetrator of assault, rape, or other trauma. Perhaps Ms. Green grew up in a country ravaged by war, or perhaps she lived in a gang environment. Perhaps Ms. Green herself was or is the perpetrator of violence. Ms. Green may have indicated earlier on that she has been exposed to violence, and if you did not pursue it, then you might now refer back to what she has told you. You might say something like this:

> "You told me earlier that your father used to beat your mother. Tell me more about this."
> "You indicated that your ex-boyfriend was 'mean' to you. Can you tell me a little more about it?"
> "You stated that your aunt used to touch you in ways that were uncomfortable to you. Can you be more explicit about this?"
> "You said that you 'let your lover have it.' What did that actually look like?" and so forth.

If this topic was not mentioned before, stay alert for an opportunity to bring it up. You might just say something like this: "Was there any violence (or abuse) in your family? In your past or current relationships?"

Be alert also for indications of Ms. Green's own potential for violence. Does she indicate that her relationships are stormy? Has she told you about slapping a lover or throwing dishes? Has she mentioned having been in a physical fight with anybody? Other indications might be her own substance abuse. People who are intoxicated might more easily engage in violent behavior than when they are sober.

Addictive Behaviors

Purpose: To collect information pertaining to addictive behaviors Ms. Green might engage in, including substance abuse, eating disorders, gambling, compulsive spending, sexual compulsions, and the like.

How to Go about It: Ask Ms. Green about her alcohol and drug intake. Does she drink? What does she drink, how often, and how much? Does she drink until intoxicated? Alone or with others? What is her view of her own drinking? Does she use drugs? Include prescription and illegal drugs. Which ones, how often, and how much? Has she had problems related to the drinking and/or drug use?
Ask if she can see an impact on any of the following areas:

- In her relationships (has she gotten into fights when intoxicated? Has she been asked to drink/use less? Has she lost a relationship because of her substance use?)
- In her work (has she been intoxicated at work? Has she been addressed at work regarding her substance use? Has she lost a job because of it? Has her performance been impaired?)
- In her physical health (has she been ill a lot? Has she ever been told that she should curb her substance use in order to improve her health? Has she noticed physical consequences because of her substance use?)

- Legal (does she have DUIs? Has she had other legal problems pertaining to her substance use?)

The answers to these questions will help you assess whether Ms. Green might have a substance abuse problem or not. If you diagnose a substance dependence, it is imperative that Ms. Green become clean and sober first. If you do work with her, a certain type of treatment is indicated—namely, supportive treatment for approximately the first year of sobriety. Insight-oriented, uncovering psychotherapy is contraindicated for a newly sober client since it will intensify the affect that the substance use is trying to numb and therefore is likely to precipitate relapse.[5]

There are other addictive behaviors besides substance use. Inquire after Ms. Green's eating patterns: Does she starve herself? Does she purge? Eating disorders can be understood as a manifestation of addictive behavior. Ongoing promiscuous behavior can be of an addictive nature, as well as gambling, compulsive buying, and self-mutilating behavior. For all of these behaviors, you can do a quick assessment following the outline given previously for substance abuse: Has there been an impact on relationships, on work, on physical health, legally? Generally, addictive behaviors are indicative of underlying personality problems and require particular attention in treatment.

Medical

Purpose: To collect information pertaining to Ms. Green's physical health to determine any impact it might have on her psychological well-being.

How to Go about It: Some of the information you elicit here might include psychiatric treatment—for example, current

---

[5]For an in-depth discussion on working with addicted persons, see Edward Kaufman, 1995, as well as Leon Wurmser, 1994 and 1987, and Joan Ellen Zweben, 1989.

treatment and current medications, as well as hospitalizations. If this is the case, you can elicit all the information pertaining to the next heading conjointly with the information regarding other medical treatment. It is for clarity's sake that I have separated these two topics here. In reality, psychiatric treatment *is,* of course, medical treatment.

Be explicit and direct. Ask about the following points:

- Current illness/disorder being treated by a physician.
- What type of physician, physician's name.
- Any prescribed medications she is currently taking (type, dosage, for how long), and if so, prescribed by whom?
- Any illness/disorder *not* currently treated by a physician (including HIV and AIDS).
- Any major illnesses in the past.
- Any major surgery in the past.
- Any hospitalizations in the past.

It will make a difference for your understanding of Ms. Green's depressive symptoms if she tells you she has had a recent abortion (surgical procedure). Likewise, if she tells you about hormone treatment she is receiving, you might consider whether her mood swings might be related to that. Overall, you are collecting data that will help you determine what the problem is, as well as the best course of treatment for Ms. Green.

Psychiatric

Purpose: To collect information regarding psychiatric treatment Ms. Green might have received in the past or in the present.

How to Go about It: Ask Ms. Green whether she is or has been in treatment with a psychiatrist, whether she has been hospitalized in a psychiatric hospital, and whether she has been prescribed psychotropic medications (like antidepressants, mood stabilizers, anxiolytica, or neuroleptics) in the past or currently. Be direct about these questions. If she has seen or is seeing a psychiatrist, ask what the reason is for her seeing this professional. Ask whether there is a formal diagnosis that she knows of. If she has or is currently taking psychotropic medications, ask for the names and dosages, as well as for the reasons why she is taking them.

This whole exchange might sound something like this:

"Are you currently taking any medications, including antidepressants and the like? You do? What are the medications? Who prescribed them? What are the reasons that you are seeing this doctor?"

"Are you currently or have you in the past seen a psychiatrist? You have? What were the reasons? Did or do you have a diagnosis that you know of? Are you taking medications that the psychiatrist prescribed? Or did you take such medications in the past? Do you feel they help you?"

"Have you ever been hospitalized, including in a psychiatric hospital? You have? When was that and what had happened that made the hospitalization necessary? Were you prescribed medications? Which ones? By whom? Are you still taking them? Are you still seeing this psychiatrist?"

You get the idea: be straightforward, open, and to the point with your questions, even though they might feel intrusive to you. This is the special situation of an anamnesis, and it is important that you get the relevant information accurately to be able to make a meaningful recommendation and plan treatment usefully.

If Ms. Green is currently seeing a psychiatrist, you might want to get a written release of information so that you can coordinate your treatment with the psychiatric treatment already established. It will behoove you in any case to establish a working relationship with her psychiatrist since what the psychiatrist does will impact your work and vice versa.[6]

If Ms. Green reports that she has been hospitalized in the past, depending on when this was and how acute it was, you might consider getting a written release of information for you to obtain hospital records. It will make a difference whether Ms. Green's hospitalization for a suicide attempt was fifteen years ago or one year ago. In the second case, you might want the hospital's documentation, as this might be helpful for your assessment and treatment planning. Likewise, if Ms. Green has a history of many hospitalizations, the need to obtain records or speak with a treating psychiatrist becomes more pressing.

On the other hand, you might find that you hear about symptoms that seem to indicate that she should be evaluated by a psychiatrist. This topic will be addressed both in the section "Mental Status Exam," as well as in Chapter 8, "Making a Recommendation."

Legal

Purpose: To collect information regarding Ms. Green's involvement with the legal system.

How to Go about It: This topic might have come up while you were collecting data for the other topics. If so, just pursue it as it arises. For example, if Ms. Green tells you that she frequently drinks, you might ask something like this: "Ever got in trouble with the law for this?"

Generally, you might ask for any convictions and time spent in jail or prison. Always ask to hear more about the reasons why. Be alert for those reasons that are being given; it makes a

---

[6]The topic of working with other professionals will be discussed under its own heading in Chapter 12.

difference for your recommendation and treatment planning whether someone tells you she is frequently in trouble because she steals compulsively, if someone tells you she has been in prison for aggravated assault, or if someone has been in jail once overnight to sleep off her alcohol intoxication. In the first case, you might be looking at someone with an impulse control disorder (more specifically, kleptomania), in the second case you might be dealing with a variety of topics (from antisocial personality disorder, to impulse control disorder, to a manic or a psychotic episode, to someone taking revenge into her own hands after having been raped, to a substance abuse problem, to name a few). In the third case you might be dealing with alcoholism. It should be clear that in any case, whatever the answer, you want to investigate further and use the information to formulate a diagnosis, make a recommendation, and devise a treatment plan.

MENTAL STATUS EXAM[7]

Part of your initial assessment will include conducting a Mental Status Exam. It is indispensable for making a diagnosis and a recommendation and devising a treatment plan.

Before I go into detail, I will give you a checklist for such a Mental Status Exam:

- ☐ General appearance
- ☐ Motoric behavior
- ☐ Attitude during interview
- ☐ Mood
- ☐ Affect
- ☐ Speech
- ☐ Perceptual disorders

---

[7]The following information is based on Kaplan and Sadock (1996), *Handbook of Clinical Psychiatry*, 2nd Edition, as well as on Zuckerman (1995), *Clinician's Thesaurus*, 4th Edition.

- [ ] Thought content
- [ ] Thought process
- [ ] Sensorium
- [ ] Memory
- [ ] Concentration and calculation
- [ ] Information and intelligence
- [ ] Judgment
- [ ] Insight

The Mental Status Exam will allow you to determine whether your client is actively psychotic, manic, or depressed, suicidal, or homicidal. It will indicate to you whether she should be seen by a psychiatrist for medication evaluation or by another physician to rule out an organic disorder. Ultimately, the Mental Status Exam will determine whether it is appropriate for you to work with this person at this time.

General Appearance

What You Are Looking for: Note how Ms. Green looks: her appearance, her dress, her grooming. Is she clean or does she appear unkempt? Does she look her stated age or does she look younger or older? How are her posture, her gestures, her facial expressions?

What It Means: You are looking here for physical indications of possible problems: stooped posture and frozen facial expression in depression; unkempt appearance in psychosis, depression, or substance abuse; and so forth.

Motoric Behavior

What You Are Looking for: Here you are observing Ms. Green's level of activity, the way she moves her body: Is there psychomotor retardation (slowing) or psychomotor agitation (speeding up), does she have tics or tremors, is there grimacing, does she mimick your movements and what you say, or is there an absence of movement? You also note her emotional appearance: Is she sad, happy, anxious, angry? You take note of the quality of her voice: Is it faint or loud? Soft or hoarse? And finally, you note the extent and quality of eye contact she gives you.

What It Means: Psychomotor retardation, including a faint voice, is commonly associated with depression; agitation and a loud voice may be associated with mania or stimulant use; tremors with anxiety; fixed posturing and odd behavior with schizophrenia; and tics and grimacing with tic disorders.

Attitude during Interview

What You Are Looking for: You are observing how your client relates to you: Is she short or angry with you? Is she seductive? Does she appear withdrawn, defensive, or guarded, or is she more indifferent, even apathetic? Does she respond sarcastically, or does she appear cooperative?

What It Means: Again, you correlate what you observe with certain pathology: suspiciousness may be linked to paranoia; apathy and withdrawal to depression or dementia; aggression and irritability might indicate either an agitated depression, mania, paranoia, or the use of certain substances.

Mood

What You Are Looking for: When we talk about mood, we are referring to a steady, long-term, underlying feeling state. That is, when you assess your client's mood, you are observing her sustained emotional state. Is she tense, resentful, hopeless, angry, happy, sad, exalted, euphoric, depressed, fearful, suicidal, grandiose, apathetic, or anhedonic? Kaplan and Sadock (1996, p. 14) suggest that you ask questions like the following:

"How do you feel?"
"How are your spirits?"

If she indicated feeling suicidal, assess her suicidality:

"Have you had thoughts of wanting to die?"
"Do you have plans to kill yourself?"

What It Means: Certain moods are associated with certain pathology. Euphoria and grandiosity are often seen in mania; sadness, anhedonia, and suicidal ideas accompany depression; anger, suspiciousness, fearfulness, and anhedonia are often seen in paranoia.

Affect

What You Are Looking for: Contrary to a person's mood (which is sustained), affect is a more momentary phenomenon, "a feeling tone associated with an idea" (Kaplan and Sadock, 1996, p. 14). Thus, a client's affect can be appropriate or inappropriate to content; it can be labile, flat, blunt, or it can be broad.

What It Means: In schizophrenia, you will sometimes see gross inappropriateness of affect (e.g., laughing uncontrollably in response to internal stimuli, when neither the external environment nor the general mood seems to warrant such behavior). Often, inappropriate affect to content indicates a conflicted area for the client that needs exploration. Note instances in which your client exhibits an affect that seems not to fit the described feeling-state; for example:

"This really makes me angry" while smiling.
"I am so happy" while appearing very angry.
"My mother just died" while laughing.
"I am so looking forward to my wedding" while crying.

Thus, when your client expresses one idea in words (content) but another in feeling-tone, it is worth exploring this discrepancy. Often in depression, your client will show you restricted or blunt affect (not expressing much, a "grayness" of affect). In schizophrenia, lability of affect is not uncommon (quick shifting among affective expressions, laughing one moment, getting angry the next, and so forth).

Speech

What You Are Looking for: You are observing your client's way of speaking. Is her speech slow or fast, pressured or stuttering, spontaneous, slurring, staccato, or stammering? Is her speech incoherent, does she speak in a stilted manner, is she mute? Is there paucity of speech or logorrhea? What are pitch and articulation like? Is there coprolalia (speaking in obscenities) or echolalia (mimicking your speech)?

What It Means: In depression, you may find paucity of speech and very slow speech. Perhaps your client is even mute (which may also indicate Selective Mutism). In mania, you often encounter pressured speech and logorrhea. Slurred speech might be indicative of organicity or substance intoxication (alcohol). Coprolalia may be indicative of a tic disorder (most notably Tourette's syndrome), while echolalia might indicate schizophrenia.

Perceptual Disorders

What You Are Looking for: Mainly, you are assessing whether your client is experiencing hallucinations (olfactory, auditory, tactile, gustatory, visual); illusions; feelings of unreality and deja vue. As suggested by Kaplan and Sacock (1996, p. 14), you might ask your client directly:

"Do you ever hear voices when you don't see anyone there?"
"Do you ever see things?"

What It Means: Auditory hallucinations may indicate schizophrenia. Visual hallucinations can be indicative of schizophrenia but can as well point to substance use (LSD, peyote). Tactile hallucinations suggest delirium tremens (DTs) or cocainism, while feelings of unreality or deja vue might be indicative of a dissociative disorder.

Thought Content

What You Are Looking for: You are assessing what your client is thinking about and screening for the different types of delusions: if she is suffering from *persecutory/paranoid* delusions, she'll express the idea that people want to harm her in some way. You might ask her directly: "Do you feel that people want to harm you?"

If she is having *grandiose* delusions, she will express the idea of having special powers like "I can read other people's mind" or "I am God" and so forth. She might be obsessed with the idea of *infidelity* of her spouse or partner, with *somatic and sensory* perceptions, complaining about strange body sensations. If she experiences *thought broadcasting*, she will tell you that others know what she is thinking, that she can hear her thoughts on the radio, and the like. In *thought insertion,* she will complain of having thoughts that are not her own but someone else's somehow inserted into her mind. She might exhibit *ideas of reference,* in which case she will be convinced that most everything has something to do with her (e.g., the show on TV really is a message to her; the woman in the waiting room has been waiting for her; when she was walking down the hallway she found a dime that was placed there for her to find; etc.).

Besides delusions, you are screening for obsessions (thoughts that your client can't get out of her mind and finds herself thinking over and over) and compulsions (acts or rituals compulsively performed, such as counting, hand washing, checking, usually performed to ward off what the obsessional thoughts are threatening), suicidal and homicidal ideation, flight of ideas (can't seem to stay with any one thought), idée fixe (fixated on one thought only), magical thinking (e.g., believes something happened because she thought it), nihilism (preoccupied with the end of the world), hypochondriasis (preoccupied with body aches and pains, illness and disease, despite medical evidence to the contrary), depersonalization (feeling of not being herself, of not knowing who she is), and derealization (feeling that the world is not real, that everything is as in a movie).

What It Means: You will find *mood-congruous delusions* (e.g., delusions of grandeur with elated mood; nihilistic ideas with depressed mood) in mood disorders, mania, or depression, respectively. *Mood-incongruous delusions* suggest schizophrenia, as do delusions concerning thought broadcasting, thought insertion, as well as ideas of reference. Obsessions and compulsions suggest obsessive-compulsive disorder, but are also often found with schizophrenia. Suicidal preoccupation suggests a depressive disorder; homicidal preoccupation may suggest a delusional disorder or schizophrenia. Derealization and depersonalization may point to a dissociative disorder.

Thought Process

What You Are Looking for: You are assessing the quality of your client's thought processes (Kaplan and Sadock, 1996, p. 15): Is she capable of goal-directed ideas? Does she seem to ramble? Does she have loose associations? Are her thoughts logical or illogical, tangential or relevant, circumstantial or to the point? Does she have the ability to abstract? Does she exhibit flight of ideas or perseverations?

What It Means: Flight of ideas and rambling might point to mania or stimulant intoxication, while loose associations and the inability to abstract may suggest schizophrenia. Irrelevant, tangential, and/or circumstantial speech might also point to schizophrenia.

Sensorium

What You Are Looking for: You are assessing your client for her level of consciousness. Is she alert or does she seem confused? Is her consciousness clear or does it appear clouded? Is she oriented to time, place, and person? In other words, does she know what the date is, where she is, and who you are? You might ask directly:

"What place is this?"
"Do you know who I am?"
"What is today's date?"

What It Means: Clouded consciousness is suggestive of delirium or dementia. Confusion can be caused by substance intoxication. Lack of orientation to time, person, and place might point to some form of psychosis.

Memory

Generally, you want to assess your client's memory (immediate, recent, and remote). Difficulties with these different types of memory suggest different pathologies. However, always make sure you rule out organic reasons for difficulties with memory.

Remote Memory (Long-Term Memory)

What You Are Looking for: You will be asking your client questions, eliciting answers related to events in the remote past (from approximately six months ago through all of the client's lifetime). You might ask:

"Where were you born?"
"Where did you grow up?"
"When did you get married?"
"What are your siblings' names?"

What It Means: Gaps in remote memory while recent and immediate memory is relatively intact (gaps for periods of time, especially childhood years) might indicate a dissociative disorder with amnesia for traumatic events. In dementia of the Alzheimer's type, remote memory is retained longer than recent and immediate memory.

Recent Past Memory

What You Are Looking for: You are assessing your client's memory of the recent past (the last few weeks up to approximately six months ago). Ask questions like the following:

"What did you do last weekend?"

"Where did you go on your last vacation?"
"What did you do during the last national holiday?"

What It Means: An inability to recall recent past memory might be indicative of dissociative disorder or a progressing dementia (moving from recent to past memory).

Recent Memory

What You Are Looking for: You will be assessing your client's recent memory (a period covering approximately the last week, including today's events). Questions to ask include:

"Where were you yesterday?"
"What did you do this morning?"
"What did you eat for dinner?"

What It Means: Gaps in recent memory might be indicative of a dissociative disorder. They might also suggest substance abuse with blackouts. In organic brain disease (e.g., Alzheimer's), memory loss progresses from recent to remote.

Immediate Memory (Short-Term Memory)

What You Are Looking for: You are testing the client's short-term memory. You might ask your client to remember three unrelated items, and then ask for these items after five minutes. Ask your client to repeat six digits forward, then backward.

What It Means: Great difficulty with short-term memory might indicate any one of the following (and therefore necessitates further investigation): organicity, dissociative disorder, anxiety, and/or substance use.

Concentration and Calculation

What You Are Looking for: You are assessing your client's ability to pay attention, her distractibility, and her ability to do simple math. You might ask her to count from 1 to 20 rapidly, or do a serial 7 test (subtract 7 from 100 and keep subtracting 7).

What It Means: You are trying to distinguish between organic disorder and depression and anxiety, all of which can seriously impact concentration.

Information and Intelligence

What You Are Looking for: You are evaluating your client's intelligence by assessing her use of vocabulary, level of education, and fund of knowledge. You might ask questions like the following:

"Who is the current president?"
"What is the biggest river of the United States?"
"How many states are there in the United States?"

However, check the level of education and whether English is the client's first language, as well as the client's nationality, before you draw any conclusions.[8]

What It Means: Use of very simple language and difficulties answering your questions might point to borderline intellectual functioning or mental retardation.

---

[8]This is something to be kept in mind for the whole Mental Status Exam.

Judgment

What You Are Looking for: You are assessing your client's ability to understand relationships between facts and to draw conclusions, as well as her response to social situations. You might ask questions like the following:

"What should you do if you find a wallet in the street?"
"What should you do before crossing the street?"
"Why do we have to put stamps on letters we mail?"
"Why shouldn't people smoke in bed?"

What It Means: In the following disorders, judgment is often impaired: organic brain disorder, schizophrenia, borderline intellectual functioning, and mental retardation, as well as substance intoxication.

Insight

What You Are Looking for: You are assessing your client's level of insight into her problem. Does she realize there *is* a problem? Does she deny her illness? Does she take responsibility or assign blame to outside factors? Does she recognize a need for treatment? Questions you might ask are:

"Do you think you have a problem?"
"Do you think you need treatment?"
"What are your plans for the future?"

What It Means: Insight is often impaired in the presence of the following disorders: psychosis, delirium, dementia, borderline intellectual functioning, and mental retardation.

8

MAKING A
PROVISIONAL
DIAGNOSIS

With the data you have collected, you are now able to make a provisional diagnosis. Your diagnosis will be provisional because you still have seen your client only a few times and your diagnosis might change with more information. However, you should have enough information now to have formed a first impression and to be able to categorize what you see in some way.

Making a diagnosis, then, means following a convention: to categorize data in a certain, agreed-upon way. Although this categorization will reveal some predictable difficulties that this particular client is most likely experiencing and may even indicate how this person experiences herself and others, while it will alert you to specific issues that you must attend to, and though it often suggests a particular treatment approach, it is important to keep in mind that the diagnosis is an artificial construct, a label first and foremost and not the person. It is your task to relate to the person, to work with the person, not the diagnosis.

There are different ways to make a diagnosis, according to the agreed-upon system of categorization. Diagnosing according to the DSM-IV[1] is widely accepted practice in the United States (and many other countries); this approach entails the collection of observable data (symptoms) and clusters them in syndromes or disorders. Many of these definitions are arbitrary, when, for example, to make a diagnosis of major depressive disorder a time requirement of two weeks of presence of symptoms has to be met. This might just as well have been three weeks, a month, or ten days as for that. Nothing about this time requirement of two weeks is inherent in the illness of depression. It is merely a convention—an agreement—to call this cluster of symptoms "depression" when it has been present for two weeks. Accordingly, the defining features of many diagnoses change with the system of categorization, and even within that system as it is updated. The major depression of the DSM-III of 1980 is not the major depressive disorder of the DSM III-R of 1987, and that in turn is not the major depressive disorder of the DSM-IV of 1994. The sufferer of the illness, however, is the same. And she would have been suffering whether diagnosed according to the DSM-III, DSM-III-R, DSM-IV, or according to another diagnostic system all together. Incidently, she would also have been suffering had she remained undiagnosed.

The most common way of diagnosing in the United States, then, is according to the convention of the DSM, currently the DSM-IV. However, other ways of diagnosing are better suited to help you understand the internal dynamics of your client, the inner world he is living in, as well as to give you some ideas and hypotheses as to the etiology of the disorder you see. To this end I will give you a short introduction to making a structural diagnosis based on Kernberg's structural interviewing technique.

---

[1] *Diagnostic and Statistical Manual of Mental Disorders*, 4th Edition.

Be aware that while every client will fall into one of Kernberg's categories of diagnosis, not every client will warrant a DSM-IV diagnosis.

A FEW WORDS ON THE DSM-IV DIAGNOSIS

The DSM has been translated into numerous languages and is used the world over. It is the most widely used diagnostic system in the mental health field at this time, and it is therefore imperative that you, too, know how to use it. Whatever you may think of the DSM, it can in effect be regarded as the common language among mental health practitioners. Thus, when you speak to your client's psychiatrist about your client's "depressive symptoms," you will both have an idea what kinds of data you are talking about. This language is also spoken by insurance agencies and government entities such as Social Security, which will request it to reimburse your efforts. Diagnosing according to the DSM will thus help you recognize what you see, will tell you about observable data, but will not tell you much about etiology and even less about understanding your client.

Do familiarize yourself with the content of the current DSM, at the time of this writing the DSM-IV.[2] To this end I have found to be very useful the newest edition of Kaplan and Sadock's *Pocket Handbook of Clinical Psychiatry*, which offers not only DSM-IV but also other defining criteria to diagnose, information on etiology, appropriate tests, epidemiology, pathology, course and prognosis, as well as offering brief introductions to various treatments of the disorders discussed.

The DSM-IV is a *multiaxial system.* This means that you are asked to categorize data along five diagnostic axes. These axes are as follows:

---

[2]I have found much value in the desk reference version of the DSM-IV for quick reference: *Diagnostic Criteria from DSM-IV*, APA, Washington, D.C. 1994.

Axis I   Clinical Disorders
             Other Conditions That May Be a Focus of Clinical
                Attention

Axis II   Personality Disorders
             Mental Retardation

Axis III   General Medical Conditions

Axis IV   Psychosocial and Environmental Problems

Axis V   Global Assessment of Functioning

While it is not always necessary to present your DSM diagnosis in the axial format, it is important that you are familiar with it.[3] For more information, peruse the literature mentioned.

SUGGESTIONS FOR REFERRALS BASED ON DSM DIAGNOSIS

I will now briefly address your course of action according to the more common DSM diagnoses you will make.

Generally speaking, whenever you make an Axis I diagnosis—that is, when you diagnose a major syndrome like schizophrenia, mood disorder, anxiety disorder, substance-related disorder, eating and sleep disorders, and the like—you should ask for the date when your client was last seen by a physician. If this date is more than a year ago and your client is not going for annual physical check-ups, consider a referral to a physician to that end. You want to make sure that you rule out organic causes for the symptoms you see.

When organic causes have been ruled out, consider having your client seen by a psychiatrist for medication evaluation.

In addition, always assess for suicidal and homicidal potential and act accordingly.

---

[3]See *DSM-IV* (1994), pp. 25–35.

In the following, I will list names of syndromes and appropriate actions to consider.

The Schizophrenias

Always refer your client to a psychiatrist for medication evaluation and medication management. She needs to be stable on antipsychotic medication if you are going to work with her at all. Moreover, with the new antipsychotic medication available, which is more effective and has fewer and less severe side effects, she has a better chance than ever of managing her symptoms.

Assess for suicidal or homicidal ideation and take steps as necessary.

Bipolar Disorder

Depending on the severity of his symptoms, refer your client to a psychiatrist for medication evaluation and management. Mood-stabilizers and antidepressants will help stabilize your client so that you can work with him. Be aware that your client might actually enjoy the mania (if he is in a manic phase when you see him) and might be resistant to seeing a psychiatrist until he enters a depressive phase. However, you will not be able to do meaningful therapeutic work with a client who is actively manic.

Assess for danger to self and others and take steps accordingly.

Major Depression

Depending on the severity of her symptoms, refer your client to a psychiatrist for medication evaluation and management. If

your client is so depressed that she cannot function, antidepressants might help her stabilize to a point where she can profit
better from her work with you.

Suicide being a great risk for depressed persons, assess suicidal potential (danger to others also must be assessed but is
usually not as great a threat) and take steps accordingly.

Anxiety Disorders

Depending on the severity of the symptoms (and the particular disorder), refer your client to a psychiatrist for medication
evaluation and management. This is particularly advisable for
a client suffering from OCD, in which case medication can be
very helpful. Other anxiety disorders may warrant medication
as well. Someone being crippled by panic attacks might feel a
lot safer with a PRN anxiolyticum available to him than he would
without it.

Usually, danger to self and others is not as great an issue in
anxiety disorders. However, especially with OCD, there may be
an obsessive preoccupation with violent thoughts. Assess carefully and take steps as necessary. If your client also suffers depressive symptoms, her potential risk for suicide is increased.
Assess and take steps.

Dissociative Disorders

Consider referring your client to a neurologist. Since dissociative disorders involve difficulties with memory and concentration, you want to make sure that there is no organic cause for
her symptoms. You might have to consider a referral to a psychiatrist as well, depending on the severity of depressive symptoms that are often present in persons suffering from a dissociative disorder.

Assess for danger to self and others (danger to self being more common) and take steps accordingly.

Eating Disorders

Depending on the severity of her symptoms, you must or you may refer your client to a physician for a physical exam. If your client is anorexic and severely underweight, she may even have to be hospitalized. In addition, a referral to a psychiatrist may be indicated if your client's concomitant depressive symptoms warrant it.

Starving oneself must certainly be seen as a danger to self. Depending on the severity of the symptoms, take steps accordingly.

Substance-Related Disorders

Depending on the severity of the symptoms, and depending on whether your client is actively using or clean and sober, consider a referral to a physician for a check-up. Substance abusers notoriously abuse their bodies and may very well need medical attention. You may also consider a referral to a psychiatrist for medication evaluation and management. If your client is newly clean and sober, do refer him to an appropriate 12-step group as an adjunct to therapy.[4]

Assess for danger to self and others (e.g., if your client is intoxicated and wants to drive his car, he is endangering himself as well as others. It is your responsibility to take reasonable steps to prevent it).

---

[4]It is important that you do not attempt expressive work with your client until he has approximately one year of sobriety. Work supportively with him; otherwise, the danger of overwhelming him with affect and consequent relapse is too great. This is where 12-step meetings can be of invaluable help.

Impulse-Control Disorders

Consider a referral to a psychiatrist for medication evaluation and management. Assess for danger to self and others and take appropriate steps.

Somatoform and Factitious Disorders

Refer your client to a physician for a medical check-up to rule out an organic disorder. Only if a physical illness is ruled out can you actually make this diagnosis. Consider a referral to a psychiatrist if concomitant depressive symptoms seem to warrant it. Assess for danger to self (rarely to others) and act accordingly.

Elimination Disorder

Refer your client for a medical check-up to rule out a physical cause for enuresis or encopresis. Particularly with enuresis in children, there might be a hormonal problem that a urologist can easily treat, rather than a psychological problem that would fall into your providence. However, even if there is a physical cause, you might still be helpful assisting your client to deal with the repercussions of the disorder.

STRUCTURAL DIAGNOSIS

The DSM is not the only way to diagnose a client, although it is the most widely used method today. Let me briefly introduce the concept of the *structural diagnosis*. Even though this is a rather theoretical chapter, I believe it will be useful in your practical work.

To make a structural diagnosis, we must assess whether a

client's internal organization (or structure) is psychotic, borderline, or neurotic (normal). Depending on the outcome of the assessment and the structural diagnosis, you can determine whether you will work with a particular client and which treatment modality to employ. Generally speaking and ideally, early on in your training you should not work therapeutically with clients whose personality organization you suspect to be borderline or psychotic. However, the reality is that trainees and interns tend to be employed in large numbers in agencies that work with greatly impaired clients. Do make sure that you receive adequate supervision and that you understand that working with such a population will inevitably give rise to pronounced countertransference feelings. I hope it will help to have a beginning understanding of such persons' ways of organizing their experience of the world and themselves in the world. You, the therapist, will be a part of their world and they will organize their experience of you accordingly.

The theoretical concepts pertaining to object relations development on which the ideas regarding structural diagnosis are based are discussed in Part III. Based on that development, we assume the existence of a continuum of experience/internal organization ranging from psychotic, over borderline, to neurotic or normal.

In the *psychotic* experience or personality organization, much of that experience is informed from the unmodified unconscious, the earliest, undifferentiated, "baby" experience. There is a poor delimination of self from others; that is, objects are not integrated, and the self is not experienced as distinct from others. Thus, the ability to distinguish between what is inside and what is outside the self is impaired (impaired reality testing).

In the *borderline* experience or personality organization, there is intact reality testing; that is, there is generally intact awareness of what is inside and what is outside the self. However, integration is not complete, and when the self or other is experienced as good (or as bad), there is no awareness and no room for ambivalence; that is, aspects of the self and other that are "not-good" (or "not-bad," respectively). Acknowledging these contradictory aspects (which are assumed to be unconscious) would threaten overwhelming anxiety. Thus, abrupt shifts in experiencing the self and others are necessary to prevent contradictory aspects from becoming conscious. This is accomplished by the employment of lower-level, or primitive, defenses.

In the *neurotic* or normal experience or personality organization, reality testing is intact. Object constancy has been achieved, that is, integrated images of the self and the objects are ambivalently held. Unconscious material is not experienced directly but in a form modified by well-functioning, higher-level defenses.

Kernberg devised a method to assess these three types of personality organization—that is, these three ways of experiencing the self and the world. In order to do so, he looks at a person's degree of identity diffusion, her type of defensive operations, as well as her capacity for reality testing.

We will now take a brief look at how to go about actually assessing a person's developmental level of personality organization, her defensive style within that level, as well as her level of reality testing. An understanding of these three dimensions will facilitate your making a treatment recommendation, as well as your treatment planning.[5] The following is based on Kernberg (1984) and Kernberg and colleagues (1989).

Degree of Identity Diffusion

The following symptoms indicate identity diffusion:

- Subjective experience of chronic emptiness
- Contradictory self-perceptions

---

[5]See Nancy McWilliams (1994), *Psychoanalytic Diagnosis: Understanding Personality Structure in the Clinical Process.*

- Contradictory behavior
- Impoverished and contradictory perceptions of others
- Inability to convey themselves and their significant interactions with others to an interviewer.

Kernberg and colleagues define identity diffusion (lack of identity integration) as "the lack of integration of the concept of the self or significant others" (Kernberg et al., 1989, p. 5). According to this group of clinicians, identity diffusion is reflected by:

- *Subjective experience of chronic emptiness:* Your client talks about being bored often; of feeling empty, despairing, as if in a black hole, alone; of not being able to find anything to do that holds his interest. Often, your client will tell you about great difficulties being alone.
- *Contradictory self-perceptions:* Your client tends to see herself as either "all good" or "all bad," "all happy" or "all sad," "totally alluring" or "totally repulsive," and so on, and is not able to bring these two concepts together. That is, when she talks about herself as "all bad" ("I am no good, I am a loser, I can't do anything right, everyone hates me, I am hateful"), she has no awareness of anything good about herself. When she experiences herself as "all good" ("I am brilliant, I really am successful, everyone loves me, I am the greatest") she doesn't seem to have any awareness or memory of anything "bad" about herself. These self-perceptions are often accompanied by severe mood swings (from depression to deep anxiety to furious anger to elation).
- *Contradictory behavior:* Your client reports (or exhibits) contradictory behavior that implies an unintegrated view of herself and others. For example, she exhibits despair over being unloved and unlovable one moment, professes her loneliness, and wonders why no one shows any interest in her, while, on the other hand, she shows elation the next

moment over having rebuked the advances of a suitor, with little understanding of how rebuking others can leave her lonely and feeling unloved.

- *Impoverished and contradictory perceptions of others:* Your client describes others in grossly contradictory terms so that it is virtually impossible for you to gain an understanding of the other person. Your client might describe someone as warm, loving, and understanding, that is, "all good" one moment, and then switch to portraying him as cold, uncaring, hurtful, and hateful, in other words, "all bad" the next moment.

- *Inability to convey themselves and their significant interactions with others to an interviewer:* This is closely related to the previous point, emphasizing the fact that you are not able to gain a clear picture, a coherent understanding about your client's interactions with others because what is related to you is so contradictory and chaotic.

In the *neurotic personality organization,* identity integration is achieved: self-representations and object representations are sharply delineated; contradictory images of self and others are integrated into comprehensive, ambivalently held conceptions.

In the *borderline personality organization,* identity diffusion is present: contradictory aspects of self and others are poorly integrated and kept apart (good self—bad self; good other—bad other).

In the *psychotic personality organization,* self-representations and object representations are poorly delineated. There is no awareness of separate self and others.

Type of Defensive Operations

The nature of a person's defensive organization is another defining factor for neurotic personality organization, on the one hand, and borderline and psychotic personality organization, on the other hand. Remember, defenses are employed to modify unconscious mental content in such a way that it can be allowed into consciousness without producing overwhelming anxiety.[6] Defensive operations can be either primitive (lower-level defenses) or advanced (higher-level defenses). The younger the child, or the less developmentally advanced the person, the more she will use lower-level defenses. The more mature and the more developmentally advanced the more she will employ higher-level defensive operations. I will now give you a list of both higher- and lower-level defenses.[7]

High-Level Defenses

Here belong repression, reaction formation, isolation, undoing, intellectualization, and rationalization.

- *Repression:* The withholding, forgetting, or expulsion of a feeling or an idea. It excludes from awareness what may once have been conscious. In this way, a person may be unaware of feelings that would be difficult to deal with, for example, of hatred toward her mother (see Moore and Fine 1990, p. 48).
- *Reaction Formation:* Changes an unacceptable feeling or idea to its acceptable opposite. For example, the feeling of hatred toward the mother might be changed into becoming overly concerned and solicitous, thus into an overt show of love for the mother.
- *Isolation:* Separates a painful idea or event from feelings associated with it. In this way, a person can have the thought of committing violence isolated from the feeling

---

[6]Please refer to the introduction of the concept of the Unconscious in Part III.

[7]I have based the following definitions for defensive operations on Moore and Fine (1990), *Psychoanalytic Terms and Concepts.*

of anger, the thought of having been left by one's lover isolated from the feeling of despair, and so forth. The result is that the thought appears alien to the person; since it is isolated from feelings, there seems to be no intent inherent in the thought, and no action following it, because it is deprived of its motivational force.

- *Undoing:* The conscious "removal" of an offensive act by atoning for it. In this case, a client may habitually commit transgressions (e.g., aggressive or sexual) and then try to undo them by self-punitive measures.

- *Intellectualization:* As in isolation, ideas are separated and isolated from their affects through intellectualization of the idea and avoidance of the affect. In this way, the potentially offensive idea is allowed into consciousness but does not have any emotional impact. A client using intellectualization might be discussing sexual practices in a highly intellectual and abstract way, perhaps even alluding to her own sexual practices as an example of it, but clearly keeping any affect attached to this topic isolated from the idea of it. Thus, you will not get a sense of what her own sexuality means to her and how she experiences it, and any conflicts she may be experiencing are thus kept at bay.

- *Rationalization:* Subjectively reasonable, conscious explanations are used to justify certain actions and attitudes, while the client unconsciously conceals other unacceptable motivations. In distinction to intellectualization, rationalization does *not* allow the objectionable ideational content into awareness (see Moore and Fine, 1990, p. 160). Thus, a client might tell you she really cannot have her sister stay at her home while she is in town because her apartment is too small for comfort, and she can't get around to clean up anyway because she is so busy, when unconsciously she is very angry at her sister and does not want her to stay over. Thus, through rationalization, she justifies her not having her sister stay at her house without having to confront the unacceptable motivation of her anger.

Overall, these high-level defenses serve the purpose of protecting the client from intrapsychic conflict. Interpretation of the defenses improves functioning in the neurotic (or normal) personality organization.

According to Kernberg and colleagues (1989, pp. 5–6) and Kernberg (1984, p. 20) *neurotic personality organization* centers on these more advanced, *high-level defensive operations*.

Lower-Level Defenses

Borderline and psychotic personality organization, on the other hand, utilizes *primarily primitive defenses.* Such primitive or lower-level defensive operations are the following: splitting, primitive idealization, projective identification, and denial, as well as omnipotence and devaluation.

- *Splitting:* The self and others are divided into "all good" and "all bad" and experienced thus, so that there are "sudden and complete reversals of all feelings and conceptualizations about one's self or views about a particular person" (Kernberg et al., 1989, p. 6).
- *Primitive idealization:* This is the tendency to see external objects as all good, the inability to tolerate any common defects, the need to preserve the image of the other as perfect. The flip-side of this defense is devaluation.
- *Projective identification:* Projection centered on splitting, where the split-off (usually "bad") part is being projected onto the other, while still being experienced in the self. This usually results in fear of the other person who is being perceived as motivated by the projected impulse (e.g., if your client is angry at you because you took a vacation but, because of a need for primitive idealization, cannot

admit that you have failed her through your absence, she may resort to projecting this anger on you. Now, she is experiencing you as angry with her and might accuse you of this. She might even act in ways that *make* you angry— e.g., she might be late, not show up without canceling, and the like—actually eliciting the very affect that she had projected onto you.)

- *Denial:* The presence of two emotionally independent areas of consciousness, when your clients are "aware that their perceptions, thoughts and feelings about themselves or others at some time are completely opposite those entertained at other times, but this recognition has no emotional relevance and cannot influence their current state of mind" (Kernberg et al., 1989, pp. 7f). For example, your client may calmly tell you that he is aware of the dangers inherent in his promiscuous, sexual behavior, but this awareness does not induce any anxiety or result in changed behavior.

- *Omnipotence and devaluation:* These relate to splitting operations, with a "highly inflated, grandiose self relating to depreciated, emotionally degrading representations of others" (Kernberg, 1984, p. 17). You might hear your client talk about most people in his life as incapable, stupid, losers, underachievers, and so on, while he portrays himself as the only one who really knows what he's doing, as intelligent, dynamic, a winner.

In *borderline personality organization,* these primitive or low-level defenses serve the purpose of protecting the client from intrapsychic conflict (similar to the way high-level defenses are being utilized by neurotics). Interpretation of these defenses improves the client's immediate functioning by integrating the ego.

In *psychotic personality organization,* these same primitive defenses serve the purpose of protecting the client from disintegration and self/object merging. Interpretation of the defenses leads to regression and deterioration of ego functioning. Thus, the client's reaction to your interpretation of her defenses yields important diagnostic information.

Capacity for Reality Testing

Capacity for reality testing is another defining feature for personality organization according to Kernberg. He states: "Reality testing is defined by the capacity to differentiate self from non-self, intrapsychic from external origins of perceptions and stimuli, and the capacity to evaluate realistically one's own affect, behavior, and thought content in terms of ordinary social norms" (Kernberg, 1984, p. 18).

Impaired reality testing is indicative of psychotic personality organization, while intact reality testing points to either borderline or neurotic/normal personality organization, depending on the assessment of the previously discussed two defining features. Symptoms indicative of impaired reality testing are hallucinations and delusions; grossly inappropriate or bizarre affect, thought content, or behavior; as well as absence of capacity to empathize with and clarify other people's observations of oneself.

Reality testing is clinically recognized by:

- *Absence of hallucinations and delusions:* You have assessed for the presence of hallucinations and delusions when you conducted a mental status exam.
- *Absence of grossly inappropriate or bizarre affect, thought content, or behavior.* You have assessed for these in your mental status exam as well.
- *Capacity to emphasize with and clarify other people's observations of what seem to them inappropriate or puzzling aspects of the client's affects, behavior, or thought content within the context of*

ordinary social interactions. Let's say your client is telling you about her mother's death, expressing how sad this makes her while she is giggling. When you make a statement regarding this fact, your client should be able to empathize with your observation. For example: "You tell me that you are sad about your mother's death, yet you are laughing. Can you see how this seems incongruous to me?"

You see impaired reality testing when your client is unable to respond appropriately to such an observation. For example, he might deny the observation: "What do you mean? I am not laughing!" or he might become angry or paranoid.

In *neurotic personality organization,* the capacity to test reality, as defined earlier, is preserved.

In *borderline personality organization,* while there may be alterations in the relationship with and feelings of reality, the capacity to test reality is preserved as well.

It is in the *psychotic personality organization* that the capacity to test reality is lost.

Generally (and simplifying), we can say that clients with a psychotic personality organization tend to have issues related to the earliest time of infancy, clients with a borderline personality organization tend to have issues related to the first three years or so (Mahler's phase of separation-individuation), and clients with a neurotic personality organization tend to have issues stemming from childhood past the age of 3. This gives you some idea as to the specific problems your client might be facing. Quite apart from a specific theory, which will determine much of what you will see as the central difficulty, you will see that in infancy problems have to do with the experience of being fed, of being held, of having had a stable primary caregiver, and of generally having been taken care of adequately. Later, the main issues might have to do with having had the opportunity to express anger, to do things on your own, to explore your world, and generally to become more independent. Issues after age 3 or so tend to have to do with triads (mother, father, child), competition, and jealousy.[8]

Practical Tips

How do you assess for these three components: capacity for reality testing, level of defensive operations, and identity diffusion?

In practice, you will not assess for these issues separately but will gather your information through observations made as you take a detailed history and mental status examination. In fact, you will use the same information but will interpret it in a different way.

You will collect information regarding preferred *defenses* by paying close attention to what information your client presents and how she presents it, particularly information related to family of origin and relationships with others, as well as information regarding sexuality. Does she primarily use higher-level or lower-level defenses, and which ones in particular? Thus, when you find your client consistently using splitting in her way of describing herself and others, you will make an interpretation of this preferred defense and observe her reaction to it. Your interpretation might sound something like this: "I notice that you are describing your father as warm and understanding, on the one hand, and as really cold and neglectful, on the other hand. I get the feeling that when you see him as cold and hurtful, you forget that there is anything good about him."

If she is organized on a borderline level, she will be able to consider this interpretation or even acknowledge it, whereas should she be organized on a psychotic level, she might become agitated, paranoid, and generally regress and decompensate.

---

[8]For more information on why this is so, see Margaret Mahler's Developmental Model.

You will get information regarding *reality testing* formally through your mental status exam and informally through all other information your client gives you. If your client does not know where she is and why, if she shows bizarre thought content, labile affect, and seems to respond to internal stimuli, you are faced with impaired reality testing.

You will elicit information on *identity diffusion* by taking your client's history. Pay close attention to how your client talks about herself and others and consider the information in light of what I have described previously.

SUGGESTIONS FOR REFERRALS BASED ON STRUCTURAL DIAGNOSIS

Referrals to other professionals based on structural diagnosis are not as clear-cut as when you have a DSM-IV diagnosis. Therefore, I will in the following make a brief suggestion as for referral according to personality organization and then briefly list DSM-IV diagnoses that might correspond to psychotic, borderline, or neurotic personality organization, respectively. Once you have assessed a person's personality functioning, please consider which DSM-IV diagnoses might be present and refer accordingly.

Psychotic Personality Organization

Always consider a referral to a psychiatrist when you find psychotic personality organization. Your client's reality testing is impaired, she is impulsive, she operates on lower-level defenses, and she lacks stability. Psychotropic medications might be very helpful to stabilize her to a point where your work with her can be more meaningful.

In the presence of psychotic personality organization, please always consider the presence of the following DSM-IV Axis I diagnoses for other referrals (see "Suggestions for Referrals Based on DSM Diagnosis" in this chapter):

- Schizophrenias
- Other psychotic disorders
- Mood disorders
- Dissociative disorders
- Anxiety disorders (particularly PTSD)
- Substance-related disorders
- Somatoform disorders

Borderline Personality Organization

Depending on the severity of the client's symptoms, you might want to consider a referral to a psychiatrist when you find borderline personality organization as well. If symptoms are more severe, your client might have occasional difficulties with reality testing, perhaps have transient psychotic episodes, or he might be very depressed, just to name a few possibilities. If that is the case, he could benefit from medication in the same way that a person with psychotic personality organization could.

Please always consider the following DSM-IV Axis I diagnoses for further referrals:

- Psychotic disorders
- Mood disorders
- Dissociative disorders
- Anxiety disorders
- Substance-related disorders
- Somatoform disorders
- Eating disorders

Neurotic Personality Organization

Even in a neurotic personality organization, you might occasionally consider a referral to a psychiatrist or other professional, depending on severity of symptoms and your clinical judgment. If your client is very depressed, suffering from OCD, a panic disorder, an eating disorder, or the like, medication might be indicated to supplement your treatment.

Consider the following DSM-IV Axis I diagnoses for further referrals:

- Substance-related disorders
- Mood disorders
- Anxiety disorders
- Somatoform disorders
- Eating disorders
- Dissociative disorders

MAKING A TREATMENT RECOMMENDATION

With all the information you have collected, you are now ready to make a treatment recommendation. Again, keep in mind that you will probably not be able to do this after your first meeting with your client, since it will take you a while to get enough information to make a considered recommendation.

Recommending Treatment with Another Therapist

This will be the first decision that you will have to make, based on the information that you have gathered: Will you actually work with this person or is it more appropriate to refer her to another clinician? You will not make this decision alone at this point in your training, but in conjunction with your clinical supervisor.

There are many reasons why you may end up not working with a particular person: perhaps you and/or your supervisor feel that you do not have enough training regarding a particular problem, perhaps you find that you are struggling with countertransference issues that cannot be quickly resolved, or perhaps you have come across information as you conduct your history and mental status exam that indicate that you are not the therapist best suited to treat her, to name only a few. If you have decided, for whatever reason that you will not be working with Ms. Green, you must now let her know about it. To that end, you might say something like the following:

> "After doing the assessment, it has become clear to me that I am not the therapist who can best help you. Let me refer you to someone who I think will be better able to treat you."
> "I am not the therapist best suited to work with you. Let me refer you to a colleague."
> "My provisional diagnosis is that you are suffering from schizophrenia. I recommend that you work with my colleague, Ms. Z, since she specializes in this area."

Be aware that, whatever your reasons, this will most likely be experienced as a rejection by Ms. Green. She has formed a connection with you, has been expecting to work with you, and will most likely not like the idea of being referred. She might want an explanation as to why you are not going to work with her.

It will depend on the reason for the referral whether you will explain more in depth to Ms. Green why you are referring her. That is to say, if the reason involves the fact that you lack training, experience, or knowledge to treat her, feel free to let her know. You might say something like this: "My initial diagnosis shows that you are suffering from severe depression. That is not one of the areas that I am experienced in treating, so I would not be the best therapist to help you. Let me refer you to a colleague who is experienced with this issue and who will be better able to help you."

If, on the other hand, your reason for referral involves countertransference issues, do *not* go into detail so as not to burden your client with the knowledge that she is "too much" for you. For example, you might find yourself extremely anxious with a particular client because she is rather hostile and you have great difficulties dealing with aggression in others. After consulting with your supervisor, the two of you come to the conclusion that you need to address your issues regarding hostility with your therapist before you can work with a client who is overtly hostile. The client does not need to know all of these issues. Let her know, as in the case described previously: "Given your issues and my level of training, I am not the therapist best suited to help you. Let me refer you to a colleague who will be better able to help you."

If she wants to know more, restrict your reasons to the fact that it is *your lack of training and experience* that prompts the referral to a more experienced therapist, who will be better able to work with her. Do not go into detail regarding *your* feelings.

As I have mentioned earlier, you will have started this assessment period by letting Ms. Green know that it *is* an assessment period. You have told her to come in so that you can get a sense of each other and you can collect information that will tell you whether you are the therapist best suited to work with her. You might now refer back to that conversation, if indicated.

It is possible that Ms. Green will now become angry or tearful. She is entitled to have an emotional reaction to the fact that you will not be working with her when she expected you to. Acknowledge her feelings and reiterate that you have her best interest at heart, that you want her to get the best treatment available, and that you will not be the one providing it.

If you have a particular therapist in mind, ask her for a release of information so that you can call that therapist and arrange for a smooth transition.

If you don't have anyone particular in mind, give her three referrals.

Perhaps Ms. Green states that she does not want to see anyone else and that she will pass on therapy. Make your treatment recommendation, that is, reiterate that you recommend that she pursue treatment and give her three referrals. It is your responsibility to make such a recommendation and give referrals, but it is *not* your responsibility to see to it that she follows your recommendation.

In either case, you may want to follow up the recommendation and referral in writing with a letter to her, listing your referrals.

Treatment with You as the Therapist

If you have decided that you will work with Ms. Green, it is now time to enter into a treatment contract. This contract will contain the mutual decision to work together, will be based on the information in the written informed consent form, and will contain any other issues that you deem necessary. For example, if Ms. Green has told you about a history of suicide attempts, your treatment contract might contain the provision that she will be hospitalized if and when she feels seriously suicidal, and that it is her responsibility to let you know about this. If she has been prescribed medication to help her deal with her depression but is not taking her medication, with the result of frequent suicide attempts—clearly a way of sabotaging her treatment—you might make treatment contingent upon her taking her medication as prescribed. In that way, you hold Ms. Green responsible for her part of the treatment process and you are able to refer back to the provisions made in the contract.[9]

---

[9]See Kernberg et al. (1989), p. 25ff.

This is also the time to establish treatment goals with your client. Those goals will be part of the contract. If you feel that Ms. Green should be seeing another professional in addition to working with you, you might make this part of the contract as well. For example, you might state that in order for you to be able to treat her, you request that she see a psychiatrist for a medication evaluation, a neurologist to rule out an organic basis for her symptoms, an internist for a complete medical check-up, and so forth.

Usually, a treatment contract will be set informally. If you do not work with seriously mentally ill clients, suicide attempts, hospitalizations, and medications will not be a part of the contract. In that case, it will most likely consist of a verbal agreement to work together and a first explication of treatment goals.

However, if you do work with more seriously disordered clients, the contract might look something like this:

> Based on the information contained in the Informed Consent Form, we are deciding to work together on the following issues: . . . , with the goal to . . . It is Ms. Green's responsibility to take her medications as prescribed. If she does not do so, treatment will be terminated until such a date when she resumes her medication, at which time there will be an evaluation to resume treatment.

It is up to you whether you want to formalize this treatment contract in writing, or whether you are comfortable doing it verbally. Whichever way you choose, it is very important that you adhere to the content of the treatment contract, since it is part of the frame you set. Thus, if the treatment contract contains the stipulation that Ms. Green must take her medication as prescribed, you may not ignore the fact that she has stopped taking it if you want to provide a consistent and trustworthy frame and thus be able to do meaningful work with her.

Also at this time you should give Ms. Green some information regarding how therapy works, as well as what is expected of her as the client and of you as the therapist respectively. For example, working psychodynamically, you will tell her that part of her responsibility, besides coming to her sessions and paying for them, will be to tell you all that is on her mind and keep you informed of all relevant issues going on in her life. Let her know that it is your responsibility to be there for her sessions, listen to her, and make interpretations (or statements) when you feel you have something useful to say. Tell her that psychodynamic psychotherapy is a long-term process and might take months to years. Give her a basic idea, in lay terms, of what the two of you will do together in therapy. There is no reason that therapy should be shrouded in mystery.

If you find it difficult to explain to Ms. Green what therapy will entail, address this with your supervisor. She or he will help you formulate for yourself what the therapeutic work is about so that you can talk to your client about it.

Recommending Consultation with a Physician/Psychiatrist/Neurologist

As mentioned previously, you might find it necessary to refer Ms. Green to another professional in adjunct to or as a prerequisite to your work with her.

Referral to a Physician

The most common referral will be that to a *physician* for a complete physical check-up. Your rule of thumb here is that if your prospective client has not seen a physician for a check-up within the last year, she should be referred for one. This is good clinical practice, since many organic disorders may express themselves with psychiatric symptoms, on the one hand, while, on the other hand, many psychiatric disorders can be aggravated or influenced by physical disorders. You may want to let Ms.

Green know the following: "Since you told me that you haven't been for a physical check-up in five years, I want you to see a doctor and get a check-up. This is necessary so we can be sure that you are physically healthy and your symptoms do not stem from anything organic."

Make sure that you have a release of information to obtain the results of the physical examination from the doctor.

Thus, one reason to refer Ms. Green to a physician for an exam is if she has not seen a physician in more than a year. Other reasons have to do with specific complaints that warrant ruling out an organic disorder, particularly since some organic disorders mimic psychiatric disorders. For example, if Ms. Green complains of symptoms of anxiety (heart palpitations, tightness of the chest, difficulties breathing, gastrointestinal distress), you should refer her for a physical to rule out heart problems or gastrointestinal problems like an ulcer before you diagnose an anxiety disorder.

I will give you here a *list of psychiatric diagnoses that always warrant a physical check-up:*

- *Anxiety disorders* (including panic attacks): To rule out heart or gastrointestinal problems.
- *Depression* (particularly atypical depression with increased sleeping): To rule out chronic fatigue syndrome or an infection.
- *Dementia:* Since all dementias are organically based.
- *Eating disorders:* To assess physical health, level of malnutrition, and aid in treatment planning.
- *Elimination disorders (enuresis and encopresis):* To rule out urological or proctological disorders.
- *Factitious disorders:* To rule out an organic basis.
- *Learning disorders and attention deficit hyperactivity disorder:* To rule out an organic basis.
- *Pervasive developmental disorders:* To ascertain the extent of organic damage, if any, and aid in treatment planning.

- *Sexual disorders:* To rule out an organic basis and aid in treatment planning.
- *Sleep disorders:* To rule out an organic basis or component.
- *Somatoform disorders:* To rule out an organic basis.
- *Substance abuse disorders:* To ascertain physical damage and to aid in treatment planning.

Overall, the aim of referring a client to a physician for a check-up is to rule out an organic component or cause to the symptoms you see. Thus, what might appear as a panic disorder could really be a mitral-valve prolapse (a heart disorder) that you are not qualified to treat. Such a client might benefit from working with you on the impact this heart disorder has on her life, but you clearly cannot treat the heart disorder itself. If, on the other hand, you have a client who has an eating disorder, you *can* usefully treat this client while she is under medical supervision at the same time. She might even have to be hospitalized in a medical (as opposed to a psychiatric) hospital to be intravenously fed if her weight drops too dramatically.

Referral to a Psychiatrist

You might also find yourself referring a client to a *psychiatrist* for medication evaluation. Many psychiatric disorders have a biological-genetic component and symptoms can be greatly alleviated with psychotropic medication. Let your client know something along those lines: "My provisional diagnosis is . . . This is a disorder that can often be substantially helped with medication in addition to psychotherapy. I will therefore refer you to a psychiatrist who can evaluate whether you might benefit from such medication. If you do, it will make our work together easier as well."

Be aware of the stigma that is often attached to "seeing a psychiatrist." Many people are very afraid of seeing a psychiatrist, not only because of what "others might think" but also because they are often afraid of what that says about them. It is worthwhile to explore with your client what your suggestion for her to see a psychiatrist means to her. You might find that she is terrified of "being crazy," and it might take several sessions' work (sometimes lasting from weeks to even months) for her to consent to follow your recommendation.

Here is a list of *diagnoses that should prompt you to refer your client to a psychiatrist.*

On a structural level, clients whom you suspect are functioning in the psychotic continuum should be referred to a psychiatrist. DSM-IV diagnoses to refer to a psychiatrist are the following:

- *Anxiety disorders (including phobias and OCD):* Depending on severity. Anxiety can be mild or debilitatingly severe. Your client might be greatly helped with an anxiolyticum.
- *Depression:* Depending on severity. Your client's base-mood might be raised with an antidepressant and your work could become more meaningful. A client with mild depression might not need medication, while a suicidally depressed client most certainly should be assessed for medication. Some depressions clear up completely with antidepressants.
- *Bipolar disorder:* Your client might become stable and mood swings might abate with a mood-stabilizer. You *cannot* achieve this effect with psychotherapy alone.
- *Schizophrenias and psychotic disorders:* Your client's thought processes might be cleared up with antipsychotic medications. You *cannot* achieve this effect with psychotherapy.
- *Tic disorders:* Tics, especially in Tourette's syndrome, can often be helped with psychotropic medication.
- *ADHD:* Can often be substantially helped with medication.

The overall aim of referring your client to a psychiatrist is to assess whether she can be helped with psychotropic medication in order to alleviate her symptoms. Such medication is most often an adjunct, not an alternative, to psychotherapy. Thus, you should always obtain a written release of information so that you can confer with the psychiatrist regarding your client. Ideally, you and your client's psychiatrist will work together. If possible, try to establish a relationship with a psychiatrist in your area and work with her or him as consistently as you can, since this will greatly facilitate your as well as the psychiatrist's work and is ultimately in your client's best interest.

Referral to a Neurologist

Finally, you might need to refer your client to a *neurologist* to determine the origin of certain symptoms—that is, either to ascertain that certain symptoms are not resulting from any damage to the brain or to ascertain the extent of such damage. Again, let your client know your concerns and be clear about your recommendation: "My provisional diagnosis is . . . The symptoms of this diagnosis are often similar to symptoms caused by some organic reason, by something not functioning correctly in the brain. Since I am not a neurologist, I cannot make sure what the cause of your symptoms is. I will therefore refer you to a neurologist who can find out for us, so that we can make sure that you will receive the appropriate treatment."

Again, be aware that your client might be afraid of seeing a neurologist. You might have to work with her on this issue for a while before she can follow your recommendation.

In the following I list *disorders that contain symptoms the origin of which might have to be determined by a neurologist:*

- *Amnesias:* To rule out the organic nature of such symptoms.
- *Dissociative disorders:* To rule out the organic nature of symptoms of cognitive difficulties, including memory.
- *Severe depresssive symptoms:* Particularly in the case of cogni-

tive difficulties (difficulties concentrating, difficulties with memory).

- *Tic disorders:* To rule out an organic origin of symptoms.
- *Psychotic symptoms* (like hearing voices, smelling odors, feeling touch) in the absence of full criteria for schizophrenia or a psychotic disorder: To rule out the organic nature of such symptoms.
- *Any history of head trauma:* To determine whether symptoms are related to head trauma and are thus organically based. This means that, whenever there is a history of head trauma in the presence of any psychiatric symptoms, the possibility of the symptoms being linked to the head injury must be taken into consideration and determined by a neurologist.

Again, obtain a written release of information so that you can confer with the neurologist as to her findings and to facilitate treatment planning.

Recommending Hospitalization

You might find yourself in the situation where you have to recommend hospitalization. Perhaps Ms. Green is suicidally depressed, perhaps she is actively psychotic and unable to care for herself, or perhaps she is suffering from anorexia nervosa and appears dangerously underweight. In none of these cases will you be able to begin work in the office with Ms. Green immediately. If you recommend hospitalization as part of your work with Ms. Green, you might want to make this hospitalization part of the treatment contract. This means, you state that in order for the two of you to work together, Ms. Green must first agree to be hospitalized. If she does not agree, treatment will not take place. On the other hand, even if you will not treat Ms. Green or if she refuses to be hospitalized, you are not free from the responsibility of keeping Ms. Green safe and of taking reasonable steps to do so. Thus, you might find that you will have to initiate an involuntary hospitalization if the severity of her symptoms warrants it.[10]

Unless you feel that it would put your client, yourself, or someone else in danger, explain to Ms. Green what you are doing. Let her know: "You are so ill that you should be in the hospital. Before we can begin our work together, you need to be stable enough to benefit from that work. Therefore, I recommend that you be hospitalized for a while until you are feeling better."

If Ms. Green is not delusional, she will most likely be able to see your point. Again, be aware that Ms. Green will probably be anxious about going to the hospital, particularly if you are suggesting a stay in a psychiatric hospital. Allow her to express her thoughts and feelings regarding these fears. However, if in your clinical judgment a hospitalization is necessary, do not under any circumstances let her talk you out of it. Show understanding of her fears but remain firm.

If Ms. Green has a psychiatrist she is working with, obtain a release of information and try to contact the psychiatrist to work with Ms. Green regarding a hospitalization. If you cannot reach her psychiatrist, leave a message regarding your actions. If Ms. Green will be your client, obtain a written release of information once she has been stabilized so that you can follow her treatment in the hospital and plan your continuing treatment accordingly. Please note that you will *not need a release of information to initiate an involuntary hospitalization.*

Recommending Detoxification and Drug Treatment

Drug or alcohol detoxification can be seen as a subtype of hospitalization. If Ms. Green is dangerously addicted, this might

---

[10]I will address the topic of an involuntary hospitalization in Chapter 11.

be the recommendation of choice. Detoxification is usually not done on an ambulatory basis, and a follow-up in a drug or alcohol rehabilitation center (or rehab center) might be indicated. If you choose to work with a recovering substance abuser, make sure that you receive adequate training and supervision.

Let Ms. Green know what your recommendation is: "You appear dangerously addicted and I recommend that you be hospitalized for a detoxification. Unless this is accomplished, we will not be able to work together."

Again, as stated earlier, if you are going to work with the client who is thus referred for detoxification and/or rehabilitation, obtain a written release of information so that you can obtain information that will be crucial for treatment planning.

9

HIERARCHY OF PRIORITIES IN TREATMENT[1]

Otto Kernberg and colleagues (1989) have devised a list of thematic priorities in treatment that is useful for work with all clients and will be valuable to help guide your work regarding which issues to address and when. For most topics I will give brief examples. More information on how to address practical issues will be presented in the following chapters.

The interventions suggested here will be readily understandable for all beginning therapists, even without any training in psychodynamic psychotherapy. However, to effectively address these issues in treatment, you should have some familiarity with making interpretations. Since this book does not cover an introduction to making interventions, please ask your teachers and supervisor to help you with this.[2]

In the following, topics are listed in descending order of importance as presented by Kernberg and colleagues (1989,

---

[1]This chapter rests heavily on Kernberg et al. (1989), pp. 54ff.

[2]See also Stark (1999), *Modes of Therapeutic Action,* regarding a lucid presentation of how to make different types of psychoanalytically oriented interventions.

pp. 54ff). That means, if Ms. Green at any given time addresses several issues pertaining to different topics in the list of thematic priority, you know to address the topic of higher thematic priority first, before addressing the other topics in order of importance.

HIERARCHY OF THEMATIC PRIORITY

1. *Suicide or Homicide Threats*
   It is obvious that if your client endangers her own or others' lives and makes a suicide or homicide threat, you must attend to this above all other issues. In fact, you have a legal obligation to do so.

2. *Overt Threats to Treatment Continuity (e.g., financial difficulties, plans to leave town, requests to decrease session frequency)*
   If your client leaves treatment, all other issues become moot. Therefore, if your client begins to speak of moving away, seems to be experiencing financial difficulties that might result in his inability to pay for treatment and thus possibly the end of treatment, if he wants to decrease frequency of sessions and is thus in fact moving to more distance and possibly preparing to end the treatment, this issue takes precedence over all following. What this means is that you will *address* these issues with your client, direct his attention to them, and explore their meaning. It does *not* mean that you will try to make sure that a certain outcome is reached.

3. *Dishonesty or Deliberate Withholding in Sessions (e.g., lying to the therapist, refusing to discuss certain subjects, silences occupying most of the sessions)*
   When you first started working with your client, you let her know that it was her responsibility to tell you all that was on her mind and to keep you informed of important developments in her life to the best of her ability. You

might begin to realize that she is deliberately withholding important information (e.g., she has been arrested for drunk driving and is facing her second DUI), outright lying to you (e.g., telling you she is employed when she is not), refusing to discuss certain issues that are relevant to her treatment (e.g. she just lost her job but refuses to talk about how she is planning to support herself, including paying for treatment), or sitting in silence during most of the session (refusing to speak when you address her, remaining stubbornly and angrily silent. This must be distinguished from your client being catatonically depressed or psychotic, in which case she has no control over the silence.) Any of these issues should be brought up immediately with your client. Thus, if she has lied to you regarding her employment, address this issue with her as soon as you find out. Do not collude with her dishonesty. It is important to say something like the following: "It has come to my attention that you lost your job a month ago. Now you have repeatedly assured me that you are still employed, which means that you have been lying to me. When we started treatment, you agreed that in order for me to help you, you would keep me informed about important developments in your life. In lying to me, you endanger our work together. What are your thoughts about this?"

Again, the idea is not to punish your client or even to keep her in treatment at all costs, but to open up the issue for discussion. In this way, you might be able to address what prompted her to lie and you may begin to reestablish the work together. Be aware of the fact that you might find yourself addressing issues like this again and again with the same client, thus assisting her along the way to more honesty with you and ultimately with herself.

4. *Contract Breaches (e.g. failure to meet with an auxiliary therapist when agreed upon, failure to take prescribed medication)*
   If part of the treatment contract included that your client

will take his medication as prescribed and he fails to do so, it is imperative that you address this breach of contract. A contract breach means in essence that you will either re-negotiate the contract, changing it in the process, or that you will terminate or suspend therapy as long as the client does not adhere to the behavior specified as a condition for treatment. You will encounter this problem mainly when you work with clients who are more seriously disturbed, which often are the very clients the less experienced clinicians in training are working with. So if your schizophrenic client is having auditory hallucinations and pronounced paranoia because he is not taking his antipsychotic medication, direct his (and perhaps his family's) attention to the fact that when you began work together, you specified that a condition for your working with him was that he takes his medications. You might say something like this: "You know that I will not be able to work with you when you are not taking your medication. Therefore, since you have stopped your medication, therapy has come to an end. You have chosen to disrupt your treatment by discontinuing your medication, and we can look at your reasons for doing so when you are once again more stable on your medication."

While such an approach does not guarantee that your client will resume his medication (and thus his therapy), it does show you to be predictable and reliable, able to maintain a secure frame, and able to protect yourself and the client.

5. *In-Session Acting Out (e.g., abusing office furnishings, refusing to leave at end of session, shouting)*
   If your client *acts out* her issues rather than talking about them, you need to address it. Thus, if she begins to kick the furniture, stop her firmly by stating that this is unacceptable behavior and not therapy, and that you will ask her to leave if she does not stop it. Then, if she does not stop it, ask her to leave your office and, if she does not

leave on her own, have her removed (by a security guard, a PET team, or the police). If your client refuses to leave at the end of the session, address it in the same manner. If she does stop her behavior upon your request, make sure you explore it with her. You might say:

> "When you began kicking the furniture, you in effect interrupted the session. Therapy does not include kicking. I wonder what was going on for you to do that?"

> "I wonder what prompted you to interrupt our session by kicking the furniture?"

6. *Between-Sessions Acting Out*

Your client engages in acting-out behavior between sessions; for example, he increases his use of drugs and/or alcohol, suddenly breaks up his long-term relationship, engages in frequent promiscuous and unprotected sex, and the like. These are issues that you need to address with your client. You might say:

> "I noticed that you have been using more cocaine in the last two weeks. I wonder what that is about?"

> "I wonder if the frequent casual sex you are telling me about has anything to do with the fact that you told me you really liked me?"

7. *Non-Affective or Trivial Themes*

If your client talks mainly about trivial matters that don't appear to be of any importance to her, be sure to address this issue. Thus, your client might be talking about how she went grocery shopping and tell you about the things she saw and what she bought, which choices she had to make, and so forth. Assuming that shopping does not have any special meaning for this client, you might say something like this:

> "I notice that you have been telling me in great detail about the things you bought, but you have not told me how the meeting with your boss went that you were so anxious about last time we met?"

> "I notice that you are spending a lot of time describing your shopping trip in detail, yet I have the impression this trip really doesn't mean much to you."

8. *Transference Manifestations*

These, simply speaking, are manifestations of the relationship between your client and yourself.

a. *Verbal references to the therapist:* Whenever your client makes implicit or explicit reference to you, be sure to address it. Imagine your client making the following statement: "All therapists are the same; they want to trick me."

It is most important that you take this up. You might say in response:

> "Well, I am a therapist. Do you believe that I am tricking you?"
> "I wonder if perhaps you feel that I am tricking you?"
> "Since I am a therapist, I imagine you feel that I am tricking you in some way."

If your client affirms this, continue with your investigation of this topic, perhaps like this:

> "How do you feel that I am tricking you?"
> "What about me makes you feel that I am tricking you?"

More directly, your client might say, "I wish I could go home with you." Don't just ignore a statement like this; explore it. You might say something like the following: "What do you imagine it would be like if you went home with me?"

b. *"Acting-in" (e.g., positioning body in overtly seductive manner)* Acting-in is another way of behavior that is nonverbal and relates to the therapist–client relationship. Thus, when your client positions herself in her chair overtly seductively, you can be sure that she is expressing something about the relationship between you and her. Address this issue. At times, you might actually have to set a limit. You might say : "I notice that you have hiked your skirt higher and higher. Please pull it down. I wonder what this is about, showing more and more of your legs to me?"

In cases of overt seductiveness, be certain to set clear limits as well as to address them with your supervisor. Document the interaction well in your files.

9. *Nontransferential Affect-Laden Material*
Your client addresses highly emotional issues that have nothing to do with the (transference) relationship between him and you. Perhaps his child is ill, perhaps his wife left him, perhaps he lost a job. These issues would be highly emotional to him and need to be addressed. Of course, any of these issues might eventually find their way into the transference and will be addressed there in due time.

This hierarchy is meant as a guidepost to help you prioritize what you will address out of the mass of statements and behaviors you are faced with during every single session with a client. This means, if Ms. Green tells you that her boyfriend left her (Number 9), that she is afraid you will leave her, too (Number 8), and that she will just leave town and not come back (Number 2), if indeed she doesn't kill herself (Number 1), you will know to address the suicidal threat (Number 1) first. Only when this topic is cleared up will you address the others in descending order of importance. That is, you will next attend to the threat to treatment, namely, Ms. Green's statement that she will leave town, next to the transference relationship— that is, her fear that you will leave her—and finally, to the precipitating event, the fact that her boyfriend left her. In actuality, there will not be a clear demarcation between the topics, and as you address one, issues pertaining to the others will most likely come up as well. However, it is important that you are clear about which topic you are aiming at, so as not to be sidetracked. Thus, as you address Ms. Green's suicidality, even if you address some of the other topics as well, it is most important that you come back to the topic of her being suicidal. Only when you have settled that topic to your clinical satisfaction—that is, either when you have ascertained that she is not acutely suicidal or when you have taken steps to keep her safe if she is—can you stay with the next topic.

10

WHEN AND HOW TO BE DIRECTIVE:
SUICIDE/TARASOFF/ABUSE SITUATIONS

Much of the following information pertains to laws governing the mental health professions in California. However, I am not a lawyer. Please make sure you are informed as to the current laws pertaining to your profession in the state where you practice. The wording of the laws changes frequently. While I am reporting as accurately as possible, it is your responsibility to stay informed!

I will now address in more depth situations in which it is necessary for you to become directive. Usually, as a therapist, you are used to being rather nondirective, to exploring issues your client is ready to address, and generally to taking your client's capacity to tolerate anxiety into consideration. However, in certain situations you are *mandated* to be directive you do not have the freedom to take your client's reactions to your interventions into consideration; in short, you are *compelled* to act in a certain way. These situations involve instances in which you are either mandated or allowed to break confidentiality because either your client's or someone else's safety is at risk. Incidently, most of these situations would be termed issues of highest priority in treatment, according to the model discussed in the preceding chapter.

What, then, do you actually say and do when your client tells you he is suicidal? What is your course of action when you become convinced your client is going to make good on threats against someone else? What do you say and whom do you contact when your client tells you she has been abused by her uncle who is now a teacher in a grade school?

A reminder: Please be sure to confer with your supervisor regarding any such issues. Your supervisor is legally as liable as you are for the decisions you make, and you will want as much input as you can get from a seasoned clinician in difficult situations such as those addressed in this chapter.

And finally: Always meticulously document all of your interventions in your client's file!

SUICIDE

It is very important that you screen for suicidality in your intake interview. People will not necessarily tell you that they feel like killing themselves flat-out without you asking for it. However, your client might become suicidal (or you might become aware of your client's suicidality) at any point during the treatment.

How to Screen for Suicidality

Ask Directly:

☐ Does the client feel like killing herself?
☐ Is this an old thought or a new thought?

☐   Does she have a plan for how she will kill herself?
☐   Does she have the means to carry out the plan?
☐   Does she have a history of prior suicide attempts?
☐   Does she have a diagnosis of mood disorder, schizophrenia, or substance abuse?
☐   Did she suffer a recent loss of any kind?

Pay close attention to what your client says. Be alert to utterances that indicate a suicidal preoccupation. Any statement like the following should prompt you to ask pointed questions regarding suicide:

"Sometimes life doesn't seem worth living."
"I wish I was dead."
"My wife/husband/boyfriend/girlfriend/mother/the world, and so forth, would be better off if I was dead."
"I wish I had never been born."
"I have a stash of sleeping pills."
"I often think of crashing my car."
"I wish I would never have to wake up again."

You get the idea. If Ms. Green makes one of those statements (or anything similar), *ask her directly whether she is thinking of killing herself.* It is important that you not be vague about this. Rather, be explicit, even though it might feel awkward and intrusive to you.

"When you say life doesn't seem worth living, have you ever thought about killing yourself?"
"You say you wish you had never been born. Have you ever thought about killing yourself?"
"You say you are keeping a gun. Have you ever thought of using this gun to kill yourself?"
"You were talking about a stash of sleeping pills. Have you thought about using them to kill yourself?"

It is unusual for us to be so direct. The fear of "putting ideas in someone's head" is prevalent. Be assured that the opposite is true: the more someone can put into words, talk about—that is, symbolize—what has previously not been expressed, the less likely he or she is to act on it, to do it, or to act it out. As a matter of fact, the opportunity to talk about suicidal feelings and plans will sometimes in itself diminish the danger of a person actually committing suicide. However, you *cannot* count on this. Instead, assess further for severity and acuteness and take action if indicated to keep your client safe.

A diagnosis or symptoms of a mood disorder, schizophrenia, substance abuse, or the presence of a recent loss of any kind should also prompt you to routinely assess for suicide. Be direct:

"You said that you feel sad and do not find life enjoyable anymore. Have you ever thought about killing yourself?"
"You said your husband left you and you feel that nothing makes sense anymore. Do you ever feel like killing yourself?"

If Ms. Green answers any of these questions in the affirmative, *assess for acuteness and severity of her suicidality.* Find out the following:

- Is this an old thought or a new thought?
- Has she made a plan as to how she will kill herself?
- Does she have the means to carry out her plan?
- Does she have a history of previous suicide attempts?

Ask her directly: "Have you thought about how you would kill yourself?"

If she answers in the affirmative, ask for specifics: "Tell me about this plan. How have you thought to do it?"

If she tells you about crashing her car, assess her means to follow through. "Do you have a car? No? Do you have access to a car? Can you drive?"

If she doesn't have a car and does not have access to a car, this plan is less likely to be carried out than if she has a car that she drives daily, and her plan involves crashing into a lamppost that she passes twice a day on her way to and from work. If her plan involves taking sleeping pills, assess whether she has access to them, and so forth.

You also want to know about previous attempts, since it becomes more likely that she will make another attempt if she has a history of doing so. As Don Freeman, a colleague of mine, is fond of saying: "The past is the best predictor of the future"— at least in regard to predicting behavior.

Once you determine that your client is suicidal, you should make a referral to a psychiatrist for an assessment for medication. You will not be able to do much meaningful work with your client as long as she is so depressed that she wants to kill herself. Instead, you will find yourself being very active to keep her safe. An antidepressant medication might help stabilize her. However, your first order of business is to keep your client safe.

Measures to Assure Your Client's Safety

- ☐ Contract for safety
- ☐ Increase frequency of sessions
- ☐ Increase phone contact
- ☐ Inform third party
- ☐ Voluntary hospitalization
- ☐ Involuntary hospitalization

When you have assessed the acuteness and severity of your client's suicidality, you must decide what *measures to take to assure your client's safety*. Depending on how severe you deem the situation, there are several ways for you to proceed. I will list them here in ascending order of structure and level of containment.

1. *Contract for Safety*

Tell your client something similar to this: "I want you to promise me that you will not kill yourself or hurt yourself in any way until you see me next."

It is important to formulate this contract in such a way that it is actually doable. This means that you should not contract for unlimited periods of time, since no one can make a meaningful commitment for "never" or "always." On the other hand, the formulation "until we see each other next" allows for a finite period of time, in which Ms. Green is asked to contain her impulses and anxieties. You may choose to write this down and have her sign it, while you sign the paper as a witness. However, this is, of course, a symbolic contract, not a legally binding one.

Do not be overly invested in her entering into this contract with you. You are offering it as a first possibility to contain the situation, but it also serves as an assessment tool as to the severity of her suicidality. If Ms. Green cannot or will not enter into this contract with you, she is making a clear statement that she feels she is unable to refrain from hurting herself until you see her next. This means that you need to enlist help to keep her safe.

An important gauge for you is purely subjective, namely, whether you actually believe her or not. If you do not believe that she is sincere about the contract she is entering into, take further steps to keep her safe.

2. *Increase Frequency of Sessions*

If you do not hospitalize Ms. Green, increasing the frequency of her sessions until she is contained and her suicidality abates is most likely indicated. If you see her once a week, a minimum of twice a week, perhaps up to four to five times a week may be indicated to contain her.

While she may not be able to stay out of the hospital when seeing you only once a week, she may be able to deal with her suicidality if she sees you more often. However, this option will depend as much on your availability—do you have the time to increase sessions to three or four times per week for a week or two?—as it does on your clinical judgment. Perhaps you deem it best to hospitalize Ms. Green without seeing her more often because you feel that an increase in sessions would amount to granting a secondary gain that would actually be detrimental to treatment. Consult your supervisor when making such decisions.

If you do increase the frequency of sessions, you have to consider the cost of doing so. Before you immediately jump to reducing your fee for a while,[1] you may want to work with Ms. Green to utilize all available support (including financial) she can get from friends and family, who may help defray the cost of keeping her out of the hospital. In any case, outpatient treatment will be less expensive than a hospital stay.

3. Increase Phone Contact
Along with an increase in frequency of sessions, I recommend an increase in phone contact. Thus, Ms. Green might check in with you once or twice a day for a limited time (or you with her) to help contain her and bridge the gap between sessions. However, it is important that these phone contacts do not become regular phone sessions. If they occur more often than once or twice a day, for more than a few days, or are longer than five to ten minutes, you should consider either increasing the frequency of sessions or hospitalization.

4. Inform Family Members, Friends, and Other Professionals
If you feel that Ms. Green will not be safe on her own, you

---

[1]Please see Chapter 16 for the topic of clients' difficulties paying the fee.

are legally allowed to breach confidentiality and notify her friends or family (the person named as the emergency contact on your intake sheet might be a good option), notify other professionals, or take whatever reasonable steps you deem necessary to keep her safe. It is preferable by far to take these steps with Ms. Green's consent. However, should she not give it, go ahead without it. Thus, you might say: "I don't feel that you will be safe on your own. Therefore, I want to call your husband (mother, sister, friend, etc.) and ask him to come get you so you won't be alone."

Be prepared that Ms. Green will not want you to call anybody. Should this be so, give her the choice of going to the hospital. Ultimately, it will be up to your professional judgment to decide what is most appropriate. This decision will also depend on your knowledge of Ms. Green and on whether you believe the people whom you call on her behalf are trustworthy and able to handle the situation. If you decide to call a family member, do it with Ms. Green present. Explain the situation, ask the person to come to your office, and when she or he arrives, meet with this person and Ms. Green. Make sure the person understands clearly that Ms. Green is suicidal and that she cannot be left alone. Ask whether the individual feels capable of handling this situation, whether he or she will be able to stay with Ms. Green, and whether anyone else can be enlisted to help. Make sure the person has your phone number and encourage him or her to call you if your help is needed. Let the person know that hospitalization is an option. Do not let Ms. Green leave without having spoken to the person who will be her support.

Again, and in addition to the steps taken, consider increasing the frequency of sessions and offer increased phone contact if you deem it appropriate.

If Ms. Green has a psychiatrist, make sure she or he is informed of what has been happening. If Ms. Green doesn't have a psychiatrist, give her the option of calling one (give her a name and phone number) or having you call one. Let her know something like this: "It is important that you be seen by a psychiatrist."

If you have a trusted psychiatrist whom you work with, you might state: "I have a colleague that I work with, whom I would like you to see. Would you like to call her yourself to make an appointment, or would you like me to call her and set up an appointment for you? Let's do it right now." Make sure that contact with a psychiatrist is made. If you do not personally know a psychiatrist to refer your client to, I suggest you have the name and number of a psychiatrist in your area recommended by a colleague you trust available for just such situations.

5. *Voluntary Hospitalization*[2]

What if there isn't anybody you can call? What if your client is alone and has not given you the name or number of an emergency contact? What if she doesn't have a psychiatrist whom you can consult with?

Now it is time to think about hospitalizing her. The aim of this is to keep your client safe in a place that will help contain and stabilize her. If you can, get her cooperation in this venture. Most likely, she will be afraid. Most likely, too, she does not know what awaits her. Give her some information to help alleviate this fear. However, it is most important for you to make clear that you believe a hospitalization is necessary and will be helpful to her. Tell her something along these lines: "I do not believe that you will be safe on your own. I believe that the best and safest place for you to be at this time is a hospital. You will not be alone. There will be people to talk to and to look after you. You will get to see a psychiatrist who will perhaps pre-

---

[2]See also Chapter 11: "How to Hospitalize a Client."

scribe a medication that can help you feel better. I am now going to make a call to . . . hospital."

You may find yourself making an initial call to a hospital from your home, after a call from your client or the person who is with her. It is a good idea for you to have the names and phone numbers of psychiatric hospitals and other referrals available at home and at work, in case you need them.

You will need information regarding the manner of payment for the hospitalization, your client's diagnosis, and the current emergency. If your client has a psychiatrist, it is hoped that you will have had contact with this professional and will know the hospital that she is affiliated with so that you can admit your client to that hospital. Try to contact your client's psychiatrist and see if she wants to admit your client personally. If you can't get a hold of her, initiate admittance yourself. Leave a message for your client's psychiatrist with the pertinent information, and give the psychiatrist's name and number to the hospital as well. Ask your client to sign a release of information (if she is in your office, ask her to sign one there) so that you can confer with the hospital personnel regarding her treatment. If you do not follow the treatment of your clients in hospital, let her know:

> "I will not have contact with you while you are in the hospital. Please let me know when you will be discharged so that we can resume our sessions."
> "I will have limited contact with you while you are in the hospital. I will call you to see how you are doing and we will resume our sessions when you are discharged."
> "I will see you in the hospital. I will get in touch with you to let you know when."

For this latter, you need to contact the hospital and apply for temporary privileges, so that you can be the therapist of record.

A word of caution: Even though you might feel tempted to do so, do not drive your client to the hospital. You will be liable if anything happens in the car, if she decides to jump out, or if you get into an accident in which she gets hurt. If you cannot find a relative or friend to come and transport her, let the hospital know that you need an ambulance for transportation. If all else fails, call a PET team or your local police station and let them know that you have a suicidal client in the office (or give them her address, if she is at home) who needs to be transported to the hospital.

6. *Involuntary Hospitalization*
If the previously discussed steps seem insufficient to keep your client safe, consider an involuntary hospitalization (also called 51/50 after Evidence Code 51/50). This means a hospitalization against her will and is truly a last resort. Be aware that you cannot actually make sure that an involuntary hospitalization will take place. Only specially trained professionals can make that decision. However, you *can* initiate this process by calling either 911 and letting the police know that you have an acutely suicidal person in your office who needs to be hospitalized but is unwilling to, or by calling a PET team (Psychiatric Evaluation Team), which will send out someone who can evaluate your client for involuntary hospitalization and make a decision whether it is necessary or not. If at all possible, let your client know what you are doing, unless you fear it would endanger her or others to do so.

You might have to initiate an involuntary hospitalization from home or when your client is not in your office. She might call you and during that conversation give you the impression that she will be in grave danger if she is not hospitalized, in which case, if she refuses to go voluntarily, you have to notify the police or a PET team. It is important that you have your client's current home address and phone number in order to accomplish this.

Be sure to let her know that you are acting out of concern for her. Be prepared that she might get angry with you for telling others and for getting her "locked up." Acknowledge her feelings and do not attempt to talk her out of them. You might say something like this: "I understand that you are angry with me. But I believe you will not be safe if you are not hospitalized, and my primary concern is to keep you safe."

On the other hand, do not waver in your endeavor to keep her safe even if she gets angry with you, or if you do not believe her when she suddenly promises not to hurt herself. Stay firmly with your best judgment and with the mandate to take reasonable steps to prevent her suicide.

What are reasonable steps? They are what we have described previously: increasing the frequency of sessions and phone contact; notifying friends, family, and other treating professionals; referring her to a psychiatrist for medication evaluation; and arranging for a hospitalization, voluntarily or involuntarily. The following are not only not reasonable but also display a dangerous degree of enmeshment that might be unprofessional and unethical: being on the phone with your client day and night; meeting with her in emergency sessions daily, or more than once daily, for weeks on end; spending time with her outside of sessions; and so forth.

Once your client is hospitalized, proceed as you would with a voluntary hospitalization regarding contact, releases of information, conferring with treating psychiatrist, and arranging for continued services after discharge.

TARASOFF

We call a "Tarasoff" situation one in which a client has made a serious threat of physical harm against an identifiable victim, after the case of Ms. Tarasoff, whose ex-boyfriend had told his therapist that he planned to kill her. Her therapist notified the police but not Ms. Tarasoff. Her ex-boyfriend did indeed kill her, as he had said he would. After this case, the Court found that a therapist is mandated not only to notify the police but also to make reasonable efforts to notify the intended victim if a serious threat to harm her has been made by a client. In fact, this is one of the "exceptions to confidentiality" that you addressed with your client at the beginning of your first meeting. Thus, a Tarasoff situation is another of those situations in which you have to become directive and in which you do not have any choice as to how to proceed.

There are several points to keep in mind:

1. Only when *your client* makes such a threat *in your presence* does the Tarasoff ruling apply. This means that if your client tells you about his wife threatening him, or a neighbor threatening another neighbor, there is no mandate. It also means that if his wife calls you and tells you that your client has threatened to hurt his boss, you cannot go ahead and warn your client's boss. First of all, you would not acknowledge to your client's wife that he is actually your client (unless you have a release of information signed by your client to speak to his wife). Second, you *must* speak to him personally and he must repeat this threat to *you* in order for you to be protected under the Tarasoff ruling to break confidentiality and notify police and the intended victim (also, of course, his wife could be angry at him and telling you a lie). However, it *would* be the appropriate course of action to get in touch with your client as soon as possible, tell him about his wife's phone call, and assess the situation. If he does repeat the threat to you, *then* you need to proceed according to the Tarasoff ruling.

2. It is important that there be an *identifiable victim*. Clearly, if your client makes a vague threat that "someday she is going to hurt somebody" without specifying who that

might be, you cannot warn the intended victim because you don't know the intended victim's identity.

3. And finally, you have to make a judgment as to whether a threat is serious or not. This means that you might find that when your client makes the threat of "one day I am going to kill my husband," she is not serious; in other words, she does not actually mean to harm her husband. On the other hand, you might find that she *is* going to hurt him. Depending on your assessment, the Tarasoff ruling applies and you have to notify law enforcement as well as the intended victim.

Assessing the Situation

Let's assume you find yourself in the situation where your client has told you that she is going to kill her husband. You must now assess, just as when your client tells you she is suicidal, the seriousness of the threat. Generally speaking, it is better to err on the side of caution. In the end, you cannot read minds and it seems better to lose a client because she is angry at your disclosure and leaves therapy, than to risk someone getting hurt because you did not take your client's threat seriously. Clearly, this is a very sticky situation without a foolproof prescription against error. However, since this disclosure is the result of what you assessed to be a Tarasoff situation and you are acting in good faith, you are most likely protected under that law against breach of confidentiality.

Pay attention to your client's expression of anger and pursue such statements. Generally speaking, always invite your client to express in more detail her feelings, whatever they are. Thus, if she is angry or is making threats, explore these statements. However, contrary to other feelings, in this case (as in the case of her being suicidal) you have an ulterior motive: you need to assess whether you have reason to believe that your client will harm another person. In order to do this, ask detailed questions aimed at eliciting concrete answers.

Be alert for expressions of great *anger directed against a specific person*, like the following:

"I hate that person."
"I want to kill that person."
"That person deserves to get hurt."
"I would like to burn down his house."
"I am so angry at her, I really want to use my gun to show her."

Make note of *general expressions of great anger* like the following:

"I'll show them!"
"One day, they'll be sorry."
"One day they'll see that I can't be pushed around."
"People are evil and deserve to be punished. I'll give them what they deserve."

Any one of those expressions, taken by itself, does not mean much. Follow up by inviting your client to elaborate. Ask detailed, pointed questions like the following, aimed at eliciting more details from your client:

"When you say you want to kill that person, have thought about how you would do that?"
"When you say that person deserves to get hurt, are you thinking about actually hurting him?"
"You said you really want to use your gun to show that person, whom you are so angry with. What do you mean by that? Are you thinking of shooting her?"
"You said you would like to burn down his house. Have you made any actual plans to do so?"

"You say that one day 'they' will see that you can't be pushed around. Who are 'they' and how will you show them?"

"You say that you will show them one day. Who will you show, and how will you show them?"

"You say that one day they'll be sorry. What do you mean by that?"

Ask specific questions that demand specific answers regarding intent and the prospective victim. Your client might go into a long tirade about how angry she is, what she would like to do to a specific person, only to say that, no, she would not really hurt that person but finds it helpful to fantasize about it. This would not be unusual and is actually what you want to have happen: you want your client to symbolize, to express her anger *in words, instead* of acting it out. So you might hear her describe at length what so and so did to her, and how she would like to burn down his house. She answers your questions regarding how and when with, "Well, no, I am not *really* going to do this, I'm just venting." In these cases, your assessment will most likely be that there is no serious harm threatening an identifiable intended victim. However, answers like the following are cause for alarm:

"Yes, I am planning to use my gun to shoot her."

"I *am* going to burn down my boss's house, you just wait and see."

"He thinks he can get away from me like that? If I can't have him, no one can. I am going to use that gun he gave me."

Sometimes you will hear a statement like this: "I am afraid I will lose control and kill him. I don't really *want* to do that, but I get so angry that I'm afraid I won't be able to stop myself."

In a case like this, it is imperative that you explore with your client ways to keep herself from acting on her impulses, including the possibility of a hospitalization. If you feel that she actually *might* lose control and become a danger, and she is not cooperative, you are mandated to take steps to prevent that from happening.

Steps to Take

We will now look at what concrete steps to take once you have assessed the seriousness of the threat.

A. No Serious Threat to an Identifiable Victim

In general, if you assess that there is *no serious threat to an identifiable victim* but you are concerned, take the steps described in the section on suicide: a nonviolence contract, increased frequency of sessions and phone calls, referral to a psychiatrist, and, perhaps, hospitalization.

If your client is very angry and you feel that there may be a threat to an "unidentifiable" victim—that is, your client might "lose it"—you should think about a referral to a psychiatrist and a possible hospitalization, preferably voluntary, but, if necessary, involuntarily as a "threat to others." This is a *permitted breach of confidentiality* (dangerous client exception) that is not mandated but is put at your disposal for cases in which you assess that it is necessary to keep your client (and others) safe.

B. Serious Threat to an Identifiable Victim

The following steps to be taken refer to your assessment of a serious threat made by your client against an identifiable victim.

- ☐ Notifying law enforcement
- ☐ Making reasonable efforts to notify the intended victim

☐ Notifying the treating psychiatrist
☐ Voluntary hospitalization
☐ Involuntary hospitalization

1. *Notifying Law Enforcement*
   Once you have assessed that there is a serious threat, you must notify law enforcement (911). You have to decide whether or not you want to let your client know that this is what you are doing before you do it. This decision will depend on your assessment of whether or not it is safer for yourself, your client, and the intended victim whether she does or does not know what you are going to do. Perhaps you feel it will calm her to know that you are taking steps, that there are limits and boundaries, that she cannot act with impunity. Perhaps she will find it soothing to know that someone is going to stop her. On the other hand, perhaps it will make her more angry and even put yourself in danger if she knows you are going to "tell on her." Perhaps she will see it as a betrayal. However, whether you tell her before or after you notify the police and the intended victim, you will eventually have to deal with the fact that you did, in fact, do so.
   In practice, you might either let her leave your session before you make those phone calls, or you might excuse yourself and call the police and the intended victim while she still is in your office. Much will depend on your actual facilities. Perhaps the only phone is in the consulting room. If you feel that it would not be safe to call in her presence, you will let her leave before you make that call.
   Be prepared to tell the police the following:

   • Your name
   • Your relationship to the client (her therapist)
   • Your credentials (MFT intern or trainee, MSW, psychological assistant, etc.)
   • Your office address and work phone

- Your client's name
- Your client's address and phone number
- The exact nature of the threat
- The intended victim's name
- The intended victim's address and phone number (if you have it).

Do not disclose more than is necessary to satisfy the Tarasoff ruling. Even though you are reporting to the police, you still want to protect your client's confidentiality as much as possible. That means, do not go into any details of the treatment or of your client's history. If the police want this information, remind them that you have told them what is necessary under the Tarasoff ruling and that you are not mandated to disclose details of your client's treatment. Politely decline to give more information. Consult with legal representation if necessary.

2. *Make Reasonable Efforts to Notify the Intended Victim*
   Even if the police tell you they will notify the intended victim, you are *mandated* to make reasonable efforts to notify him or her *yourself.* That means that you *always* must make the effort to notify the intended victim, no matter who else is notifying her or him of the threat made. If you have the intended victim's name and phone number, it will be relatively easy to make such an effort. You simply call and then notify the intended victim of the exact nature of the threat made against him or her by your client. If you cannot reach the intended victim in person, always consult with your professional organization or a lawyer specializing in these issues what will be the best course of action. For example, you may have access to a tape machine that you deem to be the intended victim's, and you may consider leaving a message on this machine, perhaps similar to the following: "This message is for . . . My name is MO. I have been notified that your former girlfriend

(or whatever the relationship is) has made a threat to your life. She plans to shoot you with her gun. Please call me at . . . "

You can see the difficulty of leaving your client's name here, since you do not know who else has access to this tape machine. Is it a "reasonable effort to notify the victim" to leave your client's name on his machine where others can hear it, or is this going beyond what is reasonable and could be considered a breach of confidentiality? This is why you should always obtain legal advice in regard to questions like these.

If you talk to someone else besides the intended victim, try to obtain a phone number that will allow you to talk directly with the intended victim (such as a work number). However, if you cannot reach the intended victim, you may consider leaving a detailed message with the person you talk to:[3] "I have knowledge of a threat against so and so's life. I am calling to notify him of this threat. When you see him, please let him know that his former girlfriend has threatened to kill him with a gun. Please also give him my phone number . . . . and ask him to call me. Tell him I have notified the police of this threat and they might be trying to get in touch with him as well."

The idea is to make a *reasonable* effort to notify the intended victim. This might, indeed, mean letting family members know so that they can tell the intended victim if you cannot reach him directly. However, it does *not* mean that you must hire a detective if you don't have the intended victim's phone number and cannot get it through information. Carefully document in your client's file what steps you have taken. For example:

> "Called information, unlisted number. Not able to contact intended victim."

---

[3] Again, obtain legal advice and act in a timely manner.

"Obtained legal advice from . . . and was advised to do
the following . . . "

"Called his home and left a message with his roommate
regarding the threat made."

"Spoke with the intended victim and notified him of
the threat made against his life."

Again, do not forget that you are your client's therapist
and, as such, have to protect his confidentiality as much
as possible. As with the police, do not disclose treatment
information or any information other than the threat
made.

3. *Notify the Treating Psychiatrist*
If your client has a current psychiatrist, notify him or her.

4. *Voluntary Hospitalization*
This may not be an option if law enforcement, which you
are mandated to inform, decides that your client must be
put on a 72-hour hold, which means in effect that she will
be involuntarily hospitalized. However, you might let your
client know that you are very concerned regarding her
state of mind and the threat she poses for others and see
whether you can't enlist her cooperation. It is in her best
interest to cooperate with law enforcement and agree to
be hospitalized. You might, if you deem it safe, say something like the following: "I don't think you are safe on your
own at this point. I think it would be best if you went to a
hospital for a while until you are more stable, and that
way no one gets hurt."
Thus, when you notify police of the threat made and
your client has already agreed to a voluntary hospitalization, let them know about it. Also, make sure that hospital staff is aware of the fact that a Tarasoff situation was
the reason for this hospitalization.

5. *Involuntary Hospitalization*
Perhaps your client needs to be involuntarily hospitalized

(51/50) because of being a danger to others. To proceed, please refer to the section on how to hospitalize a client. When you call police and notify them of the threat made, you are in fact initiating the evaluation process for such a hospitalization.

CHILD ABUSE AND NEGLECT

If your client gives you information that amounts to your knowledge or reasonable suspicion that a child is being or has been abused or neglected, you are mandated to report this information to Child Protective Services. Abusive situations are not always clear-cut, as in physical abuse or sexual molestation. Please refer to the current law to stay informed on this issue. If you are in doubt whether a situation is reportable, always call Child Protective Services for a consultation.

Assessing the Situation

Assess whether you can establish a reasonable suspicion of child abuse or gain knowledge of such abuse. Be alert to your client's statements that might hint at a child being abused and pursue those statements with further direct questions:

"My sister is really hard on her children."
"My teacher often touches me in this strange way."
"My father used to hit me, and now he is treating my nephew in a similar way."
"I don't like how my neighbors treat their children."

Ask clarifying questions, requesting concrete information regarding abusive behavior:

"What does that mean, your sister is hard on her children?
What does she do?"
"How do you mean: touches you in a strange way? What does
she do?"
"What did your father do when he hit you? How does he hit
your nephew?"
"How do your neighbors treat their children?"

Ask direct questions if you see bruises or other suspicious
wounds:

"This looks like a cigarette burn. How did you get this?"
"You broke your arm. How did that happen?"
"Where did you get that bruise?"

If your client asks you whether you will make a report if he
or she tells you, be sure to say yes, you will. You are not there to
trick your client. Remind your client that you are a mandated
reporter. Let your client know that if she is not personally involved in the abuse but only reports it to you, she can remain
anonymous if she so chooses. Let her know that in any case,
she can make the report herself, if she wants to. However, this
latter will have to take place in your presence so that you can
be sure that the report is actually being made.

Steps to Take

With the information you have gained, you now have to decide
whether you have reasonable suspicion or knowledge of child
abuse and, consequently, must make a child abuse report, or
whether you do not. Always keep in mind that it is not your job
to conduct an investigation but only to assess whether you have
reason to believe that child abuse has taken or is taking place.

A. You Have No Suspicion or Knowledge of Child Abuse

Make sure you document clearly in your client's file the information you have gained and how you came to the conclusion that child abuse did not or does not take place.

B. You Are Not Sure Whether What You Know Is Reportable

> If you are not sure whether what you know is reportable or whether you have enough information to make a report, *be sure to call Child Protective Services for a consultation.*

Let them know the facts as you are aware of them, *without disclosing your client's name,* and request information on whether or not you need to file a child abuse report.

If you are told that you need not file a report, note down the worker's name, time that you called, information you gave, and answer that you got.

If you are told that a report is necessary, that worker will most likely take your report. At this point, you will be asked to disclose your client's name if your client is involved in the abuse. You do not have to disclose your client's name (and indeed should not, if your client doesn't want you to) if your client is not involved but only tells you about child abuse she has knowledge of. In that case you might state something like this: "I am a therapist. One of my clients told me in session about her neighbors abusing their child. She gave me all the pertinent information but wants to remain anonymous."

C. You Must Make a Child Abuse Report

- [ ] Notify Child Protective Services by phone immediately.
- [ ] Notify Child Protective Services in writing within the next thirty-six hours.

☐ Let your client know what you are doing.
☐ Deal with your own feelings.

The steps to take when you must make a child abuse report are rather straightforward. The first two steps are mandated by law:

1. *Notify Child Protective Services by phone immediately.*
   This does not mean that you must excuse yourself in session to make a report the moment you hear about a child being abused. It does mean making that phone call as soon as possible: perhaps after the conclusion of that session, perhaps in your lunch hour, definitely within that working day. If your client wants to make the call herself, she has to do it in your presence. It would be best if you actually called Child Protective Services, gave a brief outline of the situation to the worker, and then gave the phone to your client. This might sound like the following: "I am a therapist and have a client here who is involved in a child abuse situation. She wants to make the report herself. Hold on, here she is."
   Don't forget to follow up her report in writing. Make sure that you have the phone number for Child Protective Services available.

2. *Notify Child Protective Services in writing within the next thirty-six hours.*
   This is as simple as it sounds. Fill out a Child Abuse and Neglect Report form and send it to the office the worker specified when you made your report on the phone. Make sure you have the appropriate forms available in your office. You can request these forms through your local office of the Department of Children's and Family Services (DCFS).

3. *Let your client know what you are doing.*
   If it seems appropriate, that is, if it would not endanger

the victim of the abuse, your client, or yourself, let your client know *before* you make the report to Child Protective Services and invite her to participate in the call. If you deem it more appropriate, let her know *after* you make the call or at least be available for discussion of the report after agents from Child Protective Services show up at her house.

Remind her that you are mandated to make that report and refer back to the exceptions to confidentiality covered in the first session. Emphasize that you are acting to keep her and others safe. Be prepared that she might be angry with you and feel betrayed by you. It is crucial that you allow her to express herself and work with her on the issues your report might bring up. If you don't, you will most likely lose her as a client. Be prepared for that, too: that you might lose her as a client anyway. Do not forget that she knew you were going to report your knowledge of child abuse *before* she chose to tell you about it and therefore, in telling you, she is enlisting your help in making this report.

4. *Deal with your own feelings regarding the report.*
It is only normal for you to have strong feelings regarding having made this report, whether or not your client stays with you or leaves. In any case, it is a good idea to take your feelings and concerns to your supervisor and your own therapist to address there, so that you won't burden your client with them. It is important that you are able to respond to your client's expression of anger at your reporting what she told you with an invitation to explore her feelings further:

> "It must have felt like a betrayal, my calling Child Protective Services. Tell me more about your anger at me."
> "You seem very angry that I called Child Protective Services. What did you imagine would happen when you told me about the child abuse?"

The work with your clinical supervisor and personal therapist will help you respond appropriately to your client.

DEPENDENT ADULT AND ELDER ABUSE

This issue is similar to the situation with child abuse. Here, you have to report knowledge or suspicion of abuse of a dependent adult or an elder.

At the time of this writing, a *dependent adult* is anyone over 18 and under 65 years of age who depends on others for his or her care and well-being. An *elder* is anyone 65 years of age or older. However, you do not have to report all instances that involve a dependent adult or elder in an abusive situation, but only those in which *you either personally observe evidence of such abuse, or in which your client tells you about it and she is involved in the abuse.* You are currently *not* mandated to report if a third person tells you about such abuse going on or if your client tells you about knowing of such abuse, which does not involve her. However, as always with legal issues, be sure to consult the current laws governing your profession for the latest updates.

Assessing the Situation

In order to determine whether or not you are dealing with a reportable instance of dependent adult or elder abuse, you need to assess the situation. Be aware that an abusive situation does not only involve clear-cut physical or sexual abuse. The following situations are considered abusive as well: your elder or dependent client is not being fed appropriately, is not being clothed appropriately, has her money withheld from her, is not being provided with appropriate medical care (including denial of needed medications), to name just a few. Please refer to the current law to stay informed on this issue.

Again, as previously described, you will need to ask direct questions and follow up on the answers your client gives you.

Be alert for *signs indicative of abuse:* Your client (who is an elder or dependent adult) has bruises, cuts, or unexplained or suspicious injuries or marks on her body. Sometimes your client will tell you outright about having been abused. Make note of *statements* like the following and follow up on them:

"My daughter won't let me have any money."
"I am always hungry. They don't give me enough to eat."
"I am afraid to be alone with my husband."
"I can't come anymore. My sister won't let me."

Ask direct questions aimed at eliciting more information:

"You said your daughter won't let you have any money. Don't you have access to your own money? How does she keep it from you? Does she ever physically restrain you? Does she hit you?"
"You say you're always hungry. Who's responsible for feeding you? How much do they give you? Do they withhold food from you?"
"What do you mean, your sister won't let you come anymore? How will she prevent you from coming?"
"What makes you afraid to be alone with your husband? Are you afraid that he will hurt you? Has he hurt you in the past? How?"
"I see that you have bruises on your legs. What happened?"

In this way you will collect information to enable you to make a clinical decision on whether or not you have knowledge or reasonable suspicion that abuse is taking place. Keep in mind that you are *not* mandated to investigate this case and decide with certainty. Leave that to the Adult Protective Services. Your job is to make the mandated report *when you have reasonable suspicion* that abuse is taking place.

If you are in doubt and cannot make up your mind whether the information you have is reportable or not, call Adult Protective Services for a consultation.

Please refer to the section on "Child Abuse" that deals with calling for a consultation and proceed accordingly.

Steps to Take

- ☐ Call Adult Protective Services immediately.
- ☐ Make a written report to Adult Protective Services within two working days.
- ☐ Notify your client.
- ☐ Deal with your own feelings.

You have made the decision that you have reasonable suspicion (or knowledge) that your dependent adult or elder client is being abused. I will now list steps for you to take to satisfy the legal requirements, as well as deal with your client professionally and responsibly.

1. *Call Adult Protective Services.*
   This is a mandated step in which you have no choice. Call Adult Protective Services as soon as possible after finding out about the abuse and make a report. This should be on the same day. If it appears appropriate—that is, if it does not endanger your client's, yours, or anyone else's safety and well-being—invite your client (whether the victim or the perpetrator) to participate in the call. Do have the phone number for Adult Protective Services available for such a case.

2. *Make a written report to Adult Protective Services.*
   This, too, is mandated and leaves you no choice. Make a

written report to Adult Protective Services within two working days of finding out about the abuse. Make sure you have the appropriate forms available. You can ask the worker to assist you with filling out the report while you are on the phone with her or him. If you do not have the forms, make sure to let the worker who is taking your report know and request that more forms be sent. Meanwhile, you may be asked to go ahead and complete a narrative report. Whatever you are instructed to do, document it in your client's file and do it.

3. *Notify your client of what you are doing.*
   If you have not already told your client, you should let her know after you made the report that this is what you have done. Again, as in the case of child abuse, remind her that you are a mandated reporter and that you discussed this exception to confidentiality in the first session. Be prepared to deal with her expressions of anger and betrayal at your having told. Be prepared as well to lose her as a client. Should she want to leave treatment with you, do try to explore this wish if at all possible, but make sure to be respectful of her decision and give her three appropriate referrals to clinicians with whom she could continue treatment, if she so chooses.

4. *Deal with your own feelings regarding the report.*
   You will no doubt feel bad if a client decides to leave treatment as the consequence of your having made a report, and you might feel tempted to try to convince her to stay with you, to make her see your good intentions, and generally to get her to stop being angry with you. Even if she does not consider any such drastic steps as leaving, you most likely have some feelings about having broken confidentiality (albeit being mandated to do so). In order for you to be able to address your client's concerns and feelings and not get caught up in your own, take them to your supervisor and your own therapy to sort them out there.

It is not appropriate to burden your client with how this situation impacts you—other than in a considered way as a clinical intervention.

DOMESTIC VIOLENCE

Domestic violence is a widespread problem in the United States that does not discriminate: it is prevalent among all socioeconomic classes; among partners of any age, race and ethnicity, gender, and sexual preference; among the able-bodied and the disabled. It is as common among the clergy, law enforcement officers, medical doctors, and attorneys as it is among blue-collar workers. You'll find it among the well educated as well as high-school drop-outs, among the rich and the poor. It's prevalent among dating youths and old couples. Whether couples are heterosexual or homosexual, domestic violence is equally likely to occur in both cases. Whether Caucasian, Black, Asian, or Latino, domestic violence is not more likely to occur in one group than in another. It occurs in connection with substance abuse, as well as among the completely abstaining. This being the case, you should routinely screen for domestic violence, particularly when you work with couples.

Let me state here that there is *currently no mandate for you to report domestic violence* to any agency unless it is a situation that involves either a minor, in which case it would be reportable as child abuse, or an elder or dependent adult, in which case it would be reportable as elder or dependent adult abuse.

Domestic violence is a problem that tends to escalate and not uncommonly ends in one partner (sometimes both) being seriously injured or even killed. In addition, in families where domestic violence occurs, the incidence of concurrent child abuse is high. In cases of domestic violence, certain treatment issues must be taken into consideration. Certain treatment modalities are indicated, while others are known to have the potential to escalate the violence and must therefore be avoided.

Thus, it is important for you to know not only whether domestic violence is occurring but also what to do once you assess its presence.

Assessing for Domestic Violence

Here is a checklist to use when assessing for domestic violence:

- ☐ Ask direct questions.
- ☐ Conduct separate assessment sessions for couples.
- ☐ Ask for instances of "house battering."
- ☐ Be alert for signs such as bruises, unexplained injuries, and the like.
- ☐ Ask for a history of violent relationships (including family of origin).
- ☐ Ask for a history of child abuse.

1. *Ask direct questions.*

    Always *ask for the presence of domestic violence in your initial consultation.* Be direct and to the point. Often, an individual or couple will tell you when asked, because often domestic violence is one of the main reasons that brings people into treatment. Overall, you want to be open to the fact that domestic violence is a possibility for anyone who is in a relationship

2. *Conduct separate assessment sessions for members of a couple.*

    If you are doing an assessment or consultation with a couple, be sure to schedule not only a joint meeting with both members but also, as part of your routine intake procedure with couples, a session with each of them separately. This might turn out to be a half-session for each partner but should not be less than that. Let them know when you first meet with them for a joint consultation: "As part of my assessment I will meet with each of you separately. After I have met with each of you, we will meet jointly again and decide together on how we want to proceed from there."

Observe how the partners handle this request. If one partner has great difficulties allowing the other partner to meet with you alone, that person is showing himself or herself to be very controlling, which is one sign of an abusive partner.

Do not agree to treat a couple that will not see you separately for your initial assessment. It is imperative for you to know whether a couple is currently engaged in a violent relationship and it is equally important that the partners be willing to follow safety rules that you will set for the treatment if you decide to work with them. If they already have difficulties with following your initial request for separate assessment sessions, it is highly likely that more problems will arise later and that those problems might actually have dangerous consequences for one or both partners, perhaps even for you. You might want to share these thoughts with the couple that is reluctant to meet with you separately.

In the separate consultation session, ask again whether violence is a problem in the relationship. Be direct about it. You might ask: "Has X ever been violent with you? Hit you, pushed you, shoved you, or the like?"

Be alert for statements like the following, indicative of the presence of a violent relationship:

"I am afraid of my partner."
"He (or she) gets very mad sometimes."
"She treats me badly."
"He is mean to me."

Always follow up with clarifying questions, asking for concrete behavior:

"What do you mean when you say he is mean to you? What does he do?"

> "How come you're afraid of your partner? What does
>   she do that makes you afraid?"
> "What does he do when he gets mad?"
> "What does she do when she treats you badly?"

3. *Ask for instances of "house battering."*
Research shows that house battering (destroying furniture, kicking holes in the wall or doors, breaking windows, and the like) often occurs either concurrently with or as a precursor to domestic violence. Ask directly for instances of "house-battering" and rages:

> "Does she ever throw anything? Break anything?"
> "Has he ever destroyed any of your possessions?"
> "Does he kick the doors or the walls when he's angry?"

4. *Be alert for bruises, unexplained injuries, and the like.*
Be alert for bruises, unexplained or suspicious injuries, or unexplained frequent absences. Be sure to ask directly when you observe a bruise or injury, or if there are unexplained frequent absences:

> "How did you get that bruise?"
> "How did you break your arm?"

Confront your client with inconsistencies if you see them:

> "You know, you keep telling me that you frequently run
>   into doors and you have also told me that your
>   partner does not want you to come here. I think
>   maybe your partner is hurting you and you are
>   afraid to tell me."
> "You say you are clumsy and that is how you got those
>   burns, while cooking. I think that your partner may
>   be hurting you and that you are afraid to tell me."
> "You've missed sessions several times now, and each time
>   when you come back you have fresh bruises. Is your
>   partner hurting you?"

5. *Ask for a history of violent relationships.*
   Be alert to a history of abuse. A history of abusive relationships, whether as the perpetrator or the victim, as well
   as a history of violence in the family of origin—domestic
   violence between parents and/or child abuse—can be
   indicative of a current violent relationship. As you do your
   assessment, do not forget to inquire about these issues.

6. *Assess for concurrent child abuse.*
   If you find out that domestic violence is an issue, be sure
   to assess whether the children in the house are being
   abused as well. If they are or if you have a reasonable suspicion that they are, you are mandated to make a child
   abuse report.

Signs Indicative of Domestic Violence

Be alert for any and all of the following signs of domestic violence, not only during the intake (of a couple or individual
alike) but also during the continuing treatment:

Statements indicating a controlling partner
- Your client has to justify her every move.
- Your client doesn't have access to money.
- Your client cannot go where she wants to go, or do what
  she wants to do, without risking a major fight.
- Your client is being cut off from friends and family.
- Your client is keeping her therapy secret because "he/she
  would disapprove."

On the other hand, *be equally alert to the possibility that your
client might be abusive* herself.

Statements indicating a possible abusiveness in your client
- She complains about her partner's involvement with
  friends and family.

- She frequently expresses anger at her partner.
- She frequently expresses suspicion as to her partner's fidelity and loyalty.
- She describes having to control her partner's moves to be certain he is faithful.
- She describes controlling the money in the household.

Note: None of these statements, by themselves, mean that there is in fact a violent relationship. However, any of these statements should prompt you to inquire further to rule out the presence of domestic violence.

Steps to Take

Once you have asserted the presence of domestic violence, there are certain steps you need to take. Those steps will vary, depending on whether you are working with the couple, with the victim, or with the perpetrator of the violence.

A. Couple Seeking Treatment or Couple in Treatment

Checklist:

- ☐ Refer the perpetrator to a peer group (batterers' groups) and/or individual treatment.
- ☐ Refer the victim to individual therapy and/or peer support group.
- ☐ Make a safety plan with the victim.
- ☐ Assess for a Tarasoff situation.
- ☐ Assess for child abuse.
- ☐ Assess for elder or dependent adult abuse.
- ☐ Make a referral for a medical check-up.

If you are either consulting with a couple that is currently actively engaged in domestic violence, or if you are working with a couple and determine during treatment that domestic violence is a current problem, tell both members that you cannot work with them conjointly. Research shows that if therapists do conjoint couples work with couples engaged in domestic violence, the therapeutic work can trigger more frequent and more violent episodes.

> It is crucial that the partners engaged in a violent relationship be seen *separately* in the appropriate treatment modalities.

Let them know that you will refer them separately for the previously named reasons: "We know that separate treatment works best in learning how to stop the violence. Once you are at a point where your therapists feel you can benefit from conjoint couples work, I will be happy to work with you."

Generally, it is best if the clinician making the assessment is not the same clinician seeing either or both of the partners in individual treatment. Thus, do not, if at all possible, see one of the partners while referring the other out. Doing so will most likely trigger feelings of competition, entitlement, envy, jealousy, abandonment, and rejection, all issues that are prevalent in such relationships anyhow and that will exacerbate the underlying problem.

If you do work individually with one of the partners, you should not be the therapist seeing them as a couple since you will have a therapeutic alliance with one of them that not only will make it difficult for the other partner to feel equally attended to, but will make it difficult for you to equally attend to the other partner. The following is the course of action of choice:

1. *Refer the perpetrator to a batterers' group and/or individual treatment.*

    Many court-approved batterers' groups deal exclusively with the issue of domestic violence. It appears that these peer groups, led by a qualified clinician, are helpful in breaking through the perpetrator's denial if he or she is not motivated in dealing with the issue. Often, the participants are court-ordered and do not believe that there is a problem.

Individual treatment is helpful when the violent partner is motivated to change, does understand that there is a problem, and does want to learn to do things differently. It can be undertaken concurrently with the group or as the treatment of choice.

2. *Refer the victim to individual therapy and/or a peer support group.*
   If the partners came originally for couples' treatment, the abused partner should be referred to another therapist to avoid the previously mentioned issues of competition, jealousy, envy, abandonment, and the like, which are likely to surface and trigger more violent episodes. If you know a therapist who has experience working with victims of domestic violence, it would be preferable. A peer support group of other victims of domestic violence, led by a qualified clinician, can also be a powerful tool to break through the denial that anything is amiss.

3. *Make a safety plan with the victim of domestic violence.*
   Give the abused partner the telephone number of a shelter, as well as of an attorney, and refer her or him to law enforcement. Educate her on restraining orders and on a safety plan, including packing important papers, staying at a friend's house, and the like. If the violence seems dangerous or imminent, assist her in contacting a shelter from your office.

4. *Evaluate whether a serious threat is being made against the partner.*
   If one of the partners makes a serious threat against the other partner in your presence, assess whether this falls under the Tarasoff ruling. Please refer to the previously discussed steps on how to proceed with this issue.

5. *Assess for child abuse, dependent adult and elder abuse.*
   Always assess for the presence of child abuse or dependent adult and elder abuse and take steps accordingly, as discussed earlier.

6. *Make a referral for a medical check-up.*
   Always assess whether a medical check-up might be necessary. If one of the partners has injuries or complains about physical pain, refer to the emergency room for a medical check-up.

B. Individual Client Seeking Treatment or in Treatment

Checklist:

- ☐ Consider peer-group support.
- ☐ Make a safety plan with the victim.
- ☐ Assess for a Tarasoff situation.
- ☐ Assess for child abuse.
- ☐ Assess for elder and dependent adult abuse.
- ☐ Make a referral for medical check-up.

In case of an individual client seeking treatment or being in treatment with you, whether she is the perpetrator or the victim, she will presumably be motivated to change since otherwise she wouldn't be in treatment with you. Also, in this case, there are no safety reasons that would warrant a referral of the client to another clinician.

1. *Recommend peer-group support in addition to individual therapy.*
   You might recommend a peer group for your client in addition to the individual treatment she is undertaking with you, especially if she is the perpetrator of the violence in the relationship, since (as mentioned previously) many have found the input of their peers helpful in learning to modify their behavior.

2. *Make a safety plan with the victim of domestic violence.*
   If your client (or prospective client) is the victim of domestic violence, always provide her with referrals to domestic violence shelters in the area, an attorney referral service, and information regarding obtaining a restraining order. Discuss the possibility of her staying with friends or family. Educate her on collecting her important papers where she can easily reach them, in case she needs to leave quickly. Encourage her to call 911 if necessary.

3. *Assess for serious threat against a partner.*
   If you are working with a client engaged in a violent relationship, whether the perpetrator or the victim, and she makes a serious threat against her partner, you must assess whether this falls under the Tarasoff ruling and proceed accordingly. Please be aware that the victim of domestic violence, too, might make such a threat on her partner's life.

4. *Assess for child abuse or dependent adult and elder abuse.*
   Assess for the presence of child abuse or dependent adult or elder abuse, and take steps accordingly, as discussed earlier.

5. *Refer for a medical check-up.*
   If your client appears injured, refer her to an emergency room for a medical check-up. Thus, your client might come to session with an injured arm, telling you her head has been hit against the floor, with facial bruises, or just in physical pain. She could have suffered broken bones or a concussion and needs to be assessed by medical professionals.

11

HOW TO HOSPITALIZE A CLIENT

I will now lead you through the mechanics of a psychiatric hospitalization. However, please also refer to the section in Chapter 10 "When and How to be Directive," which concerns itself with the assessment part of this topic.

Generally, it would be a good idea to have on hand a list of psychiatrists and psychiatric hospitals in the area, as well as the number for a local PET team, both at your office as well as at home.

CHECKLIST FOR HOSPITALIZATION

☐ Step 1: Assessment
☐ Step 2: Deciding on voluntary vs. involuntary hospitalization
☐ Step 3: Contacting the treating psychiatrist
☐ Step 4: Where to hospitalize: Contacting the hospital
☐ Step 5: Arranging for transportation
☐ Step 6: Releases of information and ongoing contact with client and hospital

Step 1: Assessment

Your first step toward a psychiatric hospitalization is your assessment that such a hospitalization is necessary. This means, in effect, that you have assessed that your client is either acutely suicidal, homicidal, a danger to self or others, or unable to care for herself. For example, if your client is floridly psychotic, even though she may not be suicidal or homicidal, she may still be a danger to herself and others and unable to care for herself.

When you have made that assessment and have not found a way to contain the situation on an outpatient basis, either by involving family members, friends, or other resources, hospitalization is the next step. Legally, you are allowed (or mandated) to breach confidentiality in these situations.

Step 2: Deciding on Voluntary vs. Involuntary Hospitalization

Once you have determined that in order to keep your client and others safe, she should be hospitalized, you must now determine whether you can hospitalize her voluntarily or whether an involuntary hospitalization is necessary. It is always preferable to have your client cooperate with you, not least because it is less likely that she will terminate therapy out of anger. Your determination of whether a voluntary hospitalization is possible rests on your client's capacity for insight, as well as on her willingness to cooperate with you. If she can see that she is in danger and needs to be in a safe place, she will be more likely to cooperate with a voluntary hospitalization than if she is psychotic, thinking people are out to get her and lock her up, and that you are part of this conspiracy. It depends on her condition whether you determine it is safe to tell her what you are planning.

Step 3: Contacting the Treating Psychiatrist

If your client has a treating psychiatrist and you get a chance to do so (as you will if the client cooperates with you for a voluntary hospitalization), get in touch with her psychiatrist. It is appropriate to tag this call as an emergency, since you have the psychiatrist's suicidal or homicidal client with you who is in need of hospitalization. Ideally, the psychiatrist should get back to you immediately. Leave a message with her assistant, her service, or her voicemail detailing the situation. Do not hesitate to use her emergency system. Ask for the hospital the psychiatrist is working with and let it know that you are initiating a hospitalization and request a call-back from the psychiatrist. It is hoped that she'll call you back soon and might be able to coordinate the admittance herself. However, if she does not get back to you in a timely manner, proceed with the hospitalization.

If this is an involuntary hospitalization, you might not get a chance to contact the psychiatrist until after your client is safely hospitalized. Be sure to do so. Your client's psychiatrist needs to know to be able to follow her treatment.[1]

Step 4: Where to Hospitalize: Contacting the Hospital

If your client has a psychiatrist, you will try to hospitalize her at the hospital the psychiatrist is affiliated with. Perhaps the psychiatrist will even do it herself. However, if she does not have a psychiatrist or if you can't get in touch with her psychiatrist and you don't know which hospital she's working with, it will be up to you to find a suitable facility. If your client is cooperating

---

[1]Make sure to have a release of information on file that allows you to exchange information with the psychiatrist.

with you, this will not be so difficult. Depending on her financial situation and whether or not she has health insurance that will cover a hospitalization, you will select a psychiatric hospital that has free beds. This might mean calling around, which, if the situation is a voluntary one, should not be a problem. Refer to your list of referrals for hospital names and phone numbers in the area.

When you call the hospital, let the staff know what the situation is and request transportation (if you are not able to contact friends or family members of your client who will transport her). Give the name of the treating psychiatrist if there is one. Educate your client as to what she can expect in the hospital (a place to keep her safe, a place to stabilize her). Let her know whether or not you will be in contact with her.

An involuntary hospitalization concerns a client who is a danger to herself or others or is gravely disabled (for example, a client who is floridly psychotic or in a full-blown manic phase) and who either does not have any insight into her situation or who just flat out refuses to be hospitalized (for whatever reason). This, in essence, is a hostile situation. As such, your first concern must be for your own safety. As in the plane where you are instructed in case of an emergency to first put on your *own* oxygen mask before attempting to help others, so here, too, must you ensure your own safety first before you can help your client. This means that if in order to initiate an involuntary hospitalization, you need to let your client leave your office, do so. Do not try to hold her back after she has made clear that she does not want to be hospitalized. It is up to your clinical judgment whether or not you want to tell her that you will initiate an involuntary hospitalization.

To initiate such an involuntary hospitalization, call 911 or a PET team and apprise them of the situation. You will most likely not have much influence over which hospital your client will be transported to. However, if there is a psychiatrist, let the psychiatrist know what you are doing and let the police or PET team know the name of the hospital the psychiatrist is affiliated with. This will not necessarily result in your client being hospitalized at that hospital, but it might.

Step 5: Arranging for Transportation

Do not, under any circumstances, transport your client yourself.

In the case of a voluntary hospitalization, contact friends or family members who might transport your client. If there are none, request transportation from the hospital or the local police department. If you do the latter, let them know that this concerns a voluntary hospitalization. You may consider a taxi as well, if you deem it safe.

In the case of an involuntary hospitalization, call 911 and let the police know what the situation is (you have a client who is a danger to herself or to others or is gravely disabled). Give them her home address or describe where she is headed. You may also want to inform family members to enlist their help. Ask them to keep you informed as to further developments. Instead of 911, you might also call a PET team. However, in the situation of an involuntary hospitalization, they will most likely want law enforcement officers to be present, since your client might become violent.

Step 6: Releases of Information and Ongoing Contact with Hospital Staff

As I mentioned previously, request a release of information authorizing you to communicate with the hospital staff. In this way you can stay apprised of new developments and may have input into the treatment. You might even request temporary privileges at the hospital and become the therapist of record if you so choose. On the other hand, you might decide not to be in ongoing contact with your client while she is in the hospital. This will depend on your policies and clinical judgment. However, you should at a minimum call your client and inform her of your plans regarding contact with her. Whenever you will see her next—whether in the hospital or after her discharge—give her an opportunity to express whatever feelings she may have in regard to the experience of the involuntary hospitalization and your role in it. You may state your motivation of keeping her and others safe, but do not expect her to be grateful or even understanding. Make sure you provide the space for her to explore what the whole episode means to her.

12

COORDINATING SERVICES WITH OTHER PROFESSIONALS

As you will have started to realize during the preceding chapters, other professionals can play a major role in your clinical practice. Thus, a very important part of your clinical work as a therapist is how you work with other professionals. We have already come across referrals to medical doctors, psychiatrists, neurologists, hospitalizations, and the like. In this chapter I will address in more depth how to go about coordinating your services with those of other professionals.

Once you have made an assessment for the need of another professional's services, the question arises as to whom you will refer your client. In your client's best interest, it is important that you are able to work with that professional cooperatively. That means, the psychiatrist (or medical doctor, neurologist, or the like) should be accessible and responsive to your calls, as well as respectful of your input. She should keep you informed as to her treatment and coordinate it with yours. It is important that you take an active role in this relationship, that you are an advocate for your client, and that you do not become intimidated by your colleague's degree. If you are not being informed or consulted to the degree you find desirable, make sure that you express this to the other professional (diplomatically, of course). Most important, the other professional should be accessible, responsive, and respectful to your client.

As simple as all of these requirements sound, none of them are to be taken for granted. Thus, once you find a professional you have success working with, cultivate that professional relationship and keep working with her.

How to Select the Professional You Will Refer to

Your first selection criteria will, of course, be the reason for referral. Depending on whether you are concerned about your client's physical health, whether you want to rule out an organic disorder, or whether you want her to be evaluated for medication, you will refer to a different specialist: perhaps an internist, a neurologist, and a psychiatrist, respectively.

If you do not already have any contacts established, your best course of action is to consult with your colleagues as to whom they have had success working with. The first person you will ask, as always, will be your supervisor. Other than that, ask your fellow therapists whom they have worked with successfully. The more you respect the work of the therapist you ask, the more likely it is that this person's referral will be what you are looking for. Make sure that you ask your colleague for permission to mention his or her name when you make contact with the professional. It will make a difference whether you speak with psychiatrist X as someone referred by a mutual colleague, as opposed to there being no connection between the two of you.

Of course, you might be lucky and hook up with a psychiatrist who is wonderful without having been referred to her. If that should be the case, make sure that you continue to work with her in the future.

Another way to get to know professionals in your area is to attend meetings and conferences. Always keep business cards of professionals in the area.

You might also need referrals to another therapist. Perhaps you are working with a woman who also wants to engage in couples' therapy. Being her therapist, you are not the appropriate person to also see her as part of a couple, so you want to be able to refer her to a professional whose work you trust. You might be assessing a prospective client whose case you do not end up taking. Again, you will want to be able to refer that person to a colleague whom you know and whose work you like. You might be working with a client who needs psychological testing. If that is not within your scope of practice, you will need to refer your client to a clinical psychologist or other professional who does conduct psychological tests.

You might want to make other referrals that will come up in your clinical practice. For all referrals that you make, be sure to note them down and keep them for future reference—perhaps in a file specifically designed for this purpose.

Make Direct Phone Contact to Refer

When you have selected the professional you want to refer to, obtain a written release of information from your client to make direct phone contact.

Let's assume you want to refer your client to a psychiatrist for medication evaluation. Make sure that you let the reception desk know the following: You are a therapist in the area who wants to refer a client to the doctor. You want to speak with the doctor to give her some background on the client before you send the client to her. You are asking for a call back. If you are not put through to the doctor just then (which is quite likely), be certain to leave a phone number where you can be reached, perhaps with the best times to reach you. If you only get a tape machine, either leave a message containing all of the information mentioned previously or call again. Give the doctor a couple of days to respond, but call again if she does not get back to you.

When you do talk to the doctor, introduce yourself and refer to the mutual colleague if there is one. For example: "My colleague XYZ referred me to you since I am looking for a psychiatrist for one of my clients."

Let her know that you want to refer a client to her and why. Thus, let her know that you have a depressed client whom you would like evaluated for medication, or a client with cognitive problems that you want to make sure are not of an organic nature, and so forth. Express your wish to be informed of the results of her examination.

With a release of information from your client, you can proceed to give the doctor your client's name. Without such a release, you cannot disclose your client's identity. However, you still can make that phone call to find out whether the doctor is taking on any new clients.

Follow-Up for Coordination of Services

Once your client has seen the specialist, send a release of information form with an accompanying letter to the doctor, requesting the results of her exam for your files. You might want to give her a call to discuss the findings in person, particularly if you have questions about anything, or you disagree about or don't understand something.

If your client will be in ongoing treatment with the psychiatrist, neurologist, or other professional, ensure a continuing relationship with that person. Particularly if your client is suicidal or psychotic and/or occasional hospitalizations are an issue, you want to make sure that you and the treating psychiatrist have a smooth working relationship.

In all of your dealings with a psychiatrist and other professionals, do not be intimidated. As a beginning therapist, particularly as a trainee and intern, it is not always easy to stand your ground vis-à-vis a licensed, credentialed professional. However, keep in mind that you are your client's therapist first and, as such, you work on her behalf. You are not an assistant to the doctor. If in doubt about a treatment issue, make sure you express your professional opinion, always with the client's best interest in mind, and document it in your client's file. With some doctors, you will have to be vigilant to set boundaries and insist on being taken seriously, as not every physician is respectful to a beginning therapist who is not yet licensed. However, be professional, courteous, and correct; maintain your role as the treating therapist; and insist on being consulted. You will most likely find that you will come to an arrangement with the treating physician.

Do consult with your supervisor regarding these issues, particularly if there are difficulties with establishing a cooperative working relationship with other professionals.

Releases of Information

Make sure you have the necessary written releases of information on file before you contact any professional with your client's identifying data. However, you can contact a professional to inquire about available space for treatment and so forth, even with information regarding a client, as long as you withhold the client's name and other identifying information.

Documentation

Be certain to document all contacts with other professionals in your client's file. Keep the releases of information in her file as well as written results of examinations the physician might send you. Keep copies of letters you might have sent to the physician as well.

Compiling a List of Referrals

Compile a list of referrals to have on hand for all of the following professionals:

Psychiatrists

- Both male and female (many clients have great difficulties working with professionals of one or the other gender).
- Who work with both adults and children (not all psychiatrists work with all age groups).
- Who accept private payment, insurance, county, state, and federal assistance: not all psychiatrists accept all methods of payment. Try to have at least one psychiatrist on your list who will accept MediCare or the like.

Neurologists

Internists

Therapists

- Male and female.
- Who work with children, adolescents, individuals, couples, and families.
- For issues that you do not work with; for example, major mental disorders like schizophrenia, substance abuse, and anxiety.
- Fee: you should be able to refer low-fee clients to a therapist as well. Make sure that at least some of the therapists on your list have a sliding scale for their fees. Perhaps a Community Mental Health Center might be of help here.

Psychological Testing

It would be a good idea to have both a male and a female psychologist to refer to, who are qualified to administer psychological tests. Again, many clients do not feel comfortable working with professionals of one or the other gender.

Psychiatric Hospital

- Private
- County

Drug and Alcohol Detoxification and Rehabilitation

For both men and women (most detox and rehab centers are not coed).

Emergency Room

Make sure you have the number for the closest emergency room on hand.

Other Referrals

You will collect more referrals suited to your specific needs as you continue to practice your profession. Over time, you will develop a network of professionals that you feel comfortable working with.[1]

---

[1]See Appendix I for a list of important phone numbers to assist you with compiling your own list of referrals.

13

WORKING WITH MINORS, COUPLES, AND FAMILIES

In this chapter we will look at some issues relating to working with minors, couples, and families that are distinct from those encountered in working with individual adults. However, these issues will not be so much clinical as they will be procedural and legal. The clinical issues of treating adults, minors, couples, and families are addressed in many publications and will be addressed in your schooling and training. Here, I will give you a brief overview of the most pertinent issues to be aware of when you begin your work with these populations.

WORKING WITH MINORS

The definition of a minor includes any person under the age of 18 who is not emancipated. I am now going to discuss several issues pertaining to work with such minors.

Whom You Can Treat

There are different situations in which you can legally treat a minor, and there are situations in which you cannot legally do so.

Minors under Age of 12 with Permission of Parents or Legal Guardian

> You *cannot under any circumstances* legally treat a minor under the age of 12 years without the permission of the parents or legal guardian.

That means that you may not *ever* legally treat a minor under the age of 12 years without permission from the appropriate persons.

Thus, if a minor under the age of 12 years comes to tell you that he or she needs therapy, you must request to speak with the minor's parent or legal guardian to obtain permission for treatment. If the parent or legal guardian withholds permission to treat, even if you deem it necessary, you may not treat this minor. However, do assess for child abuse or neglect regarding this parent or legal guardian withholding necessary treatment and make the appropriate report if you feel it is indicated. Imagine the following situation:

A minor under the age of 12 years comes to you in your capacity as a therapist and tells you he is very depressed and taking drugs, that he cannot talk to his parents, but that he feels he needs help. You talk to his parents regarding permission to treat and they withhold it. Now you might have to make a child abuse report since the parents are effectively withholding treatment that is necessary to maintain their child's health.

Another scenario:

A minor under the age of 12 comes to you in your capacity as a therapist and requests therapy but tells you that you may not contact his parents since they are abusive to him and would beat him if they knew he had talked to someone outside the family. You now must make a child abuse report.

The result of either of these two scenarios might be that Child Protective Services gets involved. If the child indeed is in need of treatment, the legal guardian (perhaps a relative or the state) will give written permission to treat so that the child can receive the necessary treatment. Thus, you will see a minor under the age of 12 years *always* with the explicit, written permission of the parent or legal guardian.

Minor Age 12 and Older with Permission of Parents or Legal Guardian

In this situation a minor who is 12 years old or older is brought to you by his parent or a legal guardian who is authorizing your treatment. Keep in mind that even when a minor of age 17 comes to see you, you usually must obtain written authorization to treat from her parents or legal guardian. Exceptions to this rule are listed in the following sections.

Minor Age 12 or Older without Permission of Parents or Legal Guardian

In some cases you *will* be able to see a minor who is 12 years or older *without* permission from the parents or the legal guardian. In order to do so, the following criteria must be fulfilled:

1. *The minor must be mature enough to intelligently participate in the treatment.*

   In addition, one of the two following criteria must be present as well:

2. *The minor would be a danger to self or others without treatment.*
3. *The minor is the alleged victim of child abuse or incest.*

The Minor Would Be a Danger to Self or Others without Treatment: Let us look at two scenarios to exemplify this situation. The first scenario regards a minor who is a danger to himself: Imagine a minor who is 12 years old or older, who comes to you and tells you he is suicidally depressed but does not want his parents to know. You now have to assess whether it would indeed be best for him not to notify his parents, and if you deem this to be the case, document your decision not to notify the parents and why you think it best in the minor's file. Clearly, the minor is a danger to himself if he does not receive treatment, and thus, if you feel he can intelligently participate in treatment, you can treat him.

However, if you feel he cannot intelligently participate—perhaps because of developmental delays that render him much more immature than his chronological age suggests—you may not treat him without parental consent and must notify the parents of the situation and obtain consent before you can treat him. Don't forget to assess for the severity of his suicidality and act accordingly.

The second scenario regards a minor who is a danger to others: Imagine that a 16-year-old with a history of impulse control problems comes to you very angry with his girlfriend who broke up with him. He does not want his parents to know that he is seeing you. Again, you have to assess whether he can intelligently participate in treatment and then whether it is indeed best not to notify his parents. Clearly, he might be a danger to others—in this case, the ex-girlfriend—if he does not receive treatment. Don't forget to assess for Tarasoff and act accordingly.

The Minor Is the Alleged Victim of Child Abuse or Incest: Imagine a case where a minor 12 years old or older comes to you and tells you she has been the victim of child abuse or incest. She does not want her parents to know that she is seeing you. Again, you must assess whether she can intelligently participate in treatment and whether it would be best not to notify the parents. Document your decision and the reasons in her file. If the parent is the abuser, as in incest, it appears clear that it would not be in the minor's best interest to notify the parents of her treatment and ask their permission to do so. However, in either case you will have to make a child abuse report.

Be aware that if you see a minor aged 12 or older without parental consent in treatment, the minor is liable for the financial obligation to you. Set the fee so that the minor can take care of it herself. However, should she not pay you, you will have no legal recourse to recover the fee, since a minor is not legally liable for debts incurred. Her parents are also not liable since you are treating the minor without their permission, and you cannot approach them due to your client's right to confidentiality.

Legally Emancipated Minor

This is the case of a legally emancipated minor—that is, a minor under the age of 18 who is legally emancipated—coming to you for treatment. A legally emancipated minor is being legally treated as an adult. Therefore, you do not need to take matters of guardianship into account and can treat this minor if it seems clinically appropriate.

Intake

Working with minors requires a modified intake and assessment procedure. Generally, you will work with minors who are being brought into treatment by their parents or legal guardian. In those cases you need to meet with both the minor and the parents, as well as with the minor and the parents separately.

Meeting with Both Parents and Minor

In your initial meeting both the minor and the parent(s) will be present, since you cannot see the minor—even in assessment—without written permission by the parent or legal guardian. Thus, your first order of business is to have the parent or legal guardian sign an *Authorization to Treat a Minor* form. Generally, go over the assessment and intake issues discussed previously. Ask both parent and minor in turn questions regarding the issues relevant to intake and assessment:

"What brings you here?"
"How long has this been going on," and so forth.

Observe the interaction between minor and parent(s) since this will give you some clues as to the family dynamics.

If the minor is old enough to read and write, make sure that she gets a chance to look over the form her parent(s) signed and that she receives and signs her own copy of the treatment contract and informed consent form. While legally such a step is meaningless, clinically it will help you—and the minor—not to lose sight of the fact that it is she who will be your client, not the parent. However, it *is* important that you establish rapport with the parents as well, since they will decide whether your minor client will continue in treatment.

This can, in fact, be a balancing act: to maintain your client's confidentiality, on the one hand—which would call for maximum distance from the parents—and to maintain a connection with the parents so that they will not take your client out of treatment, which might undermine your client's trust in the confidentiality of her therapy with you. I will discuss this point further on under the heading "Occasional Meetings with Parents."

Meeting with Parent and Minor Separately

Let both parents and minor know in your first session that you will meet with them separately as part of your assessment. This is necessary to get a clearer picture of the parents' and the minor's take on the situation and to allow them to speak freely about their concerns. Since you let them know about this right away and in fact will utilize the information gained from these meetings to assess the situation and ultimately decide whether or not you will treat this minor, these meetings should not unduly tax the relationship between you and your prospective client. On the other hand this meeting should serve to establish more of a rapport between yourself and the parent, thus, it is hoped, ensuring that the work between you and your minor client will not be disrupted unduly

Confidentiality/Parental Access to Treatment Records

A major issue in the case of treatment of minors is the issue of confidentiality. Particularly with adolescents, you will find that they will often not engage in the therapeutic process if it is not clearly established what is being reported to the parents and what isn't. It is important that you raise this issue in the first meeting, making clear that it will be the minor who will be your client and that much of the quality of the therapeutic work will depend on the degree of confidentiality that your client can be assured of. Take your time discussing this issue. These negotiations will tell you something that can be diagnostic about the family dynamics. Some parents find it easy to relinquish control, may even be eager to do so. Others might find it difficult not to be informed of everything that is happening in treatment. In any case, allow the parents to express their concerns and elicit the minor's input. Legally, the parents do have the right to know what is going on in treatment.

Ideally, you will arrive at an understanding with the parents and the minor that you will not inform the parents of anything happening in treatment without the minor's knowledge and consent unless it involves matters where the minor's health and safety are seriously endangered.

Representatives of a minor (i.e., parents or legal guardians)

are entitled to access the records of their minor child in treatment. However, legally you are allowed to refuse to give such access ". . . where the health care provider determines that access to the patient records would have a detrimental effect on the provider's professional relationship with the minor patient or the minor's physical safety or psychological well-being" (Health & Safety Code 1795.14). It is hoped that you will not come into a situation where a parent is demanding to see his child's treatment records and you feel you must refuse, to protect your treatment relationship with your client as well as your client's well-being. The danger that disgruntled parents who have been denied access to treatment records will pull their child out of treatment is quite real. Thus, you hope to forestall such problems by going over issues of confidentiality and coming to a mutual understanding regarding the importance of creating a safe space for the minor where she can express herself freely without repercussions.

Generally, in order for treatment to be effective, it is necessary that the minor trusts that his treatment will be confidential.

Occasional Meetings with Parents

I have found that occasional meetings with parents can do much to alleviate this problem. Some parents do not need or want such meetings and are completely unobtrusive, respecting their child's privacy and right to confidentiality of treatment or even being indifferent to it. However, some parents become rather anxious, perhaps even threatened regarding what is taking place in treatment and can be reassured by occasional meetings or phone contact. These meetings or phone conversations should not be lengthy and should not find you disclosing any detailed descriptions of therapy with their child.

Rather, give the parents a forum to voice their concerns, to be heard, and to get a sense of not being excluded. You might make general statements as to how their child is doing:

"She is settling in."

"She is discussing issues that are troubling her," and the like.

It is not necessary to give any details regarding what these issues are, unless your minor client wants you to. Should this latter be the case, it is advisable to have the minor participate in the session and encourage her to express directly to her parents what she wants them to know. Ask the parents to express *their* fears and concerns.

Sometimes parents will request an "emergency meeting" because they feel overwhelmed by problems involving their minor child. This might mean scheduling either a family session or a separate session for the parents. If the latter is the case, make sure that this session is used to explore their fears and their difficulties and does not center entirely on the minor as the Identified Patient. If you are conducting an occasional family session, do not forget that you are primarily the minor child's individual therapist and don't want to jeopardize this relationship. Often, a brief meeting will calm the situation.

If a request for a family or emergency meeting happens frequently, refer the parents to another therapist for family therapy, couples' therapy, or their own individual therapy, whichever seems appropriate. Often, parents try to utilize their children's therapist to address their own issues. Be alert for this possibility and make the appropriate referral. You might say something like this:

"I realize how difficult it sometimes is for you and I think you could really benefit from having your own person to talk to and to help you with some of these issues. Let me refer you to a colleague for your own individual therapy."

"I can see that you have some issues as a family that would benefit from being attended to more specifically. I want to refer you to a colleague of mine for family therapy so that you can address these issues. Since I am your child's therapist, I am not the right person to do this."

"It seems that some of the problems you experience with your
child really have more to do with what is going on between the two of you as a couple. I would like to refer
you to a colleague of mine for couples' therapy so you
can address some of these problems in more privacy.
Because I am your child's therapist, I am not the right
person to do this."

The idea is, in the service of the treatment and the best interest of your minor client, to contain the parents, to calm the
situation, and to make the appropriate referrals so that the treatment of your minor client can continue. Prepare yourself for
having to be patient. Often, parents are not ready to look at
their own difficulties—not uncommonly, this is precisely a factor in their child's difficulties. Be prepared to suggest individual
therapy, couples' therapy, or family therapy to the parents of
your minor client more than once. Be careful *how* you make
these referrals. Parents, particularly when they have issues that
need to be attended to, might become rather defensive. Do keep
in mind that most parents do the best they can with the tools
they have available. Most parents are not sadistic psychopaths.
On the contrary, they are bringing their child to you because
they realize there is a problem and want some kind of help. Be
sensitive to the parents and their needs. The following suggestions usually meet with a minimum of defensiveness on the
parents' part—even though they do not always lead to the desired result of therapy for the parents:

"I can see how upsetting this is for you and think it might be
really good for you if you had someone to talk to on a
regular basis. I would like to refer you to my colleague
XYZ."
"I see that you work very hard to make things better for your
child. What about yourself? Is there any place for you to
go where you can talk about how this feels for you?"

"You seem to be under a lot of stress and I believe it would
be helpful if you had someone to talk to on a regular
basis. I cannot be *your* therapist since I am your child's
therapist. Let me refer you to a colleague of mine."

Releases of Information[1]

Do not forget that you need the minor client's parents' or legal guardian's written authorization for release of information
before you can talk to any other professionals. If the minor has
been in prior treatment, is seeing a psychiatrist, has severe problems in school, and so forth, you should obtain releases of information that will allow you to speak with these professionals
to plan your treatment appropriately. When you do so, do not
disclose any unnecessary information about your treatment of
the minor. You want to obtain their input to facilitate your treatment, not to have a free-for-all gossip session about your client.

It helps to have your questions somewhat organized in your
head or written down, so that you don't become sidetracked so
easily. This way, you can be sure that you asked for all the pertinent information and don't find yourself having to call back
because you forgot to ask something important.

Sometimes, a former therapist of your client might ask you:
"And how is XYZ doing with you?" Do not be forthcoming with
detailed descriptions of the treatment. You have obtained a
release of information for the purpose of facilitating your treatment of your client and giving a detailed account of it to a
former therapist who is not treating her anymore does not fall
under that description. However, alienating the former therapist would not serve your purpose of facilitating your treatment

---

[1]Most of these considerations are true regarding releases of information for an adult
client as well.

and treatment planning either. Be polite, with a statement like the following:

"She's settling in."
"We are in the process of determining relevant issues," and the like.

A conversation with a currently treating psychiatrist, on the other hand, will sound quite different. In that case, your goal is not only to obtain information about past treatment but also to establish a smooth relationship where one person will alert the other to changes and new developments, as appropriate and necessary. Thus, if the treating psychiatrist asks you that same question, "And how is she doing with you," your answer will be more explicit, since facilitating treatment and treatment planning will include coordinating services with the psychiatrist now and in the future. In effect, you and the treating psychiatrist are a treatment team working with this client.

WORKING WITH COUPLES

As with minors, several special issues are to be taken into account when working with a couple that are different from those in working with individual adults.

Intake

Generally, your intake procedure when working with a couple is very similar to the intake for an individual. Your first meeting will be with both partners together, and you will obtain intake information and give all pertinent information so they can sign the informed consent form. Each partner must sign his or her own informed consent form unless you have space for two signatures on one form. That means that *you must obtain both partners' signature*, since they will both be your clients as part of the couple you are seeing.

Tell the couple that part of the intake procedure will be to *meet with each of them separately* for assessment purposes. These separate meetings might take one treatment hour each or one-half of a treatment hour each, whatever seems practical for both the couple and you. However, it should not be less than one-half a session for each partner. I have described earlier[2] what the rationale is behind this approach, as well as what to do and how to evaluate their difficulties or even their refusal to comply with your request for separate meetings. Let them know that you will meet jointly after you have met separately to decide together where to go from there.

Policies on Separate Meetings and Secrets

In the first meeting you should address your policy regarding separate meetings (aside from the intake and assessment meeting) and what you will do with "secrets" that one of them might tell you. There is really no one "right" way to handle this. Depending on how you work, you might tell them that you do not meet separately and that you do not keep any communication from one partner to you secret from the other. Or you might tell them that you do meet separately at times as needed, and that you will (or will not) keep confidential what the partner you are seeing tells you. Obviously, it will be more demanding for you to hold information that one partner has given you and not reveal it to the other *and*, most important, still work effectively with the couple. As you start out with your clinical work, it is perhaps advisable to learn the ropes by *not* meeting with the partners separately, other than for assessment purposes, and *not* keeping information "secret." However, this is really a mat-

---

[2]See Chapter 10 on issues pertaining to domestic violence.

ter of preference, ability to keep boundaries, and work effectively in ambiguous situations. Consult with your supervisor regarding this issue.

Your guideline in the end will be this: Can you still work effectively with the couple while sticking by the policy you announced at the beginning of treatment?

Here are three scenarios to illustrate what difficulties you might encounter, depending on your approach to "secrets":

You Do Not Share Information Obtained by One Partner with the Other Partner

Let's say you *allow for occasional individual meetings with one or the other partner as needed, and your policy is to keep private what you have been told privately.* You might have heard something in an individual session that you feel will prevent you from working effectively with the couple on their goal of "making the relationship work." Imagine that this couple is having great difficulties communicating and sharing any free time and interests. He is never home, and when he is, he is angry with her. They have not had sex in months. She is depressed and wonders whether she should file for divorce. He reveals in a private session that he has had an affair for over a year and does not plan to stop the affair. He does not want you to bring this up in the couples' meetings nor is he willing to work toward addressing it there. You might now be in a situation where you feel you cannot work effectively with this couple toward resolving their difficulties. However, *you may not reveal this information in the couples' session if your policy is one of keeping private what has been told to you privately.* What you may do, once you assess that you cannot work effectively with them, is just announce that: "I am not able to continue working with you effectively. It would not be ethical of me to continue to see you under these circumstances."

Do not attempt to persuade the partner with the "secret" to

share this secret. However, do let him know that you will not be able to continue working with them if this information is not shared or unless the goals of the treatment are redefined. Address with him the possibility that this might be his way of ending the treatment. However, it is not up to you to decide on the best course of action for this or any couple (as long as no one's life and safety is at stake).

You Will Share Information Obtained by One Partner with the Other Partner

On the other hand, if your policy is *to allow occasional separate meetings as needed but not to keep anything confidential that has been addressed in those meetings,* the implications of the situation described previously would be quite different. For one, you have reason to assume that the partner who reveals his affair to you actually *does* want this to be brought into the couples' session, since he already knows that you will not keep it secret. Thus, you might address in the individual meeting how this issue will be addressed in the upcoming couples' session.

You Do Not Meet Separately and You Will Share All Information

And finally, if your policy is *not to meet individually beyond the assessment meeting,* the kind of situation addressed earlier would likely not occur. It is possible that the issue of the affair will go unaddressed for a long time or will never come up. However, you will be working with the couple's dynamics as both partners present themselves to you in the room.

Keep in mind: Do not get invested in any particular outcome in your treatment. The couple you are working with might or might not stay together. It is not up to you to make a judgment about this. It is your job to facilitate the exploration of the issues the partners have. The decision as to whether they will remain a couple or not is entirely theirs.

If work with a particular couple engenders strong feelings in you, it is time to address those in supervision and your own therapy.

Confidentiality and Releases of Information

The issue of confidentiality is somewhat more complicated for a couple in treatment than when you are seeing an individual. Keep in mind that in the case of treating a couple, *your client is the couple.* Thus, generally all releases of information must be signed by both partners—even if the information pertains to only one of the partners.

Since your client is the couple, it means that if one partner wants to release the contents of the treatment records to a third party for any reason, you must obtain the written authorization for release of information of *both* partners in order to do so. For example, if one partner later in a divorce proceeding wants you to testify on his behalf, you may not do so without the written permission of the other partner as well. If one partner is suing for full custody of the children and wants you to testify on her behalf regarding the couples' therapy, you may not do so without the written consent of the other partner. On the other hand, in a situation that is nonadversarial for the couple, if one partner gets into a car accident that leaves him incapacitated, and as a result, depressed and he wants you to testify to that effect, you must also get the written release of both partners if you are to use information you gained while treating the couple. Make sure they understand this fact at the beginning of therapy.

If you receive a subpoena or other request for information regarding your treatment of the couple, you always must obtain both partners' written consent in order to disclose any information, including the fact that the partners are your clients.

You should routinely invoke the privilege in the face of any such request, perhaps similar to this: "I am sorry, but this is privileged information. I cannot tell you whether that person (these persons) are in treatment with me without a written authorization for release of information."

Always inform your clients when requests like these are being made.[3]

Converting to Individual Therapy

Sometimes, when you work with a couple, one or both of the partners may want to convert to individual therapy. They might want to see you as their individual therapist since they already know you and have built rapport with you. Again, there is no generally accepted "rule" as to how such situations should be handled. I will in this section discuss some scenarios and the issues that arise in order for you to make a clinically sound decision as to how you want to proceed. Also, it makes a difference whether you work in a large city, where you have a great number of colleagues to refer to, or whether you work in a small town, where you may be one of few clinicians serving a wide catchment area and may not have the luxury of considering referrals. In the end, you will make this decision according to your professional judgment.

Let us assume a case where one partner wants to see you in individual therapy while both partners are engaged in couples' therapy. It is easy to see how the situation would become asymmetrical, skewing the transference the couple has developed with you in couples' therapy and introducing new issues of mistrust, competition, envy, jealousy, abandonment, and the like. You might in effect set up a situation that might render

---

[3]Please see "Third Party Requests for Information" in Chapter 15 for more information on how to handle these situations.

you ineffectual with both the couple and the individual client. Thus, it is not advisable to see one partner in individual therapy while the couples' treatment is still underway. In such a situation, refer to a colleague for the individual case. Don't forget that your client is the couple and that you signed up for work with the couple when you commenced treatment with these partners. Should you find yourself wanting to work with one partner and entertaining the idea of referring the couple to a colleague, it is time to address this issue with your supervisor. Clearly, such a state of affairs would indicate countertransference issues that need to be addressed.

How about a situation where both partners want to work with you in individual therapy as well as in couples' therapy? I suggest that you not work with the individuals if you see them in couples' therapy. Even though this situation would be symmetrical, it might be difficult to contain what you know from individual sessions and not let it spill into the couples' sessions. Therefore, it is advisable that you refer both partners to see other clinicians. In this way, you keep your commitment to working with the couple.

Let us assume that you have ended treatment with the couple, and both partners approach you for individual treatment. Again, I suggest that you do not undertake work in this situation. Ideally, you would refer both partners out for treatment to avoid tainting the couples' therapy in retrospect (by preferring one partner over the other), and perhaps undoing some of the work that you have accomplished together in couples' treatment.

In the situation where the couples' therapy has ended and one partner approaches you for individual therapy, be aware that you will have to turn down the other partner's request for individual treatment should it come. You may want to discuss this issue with the partner who first approached you. Keep in mind that, should the other partner call, you cannot disclose the fact that you are seeing the first partner in therapy and you cannot use that fact as a reason for referral.

More commonly, only one of the partners is interested in

entering individual therapy. If this is the case and you feel comfortable working with him, make sure he knows that if the couple wanted to resume couples' treatment later, you would not be a good option because of the fact that by then, you would be his individual therapist and the treatment relationships would be asymmetrical.

Generally, if you are asked regarding individual treatment by a member of a couple that you are or have been seeing in couples' therapy, do not respond immediately unless it is to let them know that you will *not* see either of them individually. It is always a good idea to reserve yourself some time to think. You might say something like this: "Let me consider this possibility. I'll get back to you on this."

This gives you time to think about it and discuss it with your supervisor or obtain some consultation before you make up your mind.

WORKING WITH FAMILIES

Working with families in many ways combines issues that arise when working with minors, as well as issues when working with couples.[4]

Intake

Your intake of a family will be similar to the intake of both minors and couples. You will have an initial assessment/intake meeting in which authorizations for treatment of a minor have

---

[4]To get an understanding of the *clinical* issues pertaining to psychodynamic work with families, the following books are useful initial works with which to familiarize yourself: Scharff, D., and Savege Scharff, J. (1991), *Object Relations Family Therapy;* and Slipp, S. (1991), *The Technique and Practice of Object Relations Family Therapy.*

to be signed for each minor who will be in the family therapy and each minor who is in the room. All who can read and write should receive an informed consent form to follow along as you are explaining it and to sign. However, the adults (parents, legal guardian) *must* sign the informed consent form.

If the adults present are not the legal guardians of the child or children in the family, you may not include these minors in the treatment without receiving written authorization to do so by the legal guardian (which might sometimes be a DCFS worker who requests family therapy), and you should also obtain the signature of the legal guardian for the informed consent form before you begin treatment.

Once you have obtained all authorizations to treat all minors involved and all signed informed consent forms, let all family members know that you will conduct separate intake/assessment sessions with each of them (of course, this will exclude the 1-year-old baby on her mother's arm), and then will meet conjointly with all family members present to make a decision and a plan as to where to go from there. Again, the separate sessions might be one-half treatment hour each but should not be less, so that you have enough time to collect information. Let the family members know that information they give you in the individual meetings will be shared in the family sessions if you feel it is necessary, but it will otherwise be kept confidential unless it involves information pertaining to the legal exception to confidentiality (child abuse, danger to self and others, and so forth).

Policies on Separate Meetings and Secrets

This issue is similar in families and couples. Determine at the outset of therapy how you will handle communications that are made to you by one family member in the absence of the others and then communicate this policy to the family. Take into consideration the issues raised in the section regarding couples.

Confidentiality and Releases of Information

When working with a family, your client is the family. The issues, again, are similar to the issues raised by working with couples. Please take into consideration the issues addressed in that section.

If one family member (or that person's legal guardian) wishes you to testify on his or her behalf, you must obtain the written authorization to release information from all family members in treatment or their legal representatives. Thus, if one family member wants you to speak with his or her psychiatrist regarding his or her progress in the family therapy, obtain releases of information from all family members in treatment or their legal representatives.

If you get a request for information regarding one family member, you must get all adults' and legal guardians' signatures to be able to release any information, even though the information requested pertains to only one of the family members. However, since the information you will share was obtained in family therapy, you will have to allude to that fact and cannot do so without the authorization of the other family members or their legal representatives.

Make sure that the family members understand these issues when you begin treatment with them.

Converting to Individual Therapy

Again, the issues that arise when you consider converting clients you have seen or are seeing in family therapy into individual clients parallel those issues raised when working with couples. Please consult that earlier section regarding working with couples.

14

WORKING WITH COURT-ORDERED CLIENTS

Some of you will work regularly with court-ordered clients, and some of you will only occasionally get a referral of a client or clients that are court-ordered to receive treatment. In the following sections I will address some issues that are specific to this particular situation.

MOTIVATION FOR TREATMENT

I will only briefly address the issue of motivation for treatment in the case of court-ordered therapy. Clearly, your court-ordered client has the pressure to complete a certain amount of treatment hours so as not to incur further legal consequences. This motivation is a far cry from someone coming to you who is interested in personal growth or otherwise privately motivated for treatment. Not unusually, a court-ordered client might have a pronounced lack of insight into her problems, and treatment might sometimes feel as if you are going through the motions without being able to actually impact the client. Learning to work with resistances and defenses will be very helpful here.

In other cases, the court order for treatment might provide

an opportunity for a client who might otherwise never have considered the help of therapeutic treatment but who is well able to utilize what is offered. For children in particular, a court-order for treatment is not that different from being brought by a parent. In both cases, the client has not made the decision to engage in therapy, and you will have to address this issue early on.

Generally speaking, you cannot know beforehand whether any given court-ordered client will be able to benefit from court-ordered treatment or not.

I recommend addressing the fact of the court order at the beginning of treatment. For example:

"You are here because the court ordered you to be. What are your thoughts about that?"

"Do you have any feelings about being forced to come here?"

"I imagine you must feel angry and perhaps resentful having to come to therapy."

"How do you feel about being here, since you have not chosen to come here of your own accord?" or something to that effect.

Be prepared to engage in dialogue about their motivation. Do not assume that the court-ordered clients will trust you. In fact, trust will be a major issue, since you will in most cases have to report to the court.

YOUR QUALIFICATIONS

The initial referral might come from a DCFS worker referring either children or parents to treatment that the court ordered they receive. You might be contacted by the parents themselves, who will let you know that they are court-ordered to receive treatment or that their children are court-ordered to do so. The initial call might come from an individual who has been involved in an abusive situation, either as perpetrator or victim, and whom the court ordered to receive treatment. In fact, the court might order treatment for any number of reasons.

Whatever the case, the first issue to clarify is what qualifications you as the clinician must possess to satisfy the court requirements. If you provide treatment without meeting those qualifications, the court will not acknowledge the work you have provided. Thus, when you receive a call requesting court ordered treatment, you might say something like the following:

"What are the qualifications the court expects the therapist who provides the treatment to have?"

"What did the court order say? Who is qualified to provide such treatment for you?"

Get clarification on the following points:

- Will the court accept treatment from a therapist with your qualifications (an MFT-intern, an MSW, a Ph.D. candidate, and so forth, under clinical supervision by a licensed clinician)?
- Does the court require that you have a certain amount of experience and training, and what is it?

If the client does not know, ask her to find out and contact you again. For example, if an abusive client is court-ordered to receive group batterers' counseling, he must receive it from a therapist/counselor who is running a court-approved batterers' group.

REPORTING REQUIREMENTS

Once you have established that you are, indeed, qualified to provide the treatment the court ordered, you need to find out what your reporting requirements will be. Get clarification on the following points:

- Whom do you have to report to?
- What information do you have to report?
- How often?
- In what way (in letter, on the phone, in person)?
- Will you have to testify in court on the treatment?
- Are you required to notify the court if the client drops out of treatment?

If you work for an agency that assigns you cases, among them court-ordered cases, you will not have much choice in this matter. Otherwise, consider whether you feel capable working under these circumstances, which erode confidentiality a great deal. If you have the chance, discuss this with your supervisor before you accept the case.

PAPERWORK

You have determined that you are qualified to treat a court-ordered client, and you know what the reporting requirements are. It is now time to make sure that you have all the paperwork in place that will allow you to speak to whichever parties you must speak to regarding the treatment.

Copy of the Court Order

Request a copy of the court order for your files, to make sure that you have in writing what is expected of you and what you are required to report.

Releases of Information

Make sure you have all the necessary releases of information.

Authorization to Treat

Make sure you have the authorization to treat the court-ordered client signed by the appropriate source. For example, if you are seeing a minor who is court-ordered to receive treatment and who is with DCFS at this point, make sure you have the authorization signed by the DCFS worker and *not* by the mother, who may have called in to arrange for the treatment but who is no longer the legal guardian of her child.

REPORTS

As part of your treatment of a court-ordered client, you will most likely be expected to write regular reports on the treatment. Please refer to Chapter 17 for a detailed account of how to do that. Perhaps you will be provided with a guideline as to what is expected to appear in the report. Follow it. If the court has suspended the privilege and you are ordered to report on your treatment, you must do so.

WHO'S RESPONSIBLE IF THE CLIENT DROPS OUT?

Sometimes, a court-ordered client drops out of treatment. It is not your responsibility to keep a client in treatment. It is your responsibility to provide treatment, but it is your client's responsibility to show up for it. However, you may be required to notify the court (or DCFS worker, or other intermediary) of the fact that the client has dropped out. Be certain to have that information in place. As always, confer with your supervisor as to how to proceed should this happen.

15

THIRD-PARTY REQUESTS FOR INFORMATION REGARDING YOUR CLIENT

This is a situation that you will encounter sooner or later: a third party—perhaps a lawyer, a physician, or a spouse—contacts you regarding your client. In the following I will give you a general approach to a request for information and then discuss in some depth a few scenarios of requests for information from different sources.

GENERAL APPROACH

Generally—unless you have a written release of information from your client to speak to or release written information to a particular person, or unless the person wanting to speak to you is the parent or legal guardian of a minor client whom you are seeing with the parent's or legal guardian's consent—you may not acknowledge that the person they are referring to is your client, let alone discuss the treatment with them. Be explicit about the fact that you are guarding your client's confidentiality.

If in doubt or pressured, you can and should claim the legal privilege governing the therapist–client relationship. Also, be certain to always inform your client as soon as possible of any attempt a third party makes to elicit information from you. If indeed he wants you to speak to them, he will give you a release of information to do so.

Thus, it is best if your first response to any inquiry (be it from spouses, law enforcement, lawyers, social workers, or physicians) is a reminder of your duty to protect your clients' confidentiality, including their identity. Be prepared to say something like this: "I am sorry, but I cannot legally disclose the identity of my clients."

Be equally prepared that the caller might get angry with you and even threaten you for "stonewalling." Never mind that. As mentioned earlier, it is your legal responsibility to safeguard your client's confidentiality. In the following sections, I will discuss a few examples of possible requests for information regarding a client, as well as ways of handling such requests professionally.

WRITTEN REQUESTS FOR INFORMATION

Generally speaking, if you receive a request for information regarding a client by letter, always notify your client of it (perhaps showing her the letter) and file the request in the client's file. Do not respond to it unless it contains a release of information signed by your client. Even then, make sure you notify your client before you proceed to share any information with a third party. Your client might change her mind. Keep in mind that releases of information are revocable at any time by your client.

CALL FROM A SPOUSE OR PARTNER

Imagine that you get a call from your client's partner, stating that she must urgently speak to you about him. Let us further assume that you do not know her. Unless you have a release of information from your client permitting you to speak to the spouse, do not acknowledge that he is actually in therapy with you. Use your mantra: "I am sorry, I cannot legally disclose the identity of my clients."

Now let's assume that you *do* know her because she has brought her husband to therapy and you saw her. However, without a release of information you still may not acknowledge to her that her husband is your client.

In any case, she may become angry with you. If she becomes abusive on the phone, state calmly, "I am going to hang up now" and do so. Make sure that you inform your client of this incident and ask whether he wants you to speak to his spouse. If so, obtain a written release of information.

This scenario is somewhat different when your client's spouse calls you, stating that your client is suicidal or homicidal. Do get in touch with your client immediately and if your assessment yields that he is indeed a danger to himself or others, you may find yourself speaking to his spouse in an effort to prevent the danger. Keep in mind that if your client is a danger to himself or others, there is no privilege.

CALL FROM A SOCIAL WORKER

Imagine that you get a call from a social worker referring to your client, who is on her caseload—perhaps even referred by her. Again, unless you have a release of information signed by your client, you must state that you cannot disclose the identity of your clients. She may become annoyed with you for slowing things down, but she does, of course, know that you are legally mandated to protect your clients' identity. You may suggest something like this: "I am sorry, but without a written release of information I cannot disclose the identity of my clients. If she is a mutual client, please send me a release and I will be happy to speak to you."

This will not be new to her, although it may be inconvenient. Do not alienate the worker. The two of you need to be able to work together in your client's best interest. Verify with Ms. Green that the person who called you was indeed her social worker and let her know about the request for information.

CALL FROM A LAW ENFORCEMENT OFFICER

You might get a call from a law enforcement officer, stating that he needs information on Ms. Green, who is apparently a client of yours. The same rules apply in this situation: If you do not have a release of information from your client in hand (or if your client has not told you personally that you may speak to a particular person), you must state that you cannot legally disclose the identity of your clients. Even if the police officer threatens you with legal action, do insist on the client–therapist privilege and do not disclose anything. Law enforcement officers know that you can only be compelled by a court of law to break confidentiality (besides the other legal exceptions).

SUBPOENA OR CALL FROM A LAWYER

You might get a subpoena from a lawyer to turn over records pertaining to your client's treatment. Do not do so without your client's permission. Insist on the client–therapist privilege and state that you cannot disclose your client's identity without release of information. The lawyer might call you and let you know that a court decision has been reached to revoke privilege and that the papers are underway. However, unless you have your client's release of information or the court's notification that privilege has been revoked *in hand*, do not disclose anything. If the court actually finds that your testimony is needed, the court will suspend privilege and notify you of it. It is then that you must testify.

Especially in the cases that involve legal action and possible testimony by you, you should consider getting in touch with your professional organization and get legal advice.

CALL FROM OTHER TREATING PROFESSIONALS

Sometimes you might get a call from another treating professional requesting information on your client. Perhaps your client was even referred by that professional. If you have a written release of information in hand, go ahead and give the requested information. However, do inform your client of the exchange. If there is no written release of information, inform the other professional of that fact: "I am sorry, I cannot disclose the identity of my clients without a release of information. If this is indeed a mutual client, please send me a written release of information and I'll be happy to speak to you."

As always, make sure your client also is informed of the request by the other professional.

CALL FROM A TEACHER OR OTHER THIRD PARTY RE: A MINOR IN TREATMENT

A teacher, physician, or other third party might call you regarding a child you see in therapy. Unless you have a release of information signed by the parent or legal guardian, you may not give out any information.

When you do have such a release, make sure that your client—the minor—knows that you will be talking to a third party at her parents' request or with her parents' permission, and what you will tell that party. Clinically, it is very important that the child not be kept out of the loop of information, even though legally you do not need to inform her. It is important that the minor gets an opportunity to express her feelings and thoughts about the fact that you speak with a third party, particularly since she has no legal power to stop you from doing so, should she want to.

YOUR CLIENT REQUESTS THAT YOU SHARE INFORMATION OR PRIVILEGE HAS BEEN REVOKED

In this situation, you have received a request for information regarding your client and your client has either given a release of information, or privilege has been revoked. In either case, you must now disclose information regarding your client to a third party.

If privilege has been revoked, inform your client and let him know that you are legally compelled to disclose treatment information. Let him know what the circumstances are (if he doesn't know already) and what kind of information you will likely have to share. Make sure that you explore with him how he is impacted by the fact that you will have to disclose information (this might actually be at his request).

Generally, then, first inform your client that you have received a request for information. If there is a release of information signed by your client, verify that she still wants you to give the information and get some idea what it is for. Let your client know what kind of information you are going to disclose and what possible consequences the disclosure of this information might have, so that she can make an informed decision whether she wants that information shared or not.

Of course, you will share information truthfully.

If the sharing of information involves writing a letter, make a copy for your client to keep and keep one copy in her file.

If you receive a request for a copy of your client's file that is not a court order, start with a treatment summary[1] and not the whole file. Since it is up to your clinical judgment whether you want to release a copy of the file or write a treatment summary, you can only be compelled by a court of law to release the whole file. Usually, the treatment summary is enough to satisfy most requests.

If it is your professional opinion that the disclosure of information that your client requested would be damaging to her, it is your duty to inform your client of your opinion. For example, your client wants you to make a statement that will help her win a suit against her employer, who is, she feels, largely responsible for her depression. If in your professional opinion there was a pre-existing condition and the depression is not primarily related to her work, you will have to state so in your letter. Do let your client know what you intend to write, as well as that the court might wish to see the whole file, which might contain information that she does not want to become public. Once she introduces her mental health as evidence into a court proceeding, she has waived privilege and all information pertaining to her mental health is open to the court (and thus, likely, to the public). However, if she persists with her request, that is to say, when your client requests that you break confidentiality regarding her case, you legally must do so.

---

[1]See "How to Write a Treatment Summary" in Chapter 17.

16

SCENARIOS OF CLIENT-THERAPIST INTERACTIONS

I will now address scenarios that you will sooner or later deal with in your work with clients. These will be presented in a simple format: I will start by describing the client's behavior (verbal or otherwise) and follow it with practical tips for you to handle the situation, as well as clinical rationales for your response. In time, you will come up with your own ways to handle these and other situations. However, when you first start out, it is helpful to be able to anticipate certain interactions and to have a repertoire of possible, clinically sound responses.

CLIENT SPEAKS A LOT AND LEAVES YOU LITTLE ROOM FOR COMMENT

The Scenario: You have a client who speaks a lot and leaves you little room for comment. You might find yourself drifting off, feeling distracted or bored, or you might start feeling angry, wanting to participate in an exchange and not just listen. You also might start feeling that you are of no help to this client, since you do not get to make many interventions.

What to Do: The important distinction to make when faced with this sort of behavior is between psychotic or drug-induced and nonpsychotic, sober behavior. Is your client manic or actively psychotic or on drugs like cocaine or speed, or isn't she?

If your client is psychotic or the talkativeness is drug-induced, a referral to a psychiatrist or ER and/or a referral for assessment of detoxification/rehab is in order.

However, if your client is sober and not psychotic and habitually leaves you no room to ask questions or make any remarks, it is important that you make room for your client to continue to do so. Do occasionally remark on his style of interaction, perhaps like this: "I notice that you get irritated when I ask you a question."

It is up to your clinical judgment whether you see fit to make an interpretation like the following:

"I wonder if you feel that I am not paying attention to you when I ask you something."

"I wonder if you feel interrupted and not listened to."

"I wonder if maybe my asking you questions when you are in the middle of telling me something reminds you of how your siblings never let you finish a story. I wonder if you feel as irritated with me as you did with them."

Observe his reactions to your interpretation and remarks. Do not attempt to force your interpretations on your client. On the other hand, do not give up on introducing remarks and interpretations, either. Continue to do so judiciously, listen and observe his response carefully, and utilize this response as you continue to treat this client. Be aware that the mere fact of your benign presence on a regular basis is helpful. However, discuss your feelings, as well as how the treatment is proceeding, with your supervisor.

The basic rationale behind creating a space for your client to express himself without you yourself getting intrusive is the understanding that for some clients it is necessary to "tell their story" at length. This might be the first time they experience someone actually being interested in hearing what they have to say, the first time that there is no retribution and no punishment, the first time that there is a safe environment to do so. What is asked of you is to provide a "holding environment," a containing space, a constant object in whose presence your client can tell his story, as a child would to his mother. It can be frustrating to work in a situation like this, since you are not receiving much feedback about how you're doing. It can indeed be hard work *not* to make interventions and to contain your own anxieties and feelings while allowing the client to express himself. Do not underestimate what you *are* doing when you are sitting with a client who can't tolerate to actively engage with you yet.

CLIENT SPEAKS VERY LITTLE

The Scenario: You are in a situation where your client speaks very little. There might be protracted silences and you might find yourself working very hard indeed to receive any information from your client. This might make you anxious and might leave you feeling incompetent and unable to help this person since you seem unable to draw her out.

What to Do: Many therapists find this situation harder to deal with than the previous one. After all, in social situations, things start getting awkward when long silences ensue. However, this is not an ordinary social situation and in the therapy session all behavior (verbal communication, as well as the lack thereof) means something, even if you don't know what it is.

To start out with, allow a silence to grow. Monitor how your client is faring with this: Does she seem comfortable or does she seem to become increasingly anxious? If it seems to you that the client is becoming uncomfortable and does not know how to break the silence, do it for her. You might say something like this: "Is it difficult to say anything?"

Follow up on whatever the response is. If the silence persists you might want to ask: "What is happening? Can you tell me?"

Follow up on the response. For example, if your client shakes her head, inquire: "No? You can't tell me? Or you don't want to tell me?"

Try to get a clarification of what is going on, whether she cannot or does not want to speak. If she indicates that she cannot speak, continue clarifying until you understand the situation. If she does not want to speak, you may say something like this: "I'll be waiting right here. Let me know when you're ready to talk again."

Then wait in silence. Observe your thoughts. Do not let your anxiety prompt you to talk aimlessly. If it seems appropriate, you might comment on the situation:

"It seems as if there is not much to tell me."
"Is it hard to talk to me?"
"I wonder what makes it so difficult to talk to me."

Basically, you are explicitly commenting on the situation, inviting your client to participate more, and making an opening to explore the underlying reasons for her silence. However, if she does not go for a further exploration, give her the space to sit in silence. If this occurs with regularity, inquire after it:

"I wonder what it means that we sit here in silence."
"I wonder if there is anything you want from me that I am not providing."
"I wonder if there is anything in this silence that you want me to understand that I am not getting."

You are signaling your willingness to look at the silence as interaction. And you are letting your client know that you do not know what it means, that you need her help with it. Such silences might turn out to be hostile attacks on the treatment. If silences go on for most of the time in the majority of the sessions, it might be time to address whether the client is trying to destroy treatment (or—symbolically—you, for that matter). However, the opposite might be the case as well: something constructive is happening in the silence that cannot yet be articulated.

The basic rationale for this, as for any intervention, is that all behavior means something even when you do not understand what that is. Thus, you assume that your client's silence means something and you are trying to understand what that is. Generally, you want to address your *client's* issues and not your own. Thus, you have to learn to deal with feelings of anxiety and insecurity that might be fueled by lengthy silences. Again, do not underestimate your contribution when you are able to tolerate a long silence without having to fill it. Your client may need the space to get in touch with her reality. Also, her way of interacting with you informs you how she interacts with others.

Over time you will find it easier to distinguish between silences that are pensive, silences that are companionable, silences that are hostile or anxious, and so forth. You will learn to respond to them flexibly and with increasing ease. Until then, a good rule of thumb will be to hold back your urge to fill the silence immediately.

CLIENT CRIES

The Scenario: The situation looks deceptively simple: your client starts crying.

What to Do: Many therapists feel compelled to reassure their client when he cries, thus imparting the message that it would be best to stop crying. However, although many of us have difficulties tolerating other people's tears without feeling that we should do something about them, as therapists we are called upon to contain and later explore this expression of feeling. This means that you endeavor to provide a space where it is acceptable for your client to express his feelings, including with tears.

Your first order of business, then, when your client starts crying is to remain silent and allow him to shed his tears. Eventually, you might want to inquire:

"Can you say what the tears are about?"
"Can you tell me what hurts you so much?"
"What is so hard?"

In this way you indicate not only your empathy with the pain but also your interest in what has caused it. However, do not be too hasty with these interventions because they will, in effect, interrupt your client's expression of his feeling through tears and carry the subtle message that it is now enough of that and time to turn to the intellectual exploration of the reasons for the tears. Sometimes that is indeed the case, as when your client appears to be decompensating and needs shoring up. In cases like this, you might indeed want to interrupt the crying with questions aimed at directing your client's attention to the reasons for the tears. However, more often than not it is probably appropriate to wait for a cue from your client (such as his beginning to talk) before you inquire in this way. If your client seems inconsolable, you might consider saying something like the following:

"This is really hard."
"This is painful."

You signal that you are present, aware of his pain, and empathic to it. In this way you do not indicate that your client should now talk to you but you offer yourself as an object to talk to, if so desired.

Sooner or later everyone stops crying. This may sometimes be later and it is your responsibility to learn to tolerate this expression of unhappiness. Of course, there are all sorts of reasons for tears besides unhappiness. Whatever the case, it is important that, once the tears have stopped, you invite your client to explore their meaning with something like this:

"Can you tell me what prompted the tears?"
"What were the tears about?"
"What is it that made you cry?"

On a more sophisticated level, aiming at the transference, you might ask:

"What was it like to cry like this?"
"How did it feel to cry in my presence?"
"What is it like that I saw you like this?"

You might find that your client is angry with you for letting him cry, that he expected more "sympathy," that he wanted "solutions" from you. All these are topics well worth exploring. I will address in more detail further on how to handle situations in which your client expects specific behavior of you that is not forthcoming.

Your general assumption, as mentioned previously, is that all behavior means something. Thus, when your client begins crying, you want to provide the space for the expression of tears (step 1), as well as explore what they mean (step 2).

CLIENT IS ANGRY WITH YOU

The Scenario: In this situation, your client expresses anger with you.

What to Do: This is another situation that many therapists find difficult to handle. It is one thing when your client expresses anger at a third person, but it is quite another thing when this anger is directed at you. This often taps right into your own insecurities, your need to please, and your omnipotent wish to be seen as helpful, dedicated, and efficient. Clearly, supervision and your own therapy will be of great value in helping you to learn how to handle these situations. It is important that you not discourage the appropriate—that is, verbal—expression of anger, and, in fact, it is a sign that therapy is going well if your client is able to say to you, "I am angry with you!" *Do not justify your actions.*[1]

Your next intervention to your client's expression of anger with you should be a statement that acknowledges her anger, as well as asking for further clarification on what it is about you that has made her angry. Thus, you might want to say something like this:

"How do I make you angry?"
"What did I do to make you angry?"
"What is it that made you angry?"
"You're angry at me. Tell me more about this."

With this, you not only acknowledge your client's expression of her reality, you not only express your desire to know more about it, but you also, and most important, signal your ability to tolerate her anger. You let her know that it is acceptable for her to be angry with you and that you can handle not only the fact of her anger, but that you can and will listen to her reasons.

What if your client's reason for her anger is based on a dis-

---

[1]If the reason for her anger is the fact that you hurt your client's feelings or that you made a mistake, acknowledge it. Please see "Making a Mistake" in this chapter for a further discussion.

torted perception of you? She might say: "I'm really angry that you did not know what I was feeling."

Do not argue that you cannot be expected to read minds; do not justify your actions. Instead, invite her to explore the issue further:

"So you thought I should have known how you feel without your telling me."
"What does it mean to you to tell someone how you feel?" and so forth.

Generally, then, as long as your client's anger is expressed appropriately, make room for the exploration of it.

However, if your client becomes agitated—perhaps getting out of her chair—and you feel physically threatened, state clearly and calmly something like the following: "Please sit down again. What we do here is talk about things. Can you try to put into words what is going on?"

If your client does not calm down, assess whether she is a danger to you. If you feel that she is, you might excuse yourself and leave the office. You might initiate an involuntary hospitalization because she is a danger to others (in this case: you), or you might just give your client space to calm down. Generally, consider it diagnostic if your client decompensates into a state where she cannot control her impulses. It might indicate that she is prone to psychotic episodes. In a case like that, supportive therapy is the order of the day, *not* exploratory therapy that might move her too close to anxiety-producing material and subsequent acting-out. Be sure to discuss with your supervisor the significance of what has happened, as well as how it should inform treatment with this particular client.

I have explored the issue of your client becoming dangerously angry for completeness' sake. This is not something that usually or even often happens. However, it is something that *could* and sometimes does happen, so you should be alert to the possibility.

CLIENT POINTEDLY ASKS
YOUR ADVICE

The Scenario: This is the not unusual situation in which your client explicitly asks your advice. Perhaps he says:

"What do you think, should I take this job?"
"Do you think I should leave my wife?"
"How do I apply for SSI?"
"Do you know a psychiatrist I could see?"

What to Do: First, let us distinguish between the questions regarding life decisions, on the one hand (as in the questions regarding the job and the wife), and questions regarding practical issues, on the other hand (SSI, psychiatrist). While the latter are requests for advice regarding information you might be expected to have and share as a mental health professional, the former are requests for you to make life decisions *for* your client that he really must make on his own. This does not mean that you cannot be helpful.

Indeed, if you are being asked, "Should I leave my wife?" there are several ways to respond that are aimed at facilitating your client's exploration of that request. You might, for example, respond with: "Are you thinking of leaving your wife? What are your reasons? How do you feel about this?" and so forth.

In this way, you take the question in effect as an opening to facilitate the client's exploration of the whole idea of his leaving his wife—which might or might not lead to his actual leaving. Whatever the case, it is not up to you to make that decision. Or you might respond with:

"I wonder what makes it important what I think in this situation."
"I wonder what makes you think I should know better than you do what to do in this situation."

With these responses, you focus more on the transference relationship between you and your client. Does he see you as an authority figure? Does he generally have difficulties making important decisions on his own? Was he discouraged when growing up from having his own wishes and wants and from pursuing them?

As you see, there are many responses to a direct request for advice on topics like this without actually telling your client what you think he should do.

What if your client insists: "Yes, but what do *you* think? I want to know what *you* would do in my place."

Again, you might choose to continue exploring what seems so important about getting you to say what *you* would do. Now might also be the place to say something like this: "You know, I don't know what I would do in your place. I am not in your place. It is *you* who must make this decision, not I."

Perhaps followed up with something like this:

"It seems really hard for you to make that decision on your own, doesn't it?

"What is it like to want me to make that decision and I am not making it?"

"What is it like to directly ask me for something and not receive it?"

Your client might now move to express his anger at you and from there to an exploration of other relationships in which he asks for something that he does not receive.

In the end, you can always point to the ethical and professional mandate of not making decisions for your client: "It would not be ethical, it would be unprofessional of me to make decisions for you. This is *your* life and *you* get to decide what you want to do, not I."

However, don't use this statement to avoid exploring your client's feelings regarding the fact that you are not fulfilling his wish.

As for requests for practical information, it is always a good idea to explore the reasons behind any given question. Your client might say: "Do you know a psychiatrist I might see?"

To this question you might respond similarly to this: "Can you tell me a little more about wanting to see a psychiatrist?"

This will be good practice, in any case, since some clients do prefer to work with a male and some with a female psychiatrist, some with psychiatrists who specialize in working with particular disorders, and so forth.

Try to assist minimally to allow the client to take charge of as much of his treatment as possible. This means, give the name and number of the psychiatrist, get a release to speak with the psychiatrist and do so, but let your client be responsible for making an appointment for himself if possible. You do not want to foster an undue regression and dependency on you but, on the contrary, assist your client to increase his capacity to take care of himself, be self-reliant, and master difficult situations.

In the case of help with SSI, let your client know how to find out about his local SSI office (call information, telephone book), and encourage him to call and make an appointment. Assist with clarifying questions but do not volunteer to do the work for him.

However, it will be up to your clinical judgment to decide when your client truly needs you to take charge because he is unable to do so—as when your client is so severely depressed that he cannot rouse himself to contact a psychiatrist—versus when he is able to do so and you would deprive him of the opportunity to take care of an important issue himself. This situation highlights the fact that assessment and evaluation of the clinical situation and the treatment is an ongoing issue. Your client might at one time be able to make an appointment on his own, while at another time he might be unable to do so. It is your responsibility to decide on a clinically sound course of action at any given time.

CLIENT TELLS YOU THAT THERAPY DOESN'T HELP

The Scenario: Your client tells you in so many words that you are not helping her, that she does not feel better, that therapy is not doing for her what she expected.

What to Do: This is another situation that is prone to make many beginning therapists uneasy, tapping into their insecurities, particularly in the face of their knowledge that they are, indeed, beginners.

Imagine your client saying to you: "I have thought about it, and you are not helping me. I'm not sure I want to continue with therapy."

Not uncommonly, you will experience feelings of anxiety, perhaps about not being good enough, not being able to help, or being found wanting, or feelings of anger may arise at the client's failure to see how hard you are working, at her ingratitude, at your feeling pressured to perform. You might have an immediate reaction aimed at keeping your client, wanting to convince her of the fact that therapy is helpful, that she should stay with you, or on the contrary, if this client has made you anxious in the past, you might find yourself wishing the therapeutic relationship would end and thus you experience relief at the thought that she wants to terminate therapy. All of these are countertransference feelings. Try to be as aware of them as possible to ensure that these feelings don't translate into countertransference behavior.[2]

Generally speaking, when your client tells you that therapy does not help, treat this statement as you would any other state-

---

[2]See Chapter 18 for a more detailed discussion of the concept of countertransference.

ment that you do not quite understand, since it is a safe bet that your client is trying to communicate something that you do not yet understand. Ask for clarification, perhaps like this:

> "What do you mean when you say therapy doesn't help?"
> "What did you expect therapy would be like or what it would do for you?"

You might be even more direct and focus on the relationship between yourself and the client: "What is it that you would like from me, that you would like me to do, that I am not providing?"

And once you have some information regarding this, you might ask: "What is it like to want something from me that I am not providing?"

What you are trying to do is to elicit more information regarding what your client expected from therapy in general, from you in particular, and how she experiences not receiving what she wants from you. In the process of doing so, you might get the opportunity to clarify some notions regarding therapy, like the very common one that you, as the therapist, hold all the answers, which you then dispense to the client at will. You also might find yourself educating your client as to the collaborative nature of therapy. Overall, you will probably find yourself exploring with your client topics related to her feeling disappointed with you, being angry with you, and so forth.

Don't get too invested in keeping your client at all costs. It is entirely your client's decision whether or not she will remain in therapy, and even though you may and should make a professional recommendation, when the time comes, about whether or not you think she would benefit from continuing treatment, it is most important that you make room for her exploring the option of discontinuing therapy. So ask something like this:

> "Tell me about your wish to terminate therapy."

"You said you have thought about discontinuing therapy. Tell
me more about your thoughts regarding this."

It is important that you consult with your supervisor regarding any underlying issues that might be addressed here: perhaps your client becomes fearful at too much closeness and is
pulling back, perhaps your client expects to be terminated by
you because she is not happy with you and is trying to forestall
this event by being the one who leaves, and so forth.

Finally, be alert to and accepting of the possibility that you
might, in fact, not be helpful to your client. Explore with your
client what she expected from you and consider whether this
expectation is a reasonable one or not. It is *not* reasonable when
your client expects you to solve all her problems, tell her what
to do with her life and make her feel happy, and all of this inside of three months. It *is* reasonable when your client says she
expected to work with someone who was more experienced than
you are. Or that she wants to work in a certain treatment modality that you do not employ or are not trained or experienced
enough to employ. In these latter cases, it is important that you
acknowledge in the face of her reasonable expectations that
you might not be best suited to work with her and offer to assist with transferring her to another therapist who might be able
to work in the way she requests. However, it makes a difference
if a client tells you within the first few meetings that she really
wants to work behaviorally, and you let her know that you are
not trained to do so and you refer her out to someone who is,
as opposed to your client after six months of work suddenly
complaining about your not working behaviorally. In this latter
case, it would seem that other additional issues need to be
tended to, such as what it means that your client waited so long
to tell you this, what she hopes to gain in behavioral therapy
that she is not receiving now, and so forth.

In any case, if your client insists on termination (and, perhaps, transfer to another therapist) after exploring the meaning of this request, it is important that you oblige and assist in

terminating and transferring. If your client wants to terminate without transfer to another therapist and you think it is clinically unwise to do so, be sure to make an explicit professional recommendation for your client to continue therapy, either with you or someone else, and give three referrals. Make sure you write a letter of termination, including this recommendation and the referrals. However, you have to terminate therapy at the client's request. For more information on the issue of termination, see the next topic.

CLIENT REQUESTS TERMINATION OF THERAPY

The Scenario: As mentioned previously, this scenario consists of your client's requesting termination of therapy.

What to Do: Do not blindly act on the feelings engendered in you by your client's request for termination. We all have different ways of dealing with being abandoned and left behind (anxiety, anger, sadness, and so forth), and it is important that you keep track of how this situation impacts you to avoid acting out of unconscious countertransference material.

Ideally, a request for termination arises naturally sometime during the course of therapy and is attended to by both you and the client, who jointly explore it and come to a mutual decision as to when and how termination should occur.

However, sometimes a request for termination seems untimely and may in fact be a hostile gesture, a move to avoid closeness, or motivated by any number of reasons other than that therapy is indeed nearing its end. This means that you need to explore the request for termination, its meaning, and its message. A good way to begin is to ask for more information:

"Why do you want to terminate therapy now?"

"When did you decide you wanted to terminate our work together?" and so forth.

Also helpful might be to offer your view of the situation: "It seems to me that there are several issues worth attending to that we would not be able to work on if we terminated now. What are your thoughts on this?"

You might make an interpretation, linking the request for termination to a clinical issue:

"I wonder if your request to terminate therapy has anything to do with the fact that we started talking about your relationship to your father, and that that is frightening to you. If you leave here, you won't have to think about that anymore."

"I think when you told me last time that you are envious of me and what I have accomplished in my life, it really frightened you. Perhaps you are afraid that I will punish you in some way, like you were punished by your parents when you let them know that you were envious of your brother. Wanting to leave therapy might be your way of trying to avoid that."

Overall, you are aiming at eliciting as much information about your client's request for termination as you can. Have you begun working on an issue that is difficult or frightening? Does this client have difficulties with boundaries, does she perhaps feel threatened by increasing transference issues? Have you done or said something that makes her want to retaliate by leaving you? Is she afraid that by her feeling increasingly close to you, you might end up being hurt in some way by the feelings she has kept inside? Is she trying to protect you by removing herself? The possibilities are endless and it is up to you to provide the space to explore them. Sometimes this exploration will lead to addressing important issues, and therapy will be invigorated and proceed. Other times, termination of your work together will result.

When this latter is the case, assist your client respectfully and professionally to terminate as productively as possible. If you feel that a termination is clinically not indicated, make sure you address this with your client and offer to refer her to someone else if she feels uncomfortable continuing with you. As mentioned previously, make sure you send a letter of termination, stating your professional opinion as well as three referrals. Retain a copy of this letter in your client's file. If you are willing to work with this client in the future, make sure you let her know that she is welcome to contact you should she want to take up therapy again. In the case of termination occurring at a point in therapy where you do not foresee any clinical problems (whether or not the termination may occur prematurely), you need not give any referrals. However, if you are willing to work with this client in the future, let her know that she is welcome to return to you for continuation of treatment if she so chooses. You might also offer "booster" sessions—that is, an occasional meeting with her that she can initiate as needed.

CLIENT BREAKS OFF THERAPY

The Scenario: This is the scenario when your client either informs you that she is not continuing therapy or actually does not show up again, perhaps leaving you a message stating that she won't return.

What to Do: It is important that you try to make contact with your client to clarify what happened to prompt her breaking off treatment. Perhaps there is a possibility of addressing underlying issues and continuing the treatment (please refer to the preceding heading for more details). Begin by calling her and inviting her in for a session to assess what has happened. You might say something like the following: "I want to invite you to come in for a session so we can look at your reasons for wanting to discontinue therapy."

If she insists that there are no reasons to address, invite her in for a termination meeting. Let her know that this meeting is meant to say good-bye, to look at what you have accomplished together, and to assess what she might want to consider addressing at a later date, perhaps with another therapist if she so chooses.

If you either cannot reach her or she declines to come in, either tell her in person, leave a message on her machine if it is safe to do so (that is, if no one else has access to the machine), or write her a letter containing something like the following:

> I don't recommend that you discontinue treatment at this time. I would like for us to look at the reasons why you want to break off treatment. However, if you would feel more comfortable continuing with someone else, I will be happy to give you referrals. Whatever you decide, I wish you luck in your endeavors. Should you need a referral or decide that you would like to take up therapy again, please give me a call.

In the case of therapy being unilaterally broken off by your client, make sure you send a letter of termination that contains what I have just mentioned, as well as something to this effect:

> If I don't hear from you by . . . (two weeks from the date of sending off the letter would seem sufficient for your client to receive the letter and get in touch with you, if she so chooses), I will consider the treatment terminated. Although I don't recommend . . .

Retain a copy of the letter in her file.

The idea is to make certain that she understands that therapy will indeed be terminated and that you are no longer bound by your end of the treatment contract as of the date specified if she does not contact you. At the same time, you want to make sure that she has the referrals she needs and you want to leave the experience of ending treatment as palatable as possible. That is to say, in letting her know that you will be of assistance with either referrals or continuation of therapy (if this latter is something that you can actually offer), you are trying to leave her with an impression that endings do not have to be terrible and actually can be something that can conceivably be addressed.

In case she agrees to come in to explore what prompted her wanting to terminate, refer to the heading "Client Wants to Terminate Treatment" on how to proceed.

CLIENT HAS DIFFICULTIES
PAYING THE FEE

The Scenario: Your client cannot or does not pay the agreed-upon fee in a timely manner. This includes instances where your client complains about the fee being too high or lets you know in other ways that she has concerns regarding the fee.

What to Do: It is most important that you address this issue immediately, not least because difficulties in paying the bill could lead to termination of treatment and thus represent an issue pertaining to threats to treatment continuity, which was addressed in the hierarchy of priorities in treatment. A client who does not pay her bill several times in a row, who can pay only part of her bill, or who complains that the fee is too high may in fact be indicating that she is pulling out of treatment.

Your first order of business, then, is to directly address this issue. Be aware that you might have strong countertransference feelings regarding addressing money issues, a state of affairs that has been called by Krueger (1986) "The Last Taboo." Attend to your reluctance in your supervision and in your own therapy.

You might say for starters:

"I notice that you haven't paid your bill."
"You have said that you find the fee too high. Yet you did
    agree to this fee. What changed?"
"I noticed that you have difficulties paying the full amount
    of the fee. Let's talk about that."

In general, you want to open up the topic of the fee for discussion: Have circumstances in your client's life changed and
he hasn't told you? Has he lost his job? Has he miscalculated
his expenses? Perhaps he is angry with you for some reason and
expresses it by withholding the fee? Does he feel he is not getting his money's worth from you and has thus decided the fee
is too high? These are only a few of the reasons that might
underlie the difficulties in paying the fee. Leave enough time
to explore this area thoroughly. Perhaps you and your client
will have to go over his finances, what he owns and what he
owes, as well as look at his priorities to see whether therapy is
something he can afford and for which he is willing to make a
sacrifice in another area. Perhaps he has family members who
can help him financially?

If it turns out that he indeed cannot afford therapy at the
agreed-upon fee, it is time to renegotiate that fee. Ultimately, it
will be up to you (or the agency you work for) what fee you are
willing to accept. There are no hard and fast rules for this.
However, this is your profession and you do make your living
from it. You may find that you are able to keep a client in treatment at a low fee at one time, while at other times you may not
be able to do so. If you decide to lower the fee, make sure to
explore the meaning of this event for your client. You might
say something like this:

"What is it like for you to see me for a lower fee than we
    initially agreed upon?"
"What are your thoughts about my lowering the fee?"

You might find issues pertaining to your client feeling indebted, which might result in his having difficulties expressing negative feelings toward you openly for fear of appearing ungrateful; he might feel that he is accepting hand-outs and be angry with you for putting him in this situation; he might have thoughts that what you have to offer can't be worth much since you are selling it cheap; he might think that you are a great benefactor and begin to idealize you. These are only some of the issues that might arise subsequent to your lowering the fee. Whatever the case, be aware that your client's issues will be expressed in the treatment relationship between you and him, that is, in the transference.

If you cannot keep the client in treatment because of his inability to pay the fee, make sure you refer him to someone (or an agency) who accepts low-fee clients for treatment.

RAISING YOUR FEE

The Scenario: You are raising your client's fee.

What to Do: This situation will mainly arise with clients whom you see at a reduced fee. You have let your client know upon determining the fee during the intake meeting that this determination is to be seen as temporary and that you will either periodically raise this issue again or that the fee will be adjusted when new developments occur that make it possible for her to afford a fee closer to your full fee. Therefore, you will do just that: periodically raise the issue of increasing the fee, either on a regular basis (say, once a year), or subsequent to learning new data that indicate that your client now can afford to pay a fee closer to your full fee (for example, when she has received a raise, received an inheritance, paid off debts, or the like).

Be prepared for your own, as well as your client's, reluctance to address this matter of adjusting the fee upward. This topic often stirs strong feelings on both sides, yours and your client's.

You might fear being perceived as greedy, money-grabbing, and less than benevolently interested in your client when you do bring up the issue of raising the fee. If you don't bring it up after learning of circumstances that indicate your client can afford a raised fee, you might feel angry, resentful, taken advantage of, and the like. Your client, on the other hand, when you do raise the issue of increasing the fee, might experience you as hostile, demanding, greedy, using her, or having no "real" interest in her. If you don't bring it up, she might feel contempt at being able to "pull one over on you," she might be repeating a pattern of using others or of getting away with taking more than her share, and the like. Either way, the topic of money, and particularly of the therapist's asking for more money, will raise a multitude of issues that need to be addressed: issues pertaining to the relationship between the two of you, issues of worth, of entitlement, of who uses whom and whom owes who what, and so forth. Complicating the matter is the fact that, as mentioned previously, money issues do in fact constitute something like the last taboo in our society. This makes it difficult for therapists to address them freely. Consider how much easier it is in most cases to address issues of sexuality, sexual fantasies, and practices than to explore a client's financial situation in depth.

You might bring the issue up with something like this:

"It is time for us to re-assess the fee."
"Let's talk about your fee. In light of your recent raise, it is
    time to see how much you can realistically afford to pay
    toward my full fee."

Make room for your client's expression of her feelings. If she does not seem to have any reaction to this topic, inquire after it:

"I wonder what it is like for you, my wanting to discuss an
    increase in your fee."

"What is it like to be faced with an increase of the fee?"
"I imagine you must have some feelings regarding my increasing the fee."

Consult with your supervisor as you engage in renegotiating the fee upward. Address there and in your own therapy the issues that get stirred up for you. Do take your time with this renegotiation. You don't have to close this topic in the same session you raise it. In fact, increasing your client's fee can be a process taking weeks, sometimes months.

HOW TO END A SESSION

The Scenario: This issue seems straightforward enough: How do you best bring the hour to an end? As deceptively simple as this scenario appears to be, it is not always so. What do you do when your client is in the middle of a crying jag? When he does not seem to want to stop? When he is in the middle of an apparently important issue? When he asks for more time?

What to Do: As a rule, try always to end on time.[3] Don't run over the appointed time slot, even though it might feel tempting to do so at times. If ending on time is an ongoing problem for you, address it in supervision as well as in your own therapy. You are not doing your client a favor by demonstrating your inability to contain him and yourself and by failing to be consistent and reliable in keeping boundaries. To keep the agreed-upon time frame means keeping a boundary like any other. In addition, by running over you in effecting run into the time slot of your next client and show disrespect and lack of boundaries for her as well.

This said, there should always be room for exceptions. If an

---

[3]See Chapter 3, "The Therapeutic Frame."

emergency arises and your client seems completely decompensated and needs a few more minutes to regroup, it is important that you heed your clinical judgment and take those few minutes. Most everybody understands the concept of an exception. However, make sure you look closely at the reason for the client's decompensation so late in the session and whether there might have been ways to avoid that. It is important, in conducting a session, to stay mindful of how far along in a session you are. You would not pursue the exploration of an affect-laden, traumatic experience in the last one-third of the session, precisely for the reason of needing enough time to contain and regroup.

Generally, it seems best to adopt a fairly consistent way of ending a session. This may mean that in each session you say something similar to end it, perhaps:

"We have to end now."
"Let's leave it at that."
"Our time is up for today."

Use whatever seems fitting and comes easily to you. If your clients pay you at the end of the session, make sure that you say these words a couple of minutes before you actually want to leave the room so that your client has time to write the check or hand you the cash and for you to write a receipt and hand it to him. Don't forget, *you* set the tone and enforce the rules. One of the rules for therapy is that you begin and end on time. If you actually *do* end on time on a consistent basis, your client will not expect you to run over. The clients who will have the most difficulties in complying with a timely end of sessions are the very clients who will benefit the most by your ending on time. They obviously have difficulties containing themselves, keeping boundaries, following set rules, disengaging from contact, and so forth. Most likely, their having difficulties in ending is an illustration of these problems, and learning to end on time will simultaneously strengthen their overall capacity to contain themselves. Perhaps this is even the first time that they experienced someone following through on what they said: you said the session would last fifty minutes, and voila, it lasts fifty minutes. Be aware that clients are actually reassured to see that you are able to maintain boundaries in the face of their own difficulties and, sometimes, objections.

Thus, if your client is in the middle of an apparently important issue, you might make a statement like the following: "We have to stop for today. Since this seems really important, perhaps you could tell me more about it next time."

If your client is in the middle of a crying jag, simply state as you always do: "Our time is up for today."

Give him a minute to regroup. If the client is not decompensated, this should not pose a problem.

Sometimes you will have a client who seems to ignore your announcements of the end of the session. He keeps talking and does not seem at all inclined to get up and leave. With a client like this, it is advisable to collect your fee first thing at the beginning of the session (unless you send a bill). Doing so will allow you to actually get up and open your door for the client, even if he is still talking. Insist that the hour is up for today. Do not be engaged into continuing verbal exchanges with him. This is time for the broken record until he actually leaves: "Our time is up. You need to leave now."

It helps to close the door behind him and let him leave. For a client like this, you might consider increasing the frequency of sessions. Issues of separation obviously play a major role for this client and seeing you more often might decrease the anxiety felt over the impending long separation.

If you have a client who actually asks for more time, also consider increasing the frequency of sessions.

MISSING A SESSION

The Scenario: In this situation, a session is missed, either by the client or by you, the therapist. I will discuss the actual interventions, depending on who missed the session.

What to Do When the Client Misses a Session: When your client appears to be missing a session, that is, when you are in the office waiting for your client and she does not show up, do not immediately call her to check whether or not she is coming unless you have reason to believe that this might be an emergency. Thus, when a client with whom you have made a contract that she will not hurt herself until she sees you next does not show up for session, you may have reason to believe that she is in danger and thus should proceed with calling her.

If there is no emergency, even though you may want to know what happened, may want to remind her, may even want to be able to leave early, it is important that you leave room for your client to take the initiative to call you and let you know what has happened. She may, in fact, call you either that or the next day and let you know what has caused her to miss the session and perhaps ask to reschedule the session. If you have the time available, offer her an additional hour that week. However, do charge for the missed session.

If she does not get in touch with you, depending on the individual client and the nature of your work together, you may choose to wait until the next scheduled session to see whether she shows up, or you may choose to call her. If you choose the latter, give her at least a day to get in touch with you before you contact her. Thus, the end of the day after the missed session or the day after that are usually good times to do so. When you do call, don't forget that your actions as well as hers have meaning. It means something for the relationship between you and your client and thus for your work together that she did not show up and did not call you (unless she was unable to do so), just as it means something that you take the initiative in calling her to see what is happening. You may choose to do so for a variety of clinically sound reasons; for example, you may have reason to believe that your client will not return to therapy if you do not make contact.

When you do make contact with your client, keep it simple. Say something like the following: "You didn't appear for your session the other day. I was wondering what was going on."

Do not conduct a session on the phone. If there seems to be much to say, you might consider offering to reschedule the missed session for the same week, if you have the time. If you cannot reach your client, you might consider leaving a message for her so that she knows you called. This is usually only advisable if you think that you would otherwise lose your client or if you truly think your client might be in some danger. Thus, if you don't think your client is in any danger, you might leave a message similar to this: "You missed your session yesterday. Please call me back at my office and let me know if you want to reschedule the missed session."

If you don't hear back from your client, you may consider leaving a last message to this effect: "I will be expecting you next week at our usual time. Please let me know if you will not be able to make it."

With this, the ball is in your client's court. You now have to wait for her to contact you or appear for her next session.

If you do think your client is in danger, that is, if you have reason to believe that she might hurt herself or someone else, do call her. You may leave a message stating your concern and give her a time frame to call you back before you take steps to assure her safety. Thus, you might say: "You missed today's session and I am concerned. Please call me back at my office and let me know that you are OK. If I haven't heard from you within the hour (the next two hours, or whatever seems appropriate), I will take steps to assure your safety."

These steps may include calling family members or even the police and letting them know that you are concerned that your client might have hurt herself and might need someone to check on her. Do *not* check on her yourself.[4]

Do charge for a missed session (as you will have explained upon intake as part of your office procedures). Do not make an exception, even if there seems to be a good reason for your

---

[4]Please refer to Chapter 11, "How to Hospitalize a Client."

client's absence—her car may have broken down, she may have suddenly become ill, and so forth. This is an issue of maintaining the frame, being predictable, and observing stated boundaries. However, be prepared to address whichever feelings your client may have regarding the fact that she is being charged for a session she did not attend. Remember, you are billing for your time that you have "leased" to her. If she does not cancel within the specified time period, she has "leased" your time whether or not she uses it, or whichever way she chooses to use it.

Be prepared to explore with your client the meaning of her missing the session, as well as her feelings and thoughts regarding seeing you now, after having missed the session. Your client might feel embarrassed, angry, or sad; she might even have been reluctant to come to see you after having missed a session. She might state that she forgot the session, or she might actually have meant to break off therapy. Your client might have been angry with you for something she perceived that you did or did not do and might have intended to punish you with her absence. These are just a few possibilities that you might assist your client with expressing. You might start doing so by saying something like this:

> "Let's look at your missing the last session. Do you have any thoughts about that?"
> "I wonder what your missing last session was about?"

If the reason is more straightforward, as when your client had a flat tire and couldn't make it:

> "How do you feel about having missed that session?"
> "How do you feel about being charged for the missed session?"

What to Do When the Therapist Misses a Session: You may feel that this is an unlikely scenario, but it is definitely a possibility.

Therapists, too, may "forget" or for other reasons miss a session with a client. First off, anticipating our brief discussion regarding the unconscious in Part III, there is no such thing as "simply forgetting" a session (or anything else, for that matter), neither for you nor for your client. In the case of your client "forgetting," you would explore the underlying meaning in session. In the case of your "forgetting," you are dealing with a countertransference behavior and will examine this behavior and the underlying countertransference feelings in supervision. You will *not* do that exploration in session with your client. However, what you learn in supervision (or consultation, or self-examination) will inform your further work with this client. Thus, you might learn in consultation that you have not felt very engaged by that client in a long time and have been trying to "avoid" being bored again by "forgetting" the session. Underlying this feeling bored and avoidance of it might be an unconscious anxiety over what it might mean to be more engaged with this client. Or perhaps it really does not have to do so much with your issues but with the client's propensity not to engage others and to stay at a safe distance. These are issues that you will address in supervision and your own therapy.

Of course, you as well as your client might have had an accident, might have had to take your child to the emergency room, and so forth. If you realize that you are missing a session *after the session has already started*, try to get in touch with your office and have someone get your client. Make sure that you instruct the person doing so not to blurt out your client's name in front of others but to ask something to this effect: "Is there someone here to see MO?"

If you are in private practice, you will most likely not be able to reach your client, even though you may know that he is presently sitting in your waiting room. In that case, or when you can contact your client only after your scheduled session would have taken place, call him as soon as possible. You might leave a message on a machine where it is acceptable to do so, stating something like this: "This is MO. I apologize for missing our session today. Please call me at my office number so we can talk."

Once you have your client on the phone, apologize for your absence and let him know what happened:

"I fell suddenly ill" (if this is the case).
"I am having an emergency" (if that is so).
"My car broke down" (if it did).

You might also simply state:

"I was detained by reasons beyond my control.
"I was unable to be there."

Overall, I believe it is preferable not to be too mysterious about what happened, although, of course, you want to make sure to allow plenty of time for exploring the meaning of the missed session for your client when you do see him next. Offer a make-up session that week if you can. Do not charge for the session you missed, but do not offer the make-up session for free either. Be prepared to explore your client's feelings of anger, abandonment, doubt about your interest, and so forth.

Overall, if you miss a session, it is important that you take responsibility for that fact, that you apologize for letting your client wait in vain, and that you give your client the opportunity to explore what the experience was like.

CANCELING A SESSION

The Scenario: In this situation, either your client or you, the therapist, have to cancel a session. Again, I will look at interventions depending on whether it is the client or the therapist who is canceling.

What to Do When the Client Cancels a Session: Let us first look at the case where your client cancels an upcoming session well in advance. I recommend offering to reschedule that session, if at all possible, since I believe that any gaps in treatment should be avoided.

If your client indicates that she would rather skip a session, let her know that it is clinically best not to miss any sessions. Ask her: "Is there a particular reason for you not to want to come in?"

There might be any number of reasons for your client to want to skip a session. One that is not uncommon is financial, and if this is so, I suggest that you invite your client to come in at her regular time to discuss that issue. Obviously, as mentioned previously regarding fee setting, if your client has difficulties paying her fee, this merits looking into and addressing in depth. Money matters are never easily discussed, so I recommend that you take your time to investigate this. However, if the case is such that your client will not be able to continue with the usual schedule at the set fee, it is time for you to decide whether you will see her at a—perhaps temporarily—reduced fee, if you want to decrease the frequency of meetings (this should not be less than once weekly for effective psychotherapy), or if it is time for you to refer your client out to a colleague or an agency that will accept referrals for a lower fee than you are willing to accept.

If your client opts not to reschedule that session, make sure you explore the reasons for this in your next meeting. You might be surprised to find that your client felt she needed a "pause," some "time off," a "vacation from therapy." A wealth of information and material to work with can come from such statements.

Let us now look at the case where your client calls in and *cancels at the last minute.* It will depend on your office policy and your schedule whether you will offer a make-up time for this missed session and whether you will charge for the missed session if your client is able to make up the session. There is no one right way to deal with this issue, and my general suggestion is that whatever your policy is, be consistent and adhere to it. This means, if your policy is to offer a make-up session and not charge for the missed session if the make-up session is taken, do so every time this situation arises. If your policy is to charge for a session that has not been canceled the day before—or two days before, or whatever your policy is—regardless of whether your client schedules a make-up session or not, adhere to it. Whatever the case, you will have gone over your policy upon intake and it is now time to be consistent and maintain the frame. Whichever way you handle it, rescheduling the session will be preferable to skipping it to maintain continuity of treatment.

Overall, be certain to address the *fact* of the cancellation and ask how it impacted the client, perhaps like this:

"What was it like to realize that you had overslept and were not going to make it in?"

"What was it like not to come in at your usual time?"

"How did it feel not to be able to reschedule your missed session and be charged for it?"

What to Do When the Therapist Cancels a Session: At times you will find it necessary to cancel a session yourself. However, try to keep these instances as infrequent as possible since much of your efficacy as a therapist will depend on how reliable, how consistent, and how predictable you are.

Nonetheless, there might be the sudden stomach upset, your car might break down, or you might catch the flu. A family member might fall ill and you will be needed at home, or any number of other reasons might crop up that will occasionally prevent you from seeing your client at a scheduled time. Whatever your reason to cancel a session, try to cancel it as much in advance as you can, preferably so that there will be time to talk about the impact of this change for your client in session before the actual event. Offer a make-up time if you can (and if you can foresee that you will be feeling better if you are ill).

Do not give any elaborate explanations as to your reason for canceling. However, do not be deliberately mysterious either. Depending on your client and the nature of the case, it might be appropriate to let your client know that you are unwell or are having car trouble, when that is what keeps you from coming. Of course, this does not mean that you will elaborate on the nature of your illness or launch into a story about how your car broke down on the freeway. In other cases and with other clients it might be better to be less explicit and stick with a statement like this: "I am sorry to let you know so late (if it is late), but I will unfortunately be unable to see you at our scheduled time today."

It is really up to your clinical judgment to decide how it will impact your client to know or not to know about your reason to cancel. In any case, be sure to address the fact that you did cancel a session when you next meet. Expect a reaction, even if it is not obvious or conscious. Your client will most likely be angry with you on some level for failing to be there when you were supposed to. Facilitate her exploration and expression of her experience of the cancellation and her current feelings toward you. You might say something like this:

> "What was that like to get a phone call from me and hear that I would not be able to come in?"
> "What is it like to meet with me now after I wasn't there when you expected me?"

Or you might be more direct:

> "I wonder if it made you angry at all, the fact that I didn't show up when you expected me to?"
> "Perhaps it made you angry when I canceled the last session."

Whatever your client's experience of your absence, be certain to allow for an exploration of it.

Take notice: If you find yourself canceling a lot of sessions, be assured that it will impact your work with your clients. Unless you suffer from some definite disorder that has you housebound, requires frequent doctor visits, or the like, please be certain to address this fact with your supervisor and your own therapist. Often, it indicates countertransference issues that might be based on your own unconscious conflicts over whatever the work with your clients evokes in you or represents for you. These issues need to be addressed for you to be able to work effectively with your clients and to reduce the frequency of your cancellations.

BEING LATE FOR A SESSION

The Scenario: In this case, either your client is late, or you (the therapist) are late for a session. I will again address the interventions depending on whether it is the client or the therapist who is late.

What to Do When the Client Is Late for a Session: First, as addressed earlier, keep in mind that your client has "leased" the hour from you. This means that you should neither leave nor call your client to find out whether or not she is coming (perhaps in the hope that, if you know she will not be coming, you might be able to leave) In effect, as you wait for your client, you do *not* know whether he will show up and what happened. This might engender all sorts of feelings in you, from anger at being stood up to anxiety over your client's well-being.[5] You are asked to tolerate and contain these feelings and simply wait. It might be a good idea to bring a book to the office because

---

[5]As mentioned earlier, only when you have reason to believe that your client might be in danger or if your supervisor thinks it is indicated should you take action at this point and call her.

there will always be the occasional late client or the occasional sudden cancellation or no-show.

When your client does show up late, see what unfolds. He will probably tell you what happened and you can begin to explore what it feels like and what it means to him to have been late and have kept you waiting. If your client does not mention the fact of being late, you might do so by simply stating:

"What happened?"
"As I waited for you, I was wondering what happened?"

In any case, end your session on time. Do not run over at the end to make up for the time your client missed at the beginning. He has reserved his hour and when it is over, it is over. Charge for the full hour. This means, if your client is thirty minutes late, see him for the remaining twenty minutes and charge him for the full hour. Address his feelings about this in the next session.

What to Do When the Therapist Is Late for a Session: It is hoped that this will not happen to you. However, life being life, it is definitely a possibility.

Let us assume that when you arrive at your office, your client is still there and waiting for you. Refrain from launching into any explanations upon setting eyes on your client. It may not be necessary to get into the reasons for your lateness, but it is of great importance that you take responsibility for it. Thus, make a statement similar to this: "I apologize for being late."

Wait with any further statements until you are in your office with the door closed. If your client starts talking to you on your way to the office (assuming that you work in a setting other than a private office), say something to the effect of the following: "Let's wait until we're in my office."

Since deferring verbal exchanges until you are in your office with the door closed will be something that you have practiced from the first session, it will not come as a surprise to your client.

Once in the office, your main task will be not to exonerate yourself—you were stuck in traffic, your car broke down, and the like—but to facilitate your client's exploration and expression of the experience of your being late. In fact, depending on your client and the situation, you may never get to stating a reason for your lateness.

If you were late only five to ten minutes and you have the time to do so, I recommend that you make them up at the end of the session by extending it a few minutes until the full fifty minutes are reached. Although you are bending the frame to do that, it is something that is being dealt with in that session by addressing the whole situation and you still end the session within a sixty-minute frame.

However, for any lateness of more than ten minutes, unless your lateness precipitated an emergency that you need to attend to. As such, I recommend offering to reschedule the session or reducing the fee by the time not utilized. This means, if your client opts to see you the remaining thirty minutes of the session now instead of rescheduling the full fifty minutes, you will charge him proportionally less than if you had seen him the full fifty minutes. Thus, if his fee was $50 per session, this means that he would end up paying you $30 for this session of only thirty minutes.

Do not conduct an over-long session to make up for the time missed. That is to say, do not offer to extend the next session by the time missed so that you would end up seeing the client for seventy-five minutes to make up for twenty-five minutes missed. This might look like only a quantitative change for the session, but in fact the quality of your work changes in ways you will not be able to fathom by extending the hour by 50 percent or more, not least because of the serious breach of the frame.

PLANNED ABSENCES FROM THE OFFICE

The Scenario: In this situation, either you, the therapist, plan an absence or perhaps the client does. Again, I will discuss interventions according to whether it is the therapist or the client who plans the absence.

What to Do When the Therapist Plans an Absence from the Office: This situation will come up with regularity, since most of us take vacations and attend an occasional conference, and there are several observed holidays in the year. It is important that you plan for your absence and introduce the topic appropriately. I will propose a sequence of steps to take that will help you prepare your client for your absence.

Step 1: Consider letting your client know *upon intake* that you will be absent from the office an average of X amount of weeks (or days) per year. For example, if you know that you usually take three weeks' vacation in summer, you might say that when you introduce your office policies. I usually take one month off in late summer, and I let prospective clients know about that when we go over my office policies. These do, in fact, contain the following line: "We will meet an average of 44 weeks a year, providing for 8 weeks' absence from the office." This includes my vacation time, holidays, and any unanticipated absences such as illness and the like. In this way, a client who feels she will not be able to handle a protracted interruption of our work—as my four weeks' absence in summer certainly will entail—can make an informed choice whether she wants to work with me or whether she wants to look for a therapist who is absent for shorter periods of time.

Step 2: Arrange for emergency coverage during your absence. It is imperative that you find a qualified colleague who will take your clients' emergency calls and is willing to meet with those who may need it in your absence. It would be a good idea to have this in place before you inform your clients of your absence so that you can give them your colleague's name and phone number at the same time you give them the actual dates of your absence. Think of this as if you were letting your child know that you will not leave her alone when you go out, but that there will be a person that you trust who will look after her while you are gone.

Step 3: Approximately four weeks before your planned absense, inform your clients of the dates and the emergency coverage you have arranged. Four weeks is not a magic number, but my personal rule-of-thumb, which can and should be adjusted according to your client's needs. However, I recommend not giving dates of your absence much earlier than a month in advance, since it might cause undue anxiety and be disruptive to the work you are engaged in. On the other hand, much less than four weeks time may not be enough for many clients to familiarize themselves with the idea of your absence and to address issues that might arise from the anticipation of your leaving. Four weeks, then, seems like a workable amount of time for issues around your upcoming absence to arise and be addressed. I actually hand my clients a notice that contains the dates of my absence, the name and the phone number of the therapist available to them during my absence, and the date of our first meeting after I return. This provides them not only with a reminder that I am going to leave (before I have done so), but also with a reminder that I will return (while I am gone). Some clients experience it as comforting to have this evidence of my existence and of my plan to return in hand.

Step 4: Continue to raise the issue of your upcoming absence in session. This does not need to be more than a statement like the following: "Do you have any thoughts or feelings regarding my upcoming absence?"

Your client might or might not want to pursue this. You

might see acting-out behavior, with your client canceling, being late, or the like; your client might withdraw and become depressed; or she might show a sudden spurt into activities and more autonomy. You might want to draw your client's attention to a possible connection between these behaviors and your upcoming absence, and she may or may not be able and willing to pursue this line of inquiry. The important thing is for you to keep the issue of your absence present and to provide a space to explore what it might mean to your client. You might have clients who actually get angry when reminded that they might have a reaction to your absence. This, too, gives you much material to work with: their fear of being dependent, their indignation when thought to rely on you, and so forth. Expect your client to be angry. After all, you are going to leave her. However, she may neither be aware of this nor be willing or able to address it. Don't press your client to come up with any material around your absence; just signal that you are prepared to explore whatever might come up.

Step 5: For some clients you may have to arrange for a colleague to see them while you are gone, since some may not be highly functioning enough to do without your support *and* deal with the feelings your absence engenders. Make sure you have all this in place before you leave. For example, if you have a suicidal client, do not leave on vacation without having made sure that she has an appointment with a colleague who will see her in your absence. If she refuses to do so and you feel that she is a danger to herself, consider a hospitalization.[6] You will see that you won't be able to enjoy your vacation very much if you have to be concerned about your client's safety or well-being. I have known colleagues who found themselves on the telephone for regular sessions dur-

---

[6]See Chapters 10 and 11 on suicide and hospitalization.

ing their vacations because they had not adequately taken care of the impact of their absence on their clients. Should you find yourself feeling that no one but you can take care of your client, that you either cannot leave on vacation or feel compelled to be in contact with your client during your absence, you are dealing with countertransference issues that need to be addressed with your supervisor and personal therapist.

Step 6: If your client has a psychiatrist, inform the doctor of the dates of your absence. This is a courtesy and may be helpful for the doctor in anticipating a possible exacerbation of symptoms. Also, ask the psychiatrist to inform you of her absences in return, since this will likely engender a reaction of some sort in your client that it will be helpful to anticipate and because it is always helpful to know when parts of the treatment team are not available.

What to Do When Your Client Plans a Vacation or Other Absence: This issue is definitely less involved than when you are planning an absence. Usually, your client will let you know in advance when she is planning a vacation. Make sure that you bring up the issue of your client's upcoming vacation and absence from therapy; ask whether your client has any concerns regarding her absence and what her thoughts are regarding whether and how not seeing you will impact her. Again, your client may or may not be able or willing to pursue this line of thought, but it is important that you raise it.

If *you* have concerns regarding your client's absence, be sure to voice them. For example, if your client is currently very fragile and prone to decompensate under stress, it is important that you draw her attention to the fact that staying for two weeks at her brother's house, who she told you is having marital problems and where there are prematurely born twin daughters, might increase her stress level. Make sure you document your recommendation in your files.

RETURN FROM A VACATION OR
OTHER PLANNED ABSENCE

The Scenario: You or your client return to the office and resume therapy after a vacation or other planned absence from the office. I will discuss interventions depending on whether it is you or your client who returns from an absence.

What to Do When the Therapist Returns to the Office: When you return to the office after a planned absence, do not expect to be able to pick up just where you had left off. Your absence will have had an impact on your client and on the relationship between the two of you. Be alert for possible acting-out behavior during your absence: your client might suddenly have entered a relationship; might have been drinking and using drugs; might have become overly busy, on the one hand, or might have become more depressed and less functioning, on the other hand. Your client might or might not be aware of these issues.

Overall, it is important to make room for an exploration of how your client experienced your absence and to facilitate his expression of how he feels now that you are back. Expect issues around abandonment and loss to surface. Your client might be angry with you, might even want to "retaliate" and punish you by reducing the frequency of sessions, being late, canceling, or even requesting termination of therapy. Point out the possibility of a connection between your absence, his feelings about your absence—namely, anger, fear, hurt, desperation, and so on—and his actions. Thus, if your client returns to therapy after you have been on vacation for three weeks and tells you that he did just fine and thinks he doesn't need therapy anymore, make sure you say something akin to the following:

> "I think you got really angry with me for leaving you. Is it possible that you might want to 'pay me back' by now leaving me?"

"I wonder if you might want to prevent the possibility of my leaving you again by leaving me first."

Or, less directly: "I wonder if your plan to leave therapy might have anything to do with my having left you when I went on vacation."

Your actual words will depend on your style, on your client, and on where you are in therapy with him. But you get the idea: Make sure to address the fact that you left him, that this will have had an impact on him; make room to explore what that impact is, and for investigating the connection between it and his manifest behavior. This might be an opportunity to begin addressing underlying issues having to do with his family of origin and how loss was experienced by him and handled in his family.

Of course, it is possible that your client cannot handle abandonment and will indeed leave therapy, despite your efforts to address the issues raised by your absence. Should that be the case, be sure you make a recommendation for continued therapy and give referrals for other therapists in case he might feel more comfortable working with someone else.

Overall, your return from a planned absence poses a unique opportunity to explore in the transference issues pertaining to closeness and distance in relationships, interruptions in connectedness, and loss and abandonment.

What to Do When the Client Returns to the Office: As in the case when you left, there will be an impact on the client and on the therapeutic relationship when the client leaves for a planned absence. Upon his return, make sure you explore what the absence meant to him and what it was like not to go to therapy for the time he was gone. Feelings of loss and abandonment might still be present, particularly if you are dealing with a client who might be concerned about *your* response to his absence. You will have an opportunity to address issues pertaining to the client's experience (past and present) of being separate and different from important others (in this case, you): Does it make him anxious, does he expect you to leave him now in retaliation, does he feel depressed or angry because of the separation or because he anticipates your punishment, or does he, on the contrary, feel elated because he has mastered something on his own? Whatever the case, here again, is an opportunity to explore in the transference those issues that have to do with his experiences with his parents or early caregivers and how they manifest in his current relationships.

Of course, not all clients are willing or able to directly look at their thoughts, feelings, and fantasies as they relate to you. Some will simply state that they had a good time and did not miss you. Make note of this, follow their lead as to what they can and want to address, and consult with your supervisor as to how best to proceed.

ON GIFTS

The Scenario: Your client might offer you a gift or you consider giving a gift to your client. I will discuss interventions regarding gifts depending on who the potential gift giver is: the client or the therapist.

What to Do When the Client Wants to Give a Gift to the Therapist: First off, there is no generally accepted and followed rule as to how to handle this (or almost any other) situation. While it is clear that you should not accept any costly offering, the situation is less clear-cut when a client brings you flowers, chocolates, a book, a poem, an apple, or anything else that is not overly expensive.

Your rule of thumb should be: everything means something and needs to be explored. Depending on what that exploration yields, you might end up accepting or not accepting a particular gift.

Thus, instead of accepting a gift immediately or rejecting it out of hand, point out in so many words that you are going to look together at the meaning of this gift. After all, this is what you do in therapy: you look at the meaning of things in your client's life. Therefore, a good preliminary first answer might be something like the following: "Let's look at what it means for you to bring me this gift."

Be sure you make room to also address how the fact that you don't outright accept the gift impacts the client. Perhaps you might say something like this: "I wonder what it is like for you to have brought me this gift and not know whether or not I will accept it."

Your client might have all sorts of feelings about this; she might be angry, sad, embarrassed, and so forth.

Take your time when you explore what the gift means. You do not have to make a decision during that hour or even the next whether you will accept it, but you can ask the client either to leave the gift in your office where it will be a reminder of something that has to be addressed or to take it home and bring it next time. However, until you have formally accepted this gift from your client, do not take it home.

Consult with your supervisor regarding this issue. Perhaps, after exploring the gift and what it means, your client realizes that it was really an offering of appeasement and doesn't want to give it anymore or wants to give it for another reason. You might end up accepting it or not accepting it at the end of looking at what it means. However, whatever you end up doing, you will do it consciously and for a clinically sound reason that is in the client's best interest.

Of course, with some things, like flowers or food, you have to make a decision in that session since they will spoil. Do take your time nonetheless to look at what it means for your client to bring you flowers or to want to feed you, and do what you feel is clinically best. That means that even if you are hungry, you should *not* accept the gift of food for that reason: it is not your client's responsibility to feed you. However, it is your responsibility to explore with your client the meaning of her wish to feed you.

Once you have accepted or rejected a gift, explore with your client how she experiences your acceptance or rejection. This, too, will yield important material to understand, which will ultimately assist your client in her endeavor to lead a healthier, happier life.

In the case of your client wanting to make you an expensive gift, the only difference in the procedure is the fact that you *know* that you will not accept the offering (the law prevents you from doing so). However, you will still explore the meaning of your client wanting to make such a costly gift, as well as the impact of your rejection of it.

What to Do When the Therapist Wants to Give a Gift to the Client: Sometimes, you might feel like giving a gift to your client. Generally, I want to discourage you from doing so for the following reason: Just as it means something when your client wants to give you a gift, it also means something when you want to give a gift to your client. You might not be aware of what prompts this wish and acting on it would create a countertransference behavior, the impact of which would likely be unclear to you. This, clearly, would not be in the best interest of your client.

When you do observe an impulse in yourself to give a gift to a client, be sure to make note of this and explore it in supervision. What does that wish say about the client? About the relationship between you and the client? About therapy with this client so far? About you? All of these are issues that will be clinically useful to explore. Make use of your personal therapist as well.

If you were to offer your client a gift, he would now have to decide whether or not to accept it. In either case, there would be clinical consequences that might take a long time to explore and understand. Unless you are experienced and well versed at considering issues of transference and countertransference, as well as providing space to explore the meaning and effects of your offering a gift, I recommend that you refrain from doing so.

This does not mean that you can't at times make a considered offering as a clinical intervention. Perhaps you consider offering something to a fragile or young client as a transitional object as you are about to go on vacation, something that will help the client keep you in mind and contain himself in your absence. The point is that you should *know* why you are doing what you are doing, and you must be prepared to deal with the effects your actions have. I encourage you to obtain input from your supervisor when you find yourself thus wanting to give a gift to a client. More often than not, this will be about yourself and not about the client.

MAKING MISTAKES

The Scenario: This is the situation in which you make a mistake. It could be a blunder in a clinical intervention, such as an error in interpretation; it could be an insensitive remark that hurts your client's feelings; it could be a misunderstanding of something your client said; it could be an error regarding a meeting time, your dispensing wrong information on something, or any number of other things. What do you do when you have made a mistake?

What to Do: The first and most important step to take in this situation is for you to *acknowledge the mistake.* Do not attempt to hide it, do not attempt to justify it, do not attempt to undo it. The simple (or not so simple) fact is: You are not infallible, you are not perfect, and you made a mistake. This might be a difficult situation because it plays into your insecurities and wishes to appear knowledgeable, trustworthy, and benevolent. However, if you hurt your client's feelings, it is imperative that you acknowledge this fact. This might be the first time and the only place where your client experiences someone taking responsibility for his or her actions. It might also be the only place where she can express her feelings when her feelings have been hurt. It is important that your client gets the chance to feel her anger and hurt and express it to you; it is important that she be afforded the experience that her anger will not destroy you or sever the relationship.

For many therapists it is not easy to provide this opportunity, as we have our own issues and fears of not being liked and being rejected. Supervision and your own therapy will be indispensable tools in developing your capacity to tolerate situations like the one described here and facilitating your client's expression of her reality, as well as her experience of multifaceted, integrated whole objects that are neither all-good nor all-bad—in this case, you.

So, let's assume your client says:

"You hurt my feelings."
"You don't understand."
"This is not what I said."

As indicated earlier, your first step will be to acknowledge your client's perception. A statement like the following will be helpful:

"How did I hurt your feelings?"
"Maybe I don't understand. Tell me more about this so that I can try to understand you better."
"It is not what you said? Perhaps I misunderstood you. What did you say?"

In a second step, inquire about the impact your error or mistake has had on your client. Make a statement akin to the following:

"What is that like for you to realize that I misunderstood you?"
"How did it feel when I made that remark?"

The idea is to demonstrate your willingness and ability to tolerate your client's expression of other than "positive" feelings. Be prepared that it might take a while to appreciate the full impact of the mistake you made—or rather, of the fact that you *did* make a mistake. And be prepared for the fact that it might be less easy for you than you would like it to be. This is not unusual. Work with your supervisor and your own therapist to help you deal with these situations appropriately.

WHEN YOU DON'T KNOW

The Scenario: In this situation, your client asks you something that you might (or might not) be expected to know, and you don't know the answer.

What to Do: To a certain extent, this issue is similar to the one addressed previously. Often, not only clients believe that therapists hold all the answers, but therapists also believe that they should have all the answers. Not knowing is about your having to show yourself as less than all-knowing, as fallible, and as imperfect—in short, as human. This might be harder to admit than you think when clinical issues that you feel you *should* know about are concerned. Perhaps your client says to you: "How much longer is this going to last? When will I be well?"

Your first step, as always, will be to explore the meaning of your client's asking. This would be so even if you *did* know the answer to your client's questions. You want to know what the underlying concerns and issues are that prompted him to ask you in the first place. So you might say:

"What is it like not to know how much longer therapy will last?"

"You sound really anxious to know when you will feel better."
"What prompted you to ask now?"

Your client might or might not proceed along the lines of inquiry suggested by you. Perhaps he says: "I don't want to get into why I asked now, I want an answer!"

There are several ways to respond to this. One might simply be: "It sounds like it makes you angry that I want to know why you asked."

Or you might say:

"What is it that makes you so impatient?"
"This is what we do here, we look at what things mean. It seems that this makes you uncomfortable?"

In a second step, however, let your client know in so many words *that* you do not know. Do not be mysterious about this fact, as if your client were not supposed to ask you questions to which you have no answers, and as if he were not supposed to know that there are things that you do not know. Otherwise, you will be asking your client to collude with you in upholding the illusion that you are infallible, have all the answers, and are thus, in fact, superhuman. Therefore, you might say something like this: "You expressed that it really makes you anxious not to know when you will be well and that you want someone to tell you. But I do not know when that will be. That is something that we will try to find out together."

At this point, be sure to make room for an exploration of the fact that you don't have the information that your client wants. "What is it like to realize that I, too, don't have all the answers?"

Your client might feel terrified, he might be angry with you, he might feel that you are holding something back, or he might be relieved that there is no one "thing" to know. He might even be elated at the prospect of the two of you working together to find out what is going on. Whatever his feelings, it is your job to make room for the expression and exploration of them.

A word to the case when you *do* know: be cautious with answering questions too quickly. You might miss important underlying issues that prompted the question. Please see the next issue for more on this topic.

CLIENT ASKS YOU DIRECT QUESTIONS

The Scenario: This is the situation when your client asks you a direct question.

What to Do: Generally speaking, do not answer any direct question too quickly, lest you close off from inquiry the whole complex underlying the asking. However, do not shroud yourself in obscurity either and do not give the impression that it is not allowable for your client to ask you. In some cases, after exploring the question, you might end up answering it and in others you might not (see also the next section). In a first step you might give an acknowledgment of your client's wish to know: "I understand your question, but before looking at an answer I think we will learn more and it will be more useful if we explore your reasons for asking. Tell me a little more about what prompted you to inquire whether I have read this book?"

However, do come back to the question asked when you have explored the reason for asking, either answering it or giving a rationale for not answering it: "We have now found out more about why you wanted to know whether I have read that book. Do you still want to know?"

If your client still wants to know, either let him know and then explore what the answer and the fact of an answer means to him, or let him know that you will not answer the question and your clinical reason for it. Again, make room to explore what your answer means to your client. This latter (not answering his question) will probably not be the case when you are asked about a book, but it might be your response when asked whether or not you are married, have children, and so forth. In that case, please see the next heading.

CLIENT REQUESTS PERSONAL INFORMATION ABOUT YOU[7]

The Scenario: In this not-uncommon situation, your client asks you personal questions.

What to Do: How you respond to a request for personal information from your client will depend on the client, where you are in treatment, and the specific situation. Sometimes you *will* answer a personal question. But this should be rare and for a good, clinical reason.

Generally speaking, then, you will not answer a personal question. This does not mean that you should ignore such a question. A client who asks you whether you are married, whether you have children, whether you have siblings, and so forth, has her reasons for doing so. It is your responsibility to facilitate the expression and exploration of those reasons.

So what do you do when your client asks: "Do you have children?"

You might say simply: "Why do you ask?"

Or you might say more elaborately:

"I wonder whether you are concerned that I might not be able to understand your problems with your child if you found I had no children?"

"What would it mean to you if I did or did not have children?"

---

[7]See also Chapter 1 on self-disclosure.

You can see that all these questions are aimed at exploring your client's feelings and thoughts pertaining to the question she asked. Perhaps she really doesn't like children and is concerned that she might hurt your feelings if she said so and you had children? Perhaps she is afraid of what you might think of her? Or perhaps she fears you might get angry with her? Perhaps she identifies with you and wants you to have children because she, too, has children? Perhaps she wants to have children and cannot, and is envious at the thought that you have children? A myriad of issues could have given rise to the seemingly simple question "Do you have children?" By answering "yes" or "no," you will not be able to explore these issues, and you might prevent some of them from coming to light. Sometimes your client will say: "Yes, but I want to know! Are you going to answer my question?"

Now is the time to educate (or remind) your client regarding how therapy works. You might say: "We are here not to talk about me but to make room for you and explore what things mean in *your* life. The more you know about me, the more difficult it will be to keep this work about you. So, no, I will not answer your question, because doing so would hinder our work together."

Your client does deserve to get a straight answer regarding the fact that you will not disclose personal information. This fact is *not* a secret that your client must figure out for herself and then cannot talk about. Make sure you explore with your client the impact that your refusal to disclose personal information has. You might say something like this: "What's that like for you that I am not telling you about myself?"

Sometimes, however, you might choose to answer such a question. If you are inclined to do so, take your time to understand your reasons and make sure that you don't act out of countertransference feelings. After all, this is the place to explore what things mean in your *client's* life, not yours. If you choose to answer a personal question for whatever clinical reasons, make sure you explore the impact your answer has. Ask directly:

"What does it mean to you to know that I have children?"
"How does this strike you that I answered your question?"

In the end, you will make a decision on how to handle a situation like this based on your clinical judgment. The less experienced you are, the better it is to be more conservative with your interventions simply because you cannot know the impact they will have and may not have the knowledge to explore the impact they do have.

CLIENT INVITES YOU TO A FUNCTION

The Scenario: Your client invites you to a function like a wedding, a birthday party, a house-warming party, his graduation, and the like.

What to Do: This situation is not as uncommon as it might seem at first glance. If you work with your clients on a long-term basis, sooner or later you will be presented with an invitation to one function or another.

Again, there is no one correct way to handle a situation such as this. Generally speaking, you and your client meet for therapy in your office, which is the designated space the therapeutic relationship is usually confined to. There are ethical and legal standards pertaining to dual relationships that are aimed at preventing the development of a relationship between client and therapist outside the office. As a rule of thumb, then, I recommend declining an invitation to a function outside the office. As with gifts and requests for personal information, make room to explore not only the reason for the request but also the impact of your response.

If you choose to turn the invitation down, acknowledge the *fact* of the invitation. Say something akin to this statement: "I appreciate your wanting me to be a part of your graduation. But since the therapeutic relationship is really confined to this room, I won't actually be there."

Other statements you might make to facilitate the exploration of the meaning of both the invitation and your response to it might include something like the following:

> "It sounds like you really want me to be a part of the celebration. What is it like to know that I won't be there?"
> "What is it like to have invited me to this event that is so important to you and to have me turn down the invitation?"

Don't hesitate to let your client know that it is really not quite appropriate for you to participate in his life outside the therapy room. However, be aware that he will have feelings about that as well: he might be embarrassed for having suggested it, might be angry with you for being the occasion of his embarrassment, might feel rejected and unappreciated, and so forth. As always, explore these responses.

On a rare occasion, a therapist might make a clinical decision to accept an invitation to such a proposed function. However, leave this to the experienced clinicians who are well able to explore their countertransference feelings, as well as being skillful in addressing the impact that their actions will have on the clinical work.

If you find it particularly hard to decline an invitation, make sure you discuss this with your supervisor.

PHYSICAL CONTACT

The Scenario: A client wants to make physical contact with you, perhaps requesting a hug.

What to Do: Generally speaking, psychotherapy does not include physical contact, and of course, it never includes sex. In fact, any sexual contact whatsoever is illegal, unethical, as well as clinically most damaging, and has absolutely *no* place in your work. Keep in mind that you cannot know what a particular client will experience as sexual—particularly in light of the transference relationship. You might not think anything of putting a calming hand on your client's shoulder, while he might experience this as evidence of the fact that you are attracted to him, or that you are trying to seduce him. The rule of thumb in this area, then, is that you, the therapist, should *never* initiate any physical contact (including handshakes).

But what about the situation when a client wants to initiate physical contact? What about when your client requests a hug? Again, generally speaking, I recommend that you decline to do so. However, explore the reason for the request, as well as the impact of your response to it. This might not come easily to you if you are a physically inclined person. If that is the case, make sure you address this issue in your supervision as well as your own therapy, but do not act on it with your clients. Aside from physical contact possibly being most detrimental to their well-being, you might also invite all kinds of legal difficulties.

There is nothing wrong with stating explicitly to your client that therapy does not include physical contact. You might offer a handshake hello and good-bye instead of a proposed hug, but again, make sure that you explore the request for physical contact as well as the impact of your response to it. You might find that your client knew you were going to turn down the request for physical contact and will now be able to explore what it means for him to put you into a situation where you turn him down: perhaps he is repeating a blueprint of relating in which he asks and the other rejects; perhaps he is testing your ability to contain his request and uphold appropriate boundaries; perhaps he is reassuring himself that you will, indeed, refrain from exploiting him. On the other hand, your client might be angry with you for denying his request, sad at the perceived rejection, and so forth. There is ample material to explore in a request like this.

You might see other therapists occasionally hugging a client hello or good-bye. Refrain from doing so yourself. These other therapists may or may not have clinically sound reasons for doing so, but I recommend that physical contact, except for handshakes initiated by the client, be completely avoided.

CLIENT IS OVERTLY SEDUCTIVE

The Scenario: Your client is overtly seductive in session.

What to Do: If your client is overtly seductive in session, it is useful to view this as a manifestation of transference—that is, your client's blueprint of relating manifesting itself in the relationship between herself and you, the therapist. It is important that you address it directly.

When your client is *acting* inappropriately (perhaps touching you or positioning herself close to you in a way that is suggestive), you are faced with a frame violation that is imperative to address and mend. Thus, if your client repeatedly brushes up against you when entering the room, set a clear and direct limit and then explore the behavior. You might say something like this: "I notice that you touch me when you enter the therapy room. Therapy does not include physical contact, so it is important that you don't do this anymore."

This is the limit-setting part where you draw attention to the frame violation. Next, you might continue with something like the following: "Let's look at what this means to you, touching me."

This is when you reestablish the frame by opening the behavior up for *exploration*, instead of acting it out. Of course, you will also have to address what it is like for your client to have you set this limit. Your client might now let you know about erotic fantasies she has in regard to you. Do not be alarmed. This is not unusual and can be addressed in therapy just as any other topic would be. You might have strong countertransference feelings relating to this topic, so enlist the help of both your clinical supervisor and your personal therapist to deal with those so that you can be as helpful to your client as possible.

In general, then, addressing your client's overt seductiveness is part of doing the therapeutic work. As such, it will be helpful to the client because it will bring into the room and thus into consciousness behavior that might actually be quite automatic. On a more technical level, you show yourself as reliable, predictable, and safe when you address *all* issues and when you uphold the frame. You show yourself uncorrupted and not seduced into frame violations, which is really the best safeguard you have available to ensure that the services you offer are professional and ethical.

YOU'RE ONLY IN IT FOR THE MONEY, OR: THIS IS NOT A "REAL" RELATIONSHIP

The Scenario: Your client expresses that he thinks you only see him because he pays you, or, in a similar vein, that the therapeutic relationship is not a "real" relationship.

What to Do: These are sentiments that you will hear not infrequently expressed during your career as a therapist. These statements are often difficult for beginning therapists to deal with because they address questions you might not have answered for yourself yet: What sort of a relationship is the therapeutic relationship? What role does the money play? Let me say here again that issues of fee and money are often difficult for therapists (new and seasoned alike) to address because in our society a person's financial data seem to be more "private" than the rest of her private life (including her sexual and fantasy life).[8] Bring these issues to your supervision and your personal therapy to address in depth.

Meanwhile, consider the following thoughts: statements like "You only see me for the money" or "This is not a real relationship" refer to the nature of the relationship you and your client have and thus to the transference relationship. What does it mean to be in a relationship in general and to be in this relationship in particular? What is it like to pay for meeting with you? How is this relationship similar to other relationships and how is it different? The general sense behind these questions seems to be an awareness that this is a relationship, but that it is different. That it is different visibly because the client pays for seeing you and because it is asymmetrical. Of course, it also *feels* different because of the work you are doing in therapy. Thus, because it is different, is this relationship perhaps not quite "real"? What, then, *is* a "real" relationship in your client's eyes? You see how fruitful the exploration of a statement like this can be.

Your client might say outright:

"You are only in it for the money"
"You only see me because I pay you."

Although the money you earn is, of course, not the only reason why you have chosen this profession, this *is* your work. There is no reason to beat around the bush regarding this fact. Acknowledge the truth in the statement your client made by saying something like this:

"Yes, this is how I make my living."
"Yes, this is my profession."

If doing so is particularly difficult for you, it indicates that you should explore it in supervision and personal therapy: Why

---

[8]See Krueger, 1986.

the reluctance to state freely that you earn your living as a therapist and thus expect your client to pay for your efforts?

Be that as it may, it is equally important that you don't stop here but attempt to explore the underlying reasons for your client's statement. Did it sound hostile? Sad and despairing? Maybe even content? You might say something like the following:

> "It sounds like you don't believe I am really interested in you because you pay me money for meeting with you."
> "What is it like to pay me for meeting with you?"
> "You sound angry about having to pay me for your sessions."
> "You sounded sad when you said I only meet with you because you pay me money."
> "I noticed a little smile when you stated that this is not a real relationship."
> "What do you mean when you say that this is not a real relationship?"

Here, as always, explore what your client's thoughts, feelings, and fantasies are regarding the statement he has made. You might find yourself exploring issues relating to your client's sense of self-worth: he might feel entitled to your attention and be very angry at having to pay for something he feels should be free; he might feel essentially worthless and that no one will pay attention to him if he doesn't "pay" in one way or another. You might be dealing with issues that concern your client's comfort or discomfort with the right kind of "distance" in relationships; thus, the fact that he is paying for your services and you are "only in it for the money" might render you distant, since this is "not a real relationship" and thus makes relating to you safe. On the other hand, this might be your client's expression of a wish for more closeness.

Generally speaking, you are dealing here with a statement about the transference relationship. Don't avoid exploring it.

CLIENT REQUESTS A COPY OF HER TREATMENT RECORDS

The Scenario: Your client or her legal guardian or parent requests a copy of her treatment records.

What to Do: Be sure to always notify your clinical supervisor of a request like this and elicit her input.

Legally, your client or the parent/legal guardian of your minor client has a right to receive a written record of the treatment she receives from you. The request itself, too, must be made in writing. Once you have received the request, it is up to your clinical judgment whether you think it best to provide the client/legal guardian with a copy of the actual records or with a written treatment summary report. The actual records are the property of the agency you work for, or, if you are in private practice, your own private property—not the client's.

In case of a parent or legal guardian requesting access to the records, it is also up to your clinical judgment whether doing so would harm your minor client and whether it would damage the treatment relationship. In those cases you have a right to refuse access. However, be aware of the fact that if you do refuse access in a climate of animosity, the result might very well be that your client will be removed from treatment.

If a request for access to records is made, either by the client herself or by her parents or legal guardian, always first explore the reasons for the request. Ask directly what prompts the request:

"What prompts you to ask for the treatment records?"
"Why do you want a copy of the records?"
"Tell me about your wanting a copy of your records now."

You might find that your client wants to file a claim, but the issue also might be something like her mistrusting you and wanting to know what you might have said about her "behind her back." It might be that a parent is jealous of what you and his child are doing "in private," or it might be that a legal guardian is mistrustful of your qualifications. In all of these cases, it is useful to explore the issues raised with the persons involved. That is to say, look at the situation when a parent approaches you regarding the treatment of their child as a clinical one. The parent might say something like the following:

"I want to know what you are doing when you see my child."
"I want a report of how my child is doing in therapy."
"I want to know whether there is any progress in therapy."

Make room for the parent to express his or her fears, but do educate this person on what you think is the best clinical course of action. Thus, you might say:

"I understand that you feel unsure about what your son and I are doing when we meet for therapy. However, remember when we first met? I let you know that confidentiality for your son is a prerequisite for this therapy to be effective. If what he tells me is not private, he will not tell me what is going on with him. Do you have any particular concerns regarding what he might tell me?"
"What is it like for you to think that your child might be telling *me* things he is not telling you?"
"Is anything going on that makes you concerned at this time?"
"Do you have any particular reason for asking?"

In this way you elicit the parent's reason for asking, without divulging information regarding the treatment. Also, be sure to inform your client—the minor—of the interaction, so that there can be no doubt regarding your speaking to others without your client's knowledge.

It is also possible that a parent is trying to sabotage the treatment for a multitude of reasons. Your best course of action here would be to recommend either individual therapy for the parent or family therapy, where issues regarding the interactions between family members can be addressed directly. If you do so, remember to refer the family to another clinician. You are the *child's* therapist.

Of course, in the cases where the exploration of these issues involves persons other than your client himself, as is the case when you have to deal with parents and legal guardians, be sure to notify your client before you attempt to speak with these people.

Let your client know about the request for the meeting, elicit his input, and inform him of what you will do in that meeting, including what you will recommend regarding access to the records. If you feel that allowing access to treatment records would damage the treatment relationship or be harmful to your client, let your client know that you will not grant access to the records. Document your actions in your client's file and check with your professional organization's legal counsel.

If the requesting party is your client, your course of action is in essence the same. Explore the reason for the request. If the request results in either your giving your client a copy of the records or a treatment summary, make sure you allow plenty of time to go over either one of them with him. Enlist your supervisor's help in doing so.

17

PAPERWORK: CLINICAL NOTES AND TREATMENT SUMMARIES

As you begin your work with clients, you will also start documenting your work in your clients' files. Occasionally, you will be asked to write a treatment summary of the work you have done.

CLINICAL NOTES

First and foremost, keep in mind that the notes you write about treatment are considered legal documents, even though they are either your employing agency's or, if you are in private practice, your own private property. They can be (and at times are) subpoenaed and end up being read in court and becoming public. Therefore, be careful and conscientious about what and how you write your notes.

That said, let me also state that clinical notes are really meant for you. *Only* the court can compel you to relinquish your actual records. In all other cases, it is up to your clinical judgment whether you want to give access to the records, or whether you judge it more appropriate to submit a treatment summary report (with your client's written permission, of course). Since you write the clinical notes mainly for yourself, you will most often find yourself writing a treatment summary if there is a request for records.

At times, your client will request to see her records. However, here again, it is according to your clinical judgment whether you will either grant this request or provide her with a treatment summary.

Generally speaking, writing clinical notes can be a balancing act between safeguarding your client's confidentiality, on the one hand (by not writing too much), and satisfying the professional requirement of keeping accurate notes, on the other hand (by writing enough). Clinical notes, then, should be detailed enough so that they give an accurate picture of the course of therapy; however, they should *not* be so detailed that you report on every word that is exchanged in session. Here are a few guidelines.

A *clinical note should include*:

- The date the session took place.
- Whether client was late.
- Client's mood and affect.
- The overall theme of the session.
- Any unusual behavior (including "first times").
- The thrust of your interventions.
- Client's state of mind upon leaving.
- A brief plan for future sessions.

In effect, that might look like the following:

August 31, 1999: Client was five minutes late. Mood: depressed. Affect: congruent (tearful). Client addressed issues relating to her work environment, expressed frustration and anger. Explored options as to how to deal with her feelings in a more constructive way: speaking her mind, taking colleague aside after work, writing a letter. Appeared somewhat agitated at the beginning of the session, but seemed considerably calmer when she left. Will meet next week.

If there is something unusual such as a suicide threat, you should document that in more detail. For example:

Client expressed suicidal ideation. Upon assessment, did not appear acute (no plan, no means, only vague thoughts of "wanting the pain to end"). Contracted for safety. Client agreed to check in with me on the phone tomorrow and to call as needed. Will see her the day after tomorrow.

You might prefer to use a more formalized way of writing your notes, for example the *SOAP* concept:

S (ubjective): Theme of session. (Including: What was your impression this session was about?)

O (bjective): Actual behavior you saw the client display and your actual interventions. (Including: Was client on time or late? Any unusual behavior. What did the client say? Your interventions.)

A (ffect): What mood was the client in? What affect did she display? (Including: client's state of mind upon leaving.)

P (lan): What do you plan on doing with what was displayed in S, O, and A? (Including any referrals you might make.)

This concept is meant as a help to organize your thoughts. It is not meant to be actually written down as "S, O, A, P." Thus, it is sufficient to have in mind that you want to make mention of the theme of the sessions (S), any unusual behavior and a note regarding your interventions (O), a remark regarding your client's mood and affect (A), as well as when you will see her next and whether you made a referral, a contract for safety, and so on (P).

Many agencies have their own policies regarding the issue of record keeping. As a beginning therapist, you most likely will be required to keep records by your place of work. The suggestions you find here are meant as a starting point for you to find a way to keep records that feels comfortable to you, while keeping in mind that these notes might become public.

Generally speaking, it is good practice to restrict yourself to observations you have made, behavior you have seen, interventions you have made and, perhaps, what their result was. Do *not* speculate in your notes. Do not document what you thought or what you felt. Document what you did as well as what the client did: this could include something the client told you she thought or felt but *not* something you thought or felt. I have seen clinical notes that read more like the diary of the therapist than a documentation of the actual therapy taking place. Be as concise and to the point as you can.

TREATMENT SUMMARIES

At times, you will be asked to write a treatment summary report of your work with your client. This may come in the form of a request for your treatment records from a psychiatrist who is seeing your client, from a social worker who is working with your client, from an insurance agency that is processing a claim, from a lawyer, or from the client herself, to name just a few. Whatever the case, your first step will always be to contact your client and receive her written authorization to release the requested information. If an authorization to release information signed by your client is enclosed, make sure to contact your client and get her expressed permission personally. In this way you can make sure that she has not changed her mind, as well as demonstrate that you are not talking to third parties (unless compelled by the law) without her expressed permission.

If the request is for the treatment records, keep in mind that it is up to your clinical judgment whether you want to send a copy of the actual records or a treatment summary report. Often, the request will be for records *or* a treatment summary.

In the case of your client wanting access to her records, do not neglect to explore the reasons for this request. Often, such a request is indicative of issues of mistrust, suspiciousness, insecurities regarding the efficacy of treatment, or your personal integrity that need to be explored. This does, of course, not mean that you will withhold either the records or a treatment summary, whichever you judge clinically most appropriate to give to your client. In either case, your client must issue the request for her records in writing.

Your actual treatment summary will differ, depending on whom you are writing it for and what the reasons for the request are. Most agencies requesting a treatment summary will send you paperwork detailing the issues they want you to address. Many times they will actually send you forms to fill out but will allow the alternative of a narrative report. If you choose to do the latter, use the form to include a sentence or two on each topic mentioned.

In any case, try to go over the finished report with your client and get his explicit authorization to send out this particular report before you do so. If for whatever reason you are not able to read the report with your client before you send it, make sure you give him a copy after you send it and go over the report with him then.

Your client might change his mind and not want the report sent out after all. You must honor that request, unless you are compelled by law to send a report. However, do not neglect to explore his reasons for withdrawing his authorization to share this information, as well as explore the results this withdrawal will have. Some clients will find it hard to hear in "cold, hard, clinical terms" how you see what is going on with them. They might experience it as your being judgmental and might need time to talk it over with you and experience and express their feelings (often anger or outbursts of sadness). Sometimes, being confronted with the written report, a client might not want others to see it and decide not to send it out, which, in case of an insurance claim, might result in nonpayment. It is important that the implications of this decision are addressed in session: being responsible for paying your fee without help, possible inability to pay the fee, possible endangerment of continuity of treatment, new fee negotiations, and so forth.

In case of your being compelled by the court to submit a treatment summary report, be certain to make room for the exploration of your client's feelings regarding this issue. There might be a sense of the client feeling betrayed or violated. It is important to validate these feelings, as well as point out the limits of confidentiality. Be as open as possible to any outcome, including losing your client.

In the following list, I will give you a sample sentence or two per issue covered in a hypothetical treatment report. Please keep in mind that the actual report might cover more, less, and/or different issues than are mentioned here. Also, you will cover these issues more in depth than I have in these samples.

Your actual treatment summary report might look something like this:

- *A statement regarding why you are sending this report.*
  "Enclosed please find a confidential narrative treatment summary report as requested by you in your written communication of . . . "

- *Date you started seeing the client, frequency of sessions, as well as treatment modality* (individual therapy, couples' therapy, family therapy, etc.).
  "I have seen Ms. Green since March 1998, twice weekly, in individual psychotherapy."

- *Chief complaint* (why did client seek treatment?).
  "Ms. Green initially complained of depression and difficulties with her relationships, as well as in her work."

- *What you observed* (symptoms, behaviors, including direct quotes).

  "Ms. Green presented with symptoms of depression such as difficulties sleeping, anergia, anhedonia, chronic suicidal ideation ('I think of killing myself all the time'), weight loss, difficulties concentrating, tearfulness, as well as symptoms of obsessive-compulsive disorder such as frequent checking of locks, frequent hand-washing, intrusive obsessional thoughts, compulsion to count ('I have these thoughts and then I *must* go through this ritual to make sure everyone is safe')."

- *Some history as it relates to Ms. Green's disorder.*

  "Ms. Green has been in treatment with three other therapists prior to starting therapy with me. She reports having been hospitalized for suicidal ideation and suicide attempts five times in the last few years. In fact, she was hospitalized one time during our work together, due to severe depressive symptomatology."

- *Impairment resulting from her difficulties.*

  "Ms. Green's symptoms have resulted in her withdrawal from friends and family, as well as impairment in her ability to work (great difficulties concentrating, frequent hospitalizations due to suicide attempts). At this time Ms. Green is in danger of losing her job."

- *Referrals to other professionals you have made.*

  "Since early 1999 Ms. Green has been in psychiatric treatment with Dr. Y ."

- *Any medications Ms. Green is on.*

  "Dr. Y has prescribed Paxil 100mg 2-BID, as well as Buspar 1mg 1-TID."

- *Your diagnosis (DSM-IV axial or nonaxial).*

  "My diagnosis is Axis I: Major depression, recurrent, moderate

OBSESSIVE-COMPULSIVE DISORDER

Axis II: deferred
Axis III: none known
Axis IV: moderate (difficulties at work and at home)
Axis V: 50."

A nonaxial diagnosis might look like this:

"Ms. Green is suffering from a major depressive disorder, recurrent, moderate as well as from obsessive-compulsive disorder. There are no known physical conditions that might contribute to her disorder. Ms. Green has difficulties at her place of work as well as at home. At this time I assess Ms. Green's global functioning at 50."

- *Results of your treatment so far.*
  "Ms. Green's symptoms have slightly improved since first coming to see me. Her suicidal ideation is not diminished; however, there have been no suicide attempts in the last year."

- *Some sort of a prognosis.*
  Be careful with this one. You can't really know what is going to happen. Always qualify your prognosis with "at this time," thus leaving room for error and unforeseen changes. However, you will have a sense whether change for the better (prognosis: good at this time), no change, or change for the worse (prognosis: poor at this time) can be expected. If you feel you really don't know, state "prognosis: guarded at this time." This basically says that things don't look so good right now and might not get better, but then again, they might after all.

- *Some sort of a recommendation.*
  This will most often be a recommendation for Ms. Green to remain in treatment. It might sound something like this:

  "I recommend that Ms. Green continue treatment in order to assist her with dealing with her symptoms."

"I recommend Ms. Green continue in psychotherapeutic as well as psychiatric treatment."

"I recommend that Ms. Green, in addition to continuing in psychotherapeutic as well as psychiatric treatment, also receive couples' treatment for herself and her partner."

"Since Ms. Green has missed most of her sessions, I feel that she has not been able to benefit from the treatment made available to her. I therefore recommend that treatment be discontinued until Ms. Green makes a commitment to appear in session reliably."

PROGRESS CASE REPORTS

Some of you will find yourselves in the position not just of therapist, or perhaps not even primarily as therapist, but perhaps as case manager to a number of clients. This is particularly often the case when you work in an agency or facility that is not primarily a provider of psychotherapy but that offers psychotherapy as one service among others—such as, for example, psychiatric treatment, placement services, residential treatment, educational and vocational services, shelters for the homeless, and the like. Often, the clients are either seriously mentally ill, recipients of SSI or Disability, or placed through a government agency like the Department of Children and Family Services (DCFS) or the Department of Mental Health (DMH).

When working in such an agency—not primarily as a therapist but as a case manager—rather than writing a brief treatment summary, you will often be asked to write an extensive treatment progress report, perhaps even on a regular basis in the form of a quarterly progress report, either directly for the agency you work for or for a funding agency like DCFS or DMH.

Sometimes, the agency in question has its own format, in effect giving you a structure to follow when writing these reports. Often, however, this is not the case. I will therefore give you a formula to follow as you prepare a progress report on your client. As always, keep in mind even here that you want to protect your client's confidentiality as much as possible: give as little information as possible and as much information as is necessary to satisfy the requirements. Make sure that you have an authorization to release information on file. If your report is going to DCFS, where it will be used in court, it is likely that your client (usually a child or adolescent) will hear what you wrote. If the client is not too young, consider discussing the contents of the report with the client yourself before she hears it in court.

For the following examples, let us assume the client is our Ms. Green, who this time is a resident at a psychiatric treatment center where you work with her. You are asked to write a quarterly progress report on her to be sent to the Department of Mental Health, which is funding her stay at the Treatment Center.

Here are areas that you want to address in your report:

- *Date of report*
  Give the date when you are writing this report.

- *Name of client*
  Give the name of the client you are writing the report on.

- *Case number*
  Give the client's case number, if applicable. Sometimes, the client's DOB is used for this purpose, sometimes it is her Social Security number.

- *Date client was admitted to facility*
  Give the date the client was admitted to the facility, entered your program, or began receiving treatment.

- *Time interval this report covers*
  Give the time period you will describe in your report. For example, if the last report on this client was written on

January 1, 2000, and you are writing this current report
on March 9, 2000, you would note this as "January 1, 2000,
to March 9, 2000." If this is the first progress report on
this client, the admittance date will be noted. In this case:
"admittance date, to March 9, 2000."

- *Overall adjustment*
  Here you give a brief description of this client's overall
  adjustment during the time period described. For example:

  Ms. Green has adjusted reasonably well to her environment
  during the time of her stay. She was noticeably shy and withdrawn at first, but has warmed to her environment and is
  participating actively in the treatment program.

- *Diagnostic impression*
  In this section you can give a diagnostic impression similar to what was described in the previous treatment summary. Most likely, a complete DSM-IV diagnosis will be
  required. For example:

  Axis I: Major depression

  OBSESSIVE-COMPULSIVE DISORDER

  Axis II: deferred
  Axis III: none known at this time
  Axis IV: mild (adjustment to new living environment)
  Axis V: 65

- *Psychological*
  Here you will address issues similar to the treatment summary report described earlier, including symptoms, kind
  of treatment received, frequency of treatment, progress
  made in treatment, and referrals to other professionals.
  If client participates in a number of activities (e.g., individual therapy, group therapy, etc.), list them here.

- *Medical*
  List any medical treatment Ms. Green has received, including psychiatric treatment. State the name of the psychiatrist, if any; frequency of visits; medications prescribed; and Ms. Green's medication compliance. If she has seen any other doctors, list that fact with the date and reason why she was seen, name of doctor, medication prescribed, and result of treatment.

- *Social*
  Give a brief description of how Ms. Green is participating socially with her peers and staff. Is she well integrated, well liked, an outsider, keeping to herself? Has she made friends? Is she helpful to others, and so forth?

- *Educational and vocational*
  Make note of any involvement Ms. Green may have educationally or vocationally. State which school she is attending (if any) and briefly address her progress made. If she is working or looking for work, state it here.

- *Incident reports*
  If Ms. Green was involved in any incidents during the report period, list them here by date. Perhaps she cut herself, perhaps she did not return to the facility for two days, perhaps she got into a physical fight with a peer, or perhaps she got drunk. All of these cases would qualify as incidents at most agencies.

- *Recommendation for further treatment*
  Make a brief recommendation for Ms. Green's further treatment. This will include a recommendation that either Ms. Green remain at the facility or that a change to a facility better suited to her needs should be considered. It will include whether you recommend that Ms. Green continue with the current treatment or any changes you think necessary.

- *Date and sign*
  Date and sign the completed report.

Again, keep in mind that this sample just gives you a rough, bare-bones outline of issues to be addressed in a progress case report. Once you have written your report, show it to your supervisor and talk it over with her or him.

PART III

THEORETICAL CONSIDERATIONS:
THE PSYCHODYNAMIC APPROACH

INTRODUCTION

In Part III, I will address the theoretical concepts underlying the presentation of the preceding text. That text contains a psychodynamically oriented introduction to clinical practice for beginning therapists. It is my belief that this approach is best suited to help you understand who your clients are and to assist you in learning the art of conducting therapy, rather than just giving you a few mechanical tools to "solve problems." It will be easier, coming from the understanding and the practice of a psychodynamic model, to learn working with cognitive-behavioral interventions; to do short-term, solution-oriented psychotherapy; and to work with medical-model interventions such as medications or applying tests and the like, in the context of the therapeutic relationship. On the other hand, it will be a lot more difficult expanding into longer-term, psychodynamically (or even psychoanalytically) oriented therapy on the basis of more solution-oriented, cognitive-behavioral work. In addition, you will always be able to use interventions of the latter background with clients whom you have worked with psychodynamically, while the reverse case is not true. If you have worked cognitive-behaviorally, in a brief, solution-oriented way with a client, it can be difficult to switch to a more dynamically oriented stance.

Many theoretical orientations exist, as you are no doubt aware. Which one you choose as your own will in great measure influence the way you understand your clients, the way you conceptualize what is wrong, the way you devise a "cure" for what you have determined is wrong, as well as the way to achieve this cure—that is, which interventions you will use, why, when, and how.

Generally, it is useful to look at these theories as models to understand the human mind, as well as human experience and behavior. Quite naturally, one theory will appeal more to you than others. However, it takes time to familiarize yourself with the theories, as well as their clinical application. Much of this familiarization will consist of your own study, but more will depend on your actual work with clients; the orientation of your supervisor, who will instruct you in looking at clinical material in a certain way and making certain interventions based on her or his orientation; as well as on the orientation of your own, personal therapist, who will conduct therapy with you according to a certain theoretical model. Ultimately, what you are looking for is a certain "fit" of the theory with who you are and what appears plausible to you. This process can take years and might in fact never be finished. Be prepared that you might, over time, adopt and adapt more than one theoretical model and/or theory.

Therefore, if you don't know which theoretical orientation seems to work best for you at this time, try to settle into this "not knowing" and keep in mind that it is "normal" for you not to know. It is useful to take your time with this issue. Since your theoretical orientation will have a profound impact on the work you do, this choice is clearly not something to rush into.

There are many books on the topic of theory. Since in this text I am concerned with presenting you with ways to do practical work relatively independent of theoretical orientation, I will refrain from elaborating on this topic. Suffice it to mention a listing of literature in Appendix II that will be helpful for further study of theoretical approaches.

18

THEORETICAL CONCEPTS

In this chapter I will present a number of theoretical concepts underlying the psychodynamic theoretical approach on which this writing is based. Although this approach has not been specifically referred to as such throughout the rest of the text, it is the foundation of all you will find in the preceding.

OVERVIEW

I will give you here a quick point-by-point overview of the theoretical presuppositions underlying the rest of this text.

1. I have a "*relational developmental* bias": Human beings develop in relation with other human beings.
2. There is a predictable and necessary sequence of development for human beings, physically as well as psychologically (developmental stages).
3. The psychological development of human beings—that is, the development of the human "mind" or the development of a "self"—has to do with the nature of their external relationships to their primary caregivers during each of the developmental stages, as well as with the

child's unique way of internalizing these relationships (taking in these relationships and building structures of the mind with it).

4. Psychological disturbance results from disturbance in these external relationships according to the demands of the developmental stage, on the one hand, *and according to how this is being internalized by the child,* on the other hand.

5. What constitutes disturbed external relationships (and thus might lead to disturbed internal relationships and therefore psychological disturbance) differs with the developmental stage the child is in, as well as with the child's unique needs. Which particular psychological disturbance a child will develop thus depends on:
    *   the child's unique, constitutional structure (biology)
    *   the actual nature of the external relationships
    *   how the external relationships are experienced and internalized by the child
    *   when and how in the developmental sequence the disturbance manifests
    *   how the preceding developmental stage(s) was/were mastered

6. The thus-created psychological disturbance will manifest in a replay/re-creation/repetition of earlier relationships (and how they were experienced) in current relationships.

7. The therapeutic relationship is one of those current relationships.

8. An alleviation of symptoms or a cure is always attempted within the therapeutic relationship.

9. Your interventions as a therapist are an expression of, as well as have impact on, the relationship between yourself and your client.

10. To understand what this impact is and to judiciously place your interventions, it is necessary to understand the na-

ture of the relationship between yourself and your client.

To put it simply: My bias is that you, the therapist, and your client have an impact on each other as real human beings. This being the case, it matters what you say and how and when you say it. Having developed a mind in interaction with other human beings, interactions with other humans impact our minds, on the one hand, and we will play out the structure and content of our minds with other humans, on the other.

However, even if you do not practice a dynamically oriented psychotherapy and therefore do not actively address this impact that the two (or more) of you have on each other, the fact still remains that there *are* two or more real human beings in a room, meeting on a regular basis. It stands to reason to assume that this fact will have an impact on both you and your client/s—even if you choose not to work with that impact. As Lucia Towers stated in 1956 (Towers in Langs, 1990, p. 166): "I simply do not believe that any two people, regardless of circumstance, may close themselves in a room, day after day, month after month, year after year, without something happening to each of them in respect to the other."

WHAT DOES "PSYCHODYNAMIC" MEAN?

The psychodynamic approach refers to an understanding of the human psyche as a "thing" in motion, a *dynamic* (as opposed to a static) structure, even a process, if you will. With Moore and Fine (1990, p. 152), psychodynamic theory explains "(. . .) mental phenomena, such as thoughts, feelings, and behavior, as the result of interacting and opposing goal-directed motivational forces."

Psychodynamic theory is based on Freudian psychoanalytic theory, assuming a structure of the mind composed of Id (impulses, wishes), Ego (the part of the mind that is in touch with reality and the Superego, the executive agency responsible for actions), and Superego (conscience and ideals). A wish thought to originate in the Id may not lead directly to its satisfaction in reality, because the Ego judges it to be in conflict with the demands of the Superego—for example, with a societal ideal. In other words, the wish to possess my neighbor's car will not result in my taking that car because (among other things) stealing is unacceptable behavior in the society I live in. I may even push this wish out of awareness, so that I don't consciously experience it.

Thus, in psychodynamic theory, mental content (feelings, thoughts, wishes, etc.) may move from being conscious to being unconscious; impulses originating in what is unconscious may either become conscious, get discharged, or reach consciousness in a disguised form, perhaps as symptoms or not at all.

There are many different theories as to how the structures of the mind get laid down, where mental content originates, and what it is composed of. The important issue for us here is understanding the mind to be dynamic and mental content to be conscious or unconscious.

A WORD ON THE CONCEPT
OF THE UNCONSCIOUS

As you have seen, this text assumes that there is "(. . .) mental content that is not available to conscious awareness at a given time, as demonstrated by parapraxes, dreams, and disconnected thoughts and conclusions" (Moore and Fine 1990, p. 201). Without going into any detail about the classical Freudian concepts of the systems of Conscious and Unconscious—in any case, a reification of a theoretical construct—assuming that much (if not most) mental content is unconscious means that we assume that we humans are unaware of many of our motivations, feelings, memories, and wishes. It means that what we see is not necessarily all there is to see; that all we do and do not do not only has meaning but may actually have meaning that is distinct from the obvious. In fact, it means that many of our actions are a disguise for deeper-lying, unconscious meanings. Assuming that there is unconscious mental content in fact gives us a rationale for exploring all we are presented with in therapy for such additional, underlying meaning.

Depending on one's theoretical orientation, the assumption of the actual content of the unconscious, as well as the reason for its being unconscious, differs. However, there is a general understanding that some areas of unconscious mental content, if conscious, would produce intolerable levels of anxiety and are therefore defended against by way of the various defense mechanisms. Such areas of unconscious mental content that threaten overwhelming anxiety are said to be "conflicted": there is a conflict between the "push" of the unconscious mental content into consciousness, on the one hand, and the threatened overwhelming anxiety if the now-unconscious mental content were to become conscious, on the other hand. That means, the purpose of defense mechanisms is to prevent unconscious, anxiety-threatening mental content from becoming conscious. Much pathological behavior can be seen as defensive in this sense.[1]

Believing that there is unconscious mental content, then, is tantamount to believing that there is more to us humans than meets the eye. That it is possible to make at least some of what is unconscious conscious and, in so doing, broaden the range of choices and improve the quality of life for the person concerned.

You will see that many of my suggested interventions can be paraphrased as a search for more, additional, not obvious, un-

---

[1]For more information on these concepts, see Moore and Fine (1990), as well as A. Freud (1946), *The Ego and the Mechanisms of Defense.* See also Chapter 8 ("Making a Structural Diagnosis") on more information regarding defense mechanisms.

derlying meaning; that much of what I suggest you pursue with your client is really the question: "What does this mean to you?"

This question is firmly based on the belief that there is unconscious mental content and that in pursuing the meaning of words, thoughts, and behaviors, we come closer and closer to additional, unconscious meanings, of which there are many.

The concepts addressed in "Transference" and "Countertransference" also assume the presence of unconscious mental content. In the former (transference) we are looking at the client's unconscious, while in the latter (countertransference) we are dealing with the therapist's unconscious mental content.

TRANSFERENCE

"Transference" is a technical psychoanalytic term referring in its wider sense to "the displacement of patterns of feelings, thoughts, and behavior, originally experienced in relation to significant figures during childhood, onto a person involved in a current interpersonal relationship" (Moore and Fine 1990, p. 196). It is understood to be an unconscious, automatic repetition. In its narrow sense, such transference is assumed to be taking place solely in psychoanalysis, with the analyst being the person onto whom the patterns of feelings, thoughts, and behavior are displaced. In its wider sense—and that is the way I am looking at it here—it is generally assumed that there is extra-analytic transference taking place in other types of psychotherapy, even in social interactions. To this day, there is no generally accepted, agreed-upon definition of the term.

For our purposes, it is important to understand that in the relationship between therapist and client you will see a replay of your client's usual ways of relating to others, a replay that is based on your client's part on the blueprint of her primary relationships when growing up. As stated by Moore and Fine (1990, p. 197), it is important to keep in mind that not all of your client's reactions to you are based on transference but also are based in part on your actual behavior and your attitudes. However, the way your clients perceive your actions and behaviors, what meaning they attach to these, and how they choose to respond to your actions will be based on their blueprint of relating.

Therefore, it is most important that you are aware of the fact that what you do and say (and what you do not do and do not say) have meaning that can potentially be explored in the therapeutic setting.

This book is not meant to teach you how to work with the transference. Many other books, as well as your supervised clinical practice and the experience of your own therapy, will do that. However, I do want to direct your attention to the relationship between you and your client and the fact that it is of significance. This understanding is the basis for many of my recommendations regarding such seemingly disparate issues as the recommendation to abstain from self-disclosure, to end sessions on time, and how to handle therapist vacations, client cancellations, and so forth.

COUNTERTRANSFERENCE

In many ways, the concept of "countertransference" is the theoretical counterpart to the concept of "transference." Again, as with transference, there is no general consensus as to the definition of this term. In its narrow sense, it refers to the analyst's (or therapist's) unconscious specific reactions to the client's transference. In the wider sense—in which I use it here—it reflects the therapist's emotional reactions (conscious and unconscious) to the client. In either case, as explicated by McClure and Hodge (1987, p. 326), it refers to the process of transferring onto the person of the client thoughts, feelings, and attitudes based on images of the therapist's internal world rather than those of the client.

Countertransference was initially seen as a manifestation of a problematic nature, to be avoided and eliminated. In recent years there has been much discussion regarding this issue, and the general attitude now includes the notion that countertransference is something that always and of necessity takes place in the therapist when conducting therapy, as well as the notion that it is a useful and indispensable tool for the therapeutic work.

A most useful distinction has been made by Robbins and Jolkovski (1987) between *countertransference feelings* (the complex of feelings and thoughts a therapist has in response to a client, conscious and unconscious) and *countertransference behaviors* (actions a therapist takes based on countertransference feelings that arise from internally conflicted, unresolved areas). Applying McClure and Hodge's (1987) concept of facilitative and nonfacilitative countertransference, we can understand countertransference feelings as inevitable therapist responses that can be facilitative, aiding the therapist's understanding of the client. On the other hand, countertransference behavior can be seen as nonfacilitative and resulting in misperceptions and inappropriate responses to the client, based on those perceptions.

It is clear that what we want to avoid is nonfacilitative countertransference manifested in countertransference behaviors. An example of nonfacilitative countertransference would be the following case:

> A client misses several sessions. You feel angry, then anxious (countertransference feelings). You choose not to address the fact of the cancellations with your client (countertransference behavior) because of your own fear of confronting your client— that is, because of your own issues about making others angry and not being liked. Your client in fact gets deprived of the experience of exploring the reasons that led to the cancellations, reasons that might, in fact, contain anger at you, the therapist, and would require your dealing with these issues, the very issues that your behavior avoids.

Rather, we want to be able to utilize such countertransference feelings in facilitative countertransference, in fact avoiding countertransference behavior. An example for facilitative countertransference we can find in that same situation:

> Your client canceled several sessions in a row and you did not address this fact. You might find yourself feeling angry at your client (countertransference feeling). If you can allow yourself to become aware of this fact and if you have a place where you can explore this further (in supervision and your own therapy), you might arrive at the realization that this anger at your client tells you something about the interaction between the two of you that you can use. You might find that your own anger is indicative of the anger your client feels, you might find that your anger is a useful sign that you have neglected to attend to an issue (in this case, having been stood up), and so forth. If you have resolved your own issues enough in your own therapy, you will be able to utilize these countertransference feelings and begin to address with the client the meaning of her missing the sessions.

Of course, in order to use our countertransference feelings, we must first become conscious of our internal responses to our clients, quite aside from the fact of having to learn how to utilize what we have become aware of. Your clinical supervision will be the place to become aware of your countertransference behaviors and begin looking at some of your countertransference feelings. Also, it will be here that you will learn what to do with the information these countertransference issues give you. I recommend your own personal therapy as the place to explore these feelings, as well as your personal issues that give rise to them. As you do so, you will see how your awareness of countertransference issues will expand analogous to the resolution of your own internal conflicts.

19

MARGARET MAHLER'S DEVELOPMENTAL MODEL

The human infant develops psychologically as well as physically. Such development is intimately connected with the care and interaction the infant and child receives from her or his caregivers. The idea is that such interactions get internalized and in fact are the building blocks (along with constitutional factors) for the development of psychical structure or, in other words, a mind. I will now give you a brief explication of the developmental bias mentioned previously by introducing Margaret Mahler's developmental model.[1] Please note that there are other models of human development, for which Appendix II will offer suggested reading. I chose Mahler's developmental model because it is a good introduction to the concept of object relations development, as well as for its relevance for clinical work with adults and children.

The theory of object relations grew out of classical psychoanalytic theory and practice. It refers to a particular understanding of human psychological development. The main under-

---

[1]See Horner (1991, pp. 11–37) for an excellent brief introduction to this topic as well.

standing of this theory is that the human mind is composed of elements taken in (internalized) from the outside—that is, that the human mind develops in interaction with other human beings. That which is internalized are primarily experiences of the infant and child with her primary caregivers, including the feelings evoked by these experiences. These internalized experiences of relating are called internal objects, as opposed to external objects, a term that refers to the actual person (mother, father, other primary caregiver). If these internalized experiences are integrated—that is, if all experiences, good and bad, belonging to one caregiver are felt to belong to that caregiver—we speak of a "whole object." Otherwise, if the internalized experiences are not integrated, we speak of "part objects."

To put it differently: the interaction of an infant and child with her primary caregivers will be internalized by the child and will serve as a blueprint for all relating that will take place later. These internal object relations (the "blueprint") are in part conscious and in part unconscious. They are enduring but modifiable.

Margaret Mahler's model of psychological development, which she called "The Psychological Birth of the Human Infant," is a model of object relations development.[2] It is based on observations of healthy mother–child pairs and has been found to coincide with many clinical cases since she posited it in the 1970s.

Mahler assumes a psychological development that takes place in the following phases:

Normal Autism (0–2 months)
Symbiosis (2–6 months)
Separation-Individuation (6–24 months)
    Hatching Subphase (6–10 months)

---

[2]Mahler saw herself as an ego-psychologist. However, her theory effectively describes object relations development.

Practicing Subphase (10–16 months)
Rapprochement Subphase (16–24 months)
Developing Object Constancy (24–36+ months)

Depending on how the development of the phases are mastered, as well as difficulties and disruptions experienced during the different phases, different pathological development might result. The following explications of Mahler's developmental model rely heavily on Hamilton's work *Self and Others: Object Relations Theory in Practice* (1992).

NORMAL AUTISM (0–2 MONTHS)

During the phase that Mahler and her colleagues call "normal autism"—that is, during the first two months of life—the infant is thought to form a one-person, monadic system with a lack of differentiation between self and other and only rudimentary reactivity towards the environment. In other words, the child is assumed to be not yet aware of the environment, including the primary caregiver. This phase predates the capacity for relationships with an "other" who is perceived as distinct from self. All experiences are assumed to be centered around the body, in other words, they are physiological and inward-directed. The child does, however, display innate attachment-seeking behavior that secures the primary caregiver's attention. Attachment in this phase is assumed to be largely one-sided from parent to child. Remember that the child does not yet have the mental capacity for reciprocal relating, since he or she is not able to differentiate between self and other. As a matter of fact, it can be said that the infant is in a sleep-like state during that phase—that is, he or she is psychologically withdrawn. Indeed, infants spend much time in sleep or half-sleep at that age. This can be said to approximate the isolation of intrauterine life.

Serious disruptions during this phase, which include severe neglect and abuse, might lead to a "failure to thrive" and even death. If the results are not as drastic, they can nevertheless result in a pervasive developmental disorder and mental retardation, as well as a compromised further development. Erickson's "basic trust" never gets developed if the early environment is not attentive and trustworthy: the world is experienced as dangerous and not to be trusted, and the person might develop great difficulties in distinguishing between what is inside and what is outside (psychosis), as well as be rather paranoid in her or his outlook.

SYMBIOSIS (2–6 MONTHS)

With the maturation of the nervous system and the gathering of experience, infants begin to develop a "dim awareness of the need satisfying object" (Mahler et al., 1975, p. 44)—that is, of the primary caregiver. The mother (or other primary caregiver) and the infant are experienced by the infant as part of "the same omnipotent system, a dual unity within one common boundary" (Mahler et al., 1975, p. 44). This is because of poor self–other differentiation, where the infant experiences him or herself as "omnipotent": she's hungry, the breast appears, she cries, she gets picked up, and so forth.

As the infant gets older, her ego functions unfold (memory, cognition, motor coordination). She can now begin to organize experiences like being hungry, being fed, being held, seeing, feeling, smelling, self, and mother. These perceptions provide a budding sense of self in relation to mother (other/object). Overall, it can be said that the unfolding ego functions allow for relationship with the primary caregiver. In turn, the relationship with the primary caregiver enhances the unfolding ego functions. As we now know, the newest infant research verifies Mahler's theory: interaction between infant and parent allows for the actual physical development of the brain. With

Hamilton: "There is a vital, circular interaction between the development of mother–child relationships and the maturation of ego-functions" (Hamilton 1992, p. 39).

Also during that time we see the smiling response that heralds this dawn of relationship development.

The infant now has the beginning cognitive capacity to accumulate memory traces of pleasurable (good) and unpleasurable (bad) experiences. This becomes a second polarity, next to the self–other polarity, around which the child organizes her world.

Serious disruptions during the symbiotic phase might make for a rather paranoid or schizoid personality organization: the child withdraws, the world is "bad" and "dangerous," "out to get me."

SEPARATION-INDIVIDUATION (6–24 MONTHS)

This is a phase characterized by three subphases (hatching, practicing, and rapprochement). Overall, we can say that in the separation-individuation phase the "psychological birth of the human infant" takes place, in that the infant moves beyond symbiotic union with the primary caregiver (mother/other) and individuates into a psychological entity separate and distinct from mother.

Subphase 1: Hatching/Differentiation (6–10 months)

In this first subphase, which Mahler aptly called "hatching," the infant begins to differentiate between self and object (mother/primary caregiver): the child is literally "hatching" out of the orbit of undifferentiation. The child directs attention away from the "mother-me" unit, and mother is increasingly experienced as separate from self. Witness a 6- to 10-month-old exploring his mother's body: pulling her hair, touching her eyelids, leaning away from her and looking at her as a separate object. This development goes hand in hand with the increasing development of ego functions, especially motility, which allows the infant to move away from the mother in some measure and facilitates the experience of a differentiation between self and object. During this development, the primary caregiver (mother) continues as a frame of reference or point of orientation.

Subphase 2: Practicing (10–16 months)

With increasing age, the child practices autonomous ego functions over and over. The autonomous ego functions are: motility, perception, intention, intelligence, thinking, speech, and language. The activities little children engage in and the games we play with them all aim at exercising these functions: pat-a-cake, peek-a-boo, crawling, creeping, walking. The child is now able to literally physically separate from the primary caregiver and is said to "orbit around mother," to whom s/he returns for emotional "refueling" (Hamilton, 1992, p. 44). Thus, 10- to 16-month-olds "practice" small separations. This is a time of omnipotence and grandeur for the youngster, since she is suddenly able to propel herself by her own volition to explore the world. As long as mother is nearby and available to return to for refueling, the small child will most likely feel pretty much "on top of the world."

Subphase 3: Rapprochement (16–24 months)

Of course, development of motor skills and cognitive skills continues, and within a few more months the same child who had felt that "the world is her oyster" now has developed the cognitive capacity to recognize and remember failure: the sense of omnipotence shatters, closeness and distance become conflictual. This is the time when the toddler manifests dependency needs and needs for independence simultaneously: wanting to tie her shoes on her own and throwing a tantrum when she cannot do it. Needing her mother's help and rejecting it at the same time. "No" is the big word during this time. The primary caregiver (mother) is increasingly seen as separate, and Hamilton states: "Mother must go through a prolonged push-pull separation process at the child's pace and according to the needs of the child" (Hamilton, 1992, pp. 51f).

Now is the time that the second attachment figure (father) becomes increasingly important to help mother and child disengage from the symbiotic dyad.

Many things can go wrong during this separation-individuation phase: there might be a primary caregiver who cannot wait for the child to be separate and autonomous, hurrying the toddler along toward greater independence and discouraging the fall-back behavior to dependence and clinging. A child like this might well develop difficulties with allowing for weaknesses and failures later—that is, might develop a narcissistic personality structure. On the other hand, the child might on the contrary be overly clinging and unable to separate, developing a dependent personality structure. Another, not uncommon, scenario is the one in which the primary caregiver discourages autonomy and separateness: the message is that it is not acceptable to be your own person, to develop your own strengths, to be independent from mother (or father, or whoever the primary caregiver happens to be). That maternal love will be withdrawn if you move away too far, that in order to receive the primary caregiver's approval the child must remain symbiotically merged.

The actual back-and-forth behavior of this phase of separation-individuation is duplicated in the features of borderline personality organization, with its separation of "good" and "bad," "black" and "white," "pick me up" or "no, put me down." Borderline personality organization is, in fact, one of the possible consequences for disruption during this phase.

Toward Object Constancy and beyond (24–36+ months)

This last developmental phase contains the integration of good and bad *object-images* into a single, ambivalently experienced *object*, which Horner aptly describes as "unified under the concept 'Mama'" (Horner 1984, p. 77), as well as the integration of good and bad *self-images* into a single, ambivalently experienced *self,* "unified under the concept 'I'" (Horner 1984, p. 78).

This last phase is open-ended and continues all through life. With the move toward object constancy, and particularly with the achievement of object constancy, the greatest danger threatening the child is loss of the love of the object (primary caregiver, mother, father). Before object constancy, the greatest danger was loss of the object itself: if mother was not present, she might never return. Now, however, the threat is more in the rank of: If mother is angry, she might not love me anymore.

Pathology during this subphase might result in more or less ego and object integration. A profound lack of such integration will result in a borderline personality organization, where there is a constant and absolute switch between the experience of an object or the self as "good" and "bad." If object constancy is not achieved or is compromised, the experience and resolution of the now dawning oedipal phase, with its attendant development of the Superego, will be compromised as well.[3]

This introduction to Margaret Mahler's model of developmental theory is aimed at giving you a glimpse of how we humans develop in relational networks that we internalize and that provide the building blocks for our personalities.

---

[3]The concept of this development is based on classical psychoanalytic theory. See Moore and Fine (1990) for an introduction to these concepts.

APPENDIX I

LIST OF IMPORTANT PHONE NUMBERS

This list is meant to assist you in compiling your own referral base. Use it by filling in pertinent phone numbers and addresses and by adding new ones and new categories over time.

Child Abuse Hotline

Dependent Adult and Elder Abuse Hotline

National Domestic Violence Hotline

Your Local Domestic Violence Hotline

Your Local Domestic Violence Shelter

Info-Line

Your Local Homeless Shelter

National HIV/AIDS Hotline

Local HIV/AIDS Hotline

Board of Behavioral Services

American Association of Marriage and
    Family Therapists

Your State Association of Marriage and
    Family Therapists

American Association of Clinical Social Workers

Your State Association of Clinical Social Workers

American Psychological Association

Your State's Chapter of the APA

Psychiatrist:

   Male

   Female

Psychologist

   Male

   Female

Psychiatric Emergency Team (PET)

Local Emergency Room

Neurologist

Internist

Therapists

  Working with adults (individuals)

   Male

   Female

  Working with adolescents and children

   Male

   Female

  Working with couples

   Male

   Female

Working with families

Male

Female

Psychological Testing

For children

For adults

Local Psychiatric Hospital

Private:

County:

Drug and Alcohol Detoxification

Drug and Alcohol Rehab

For men

For women

HIV Testing

Local HIV/AIDS Services

Other Referrals

Appendix II

SUGGESTED READING ON TOPICS OF INTEREST

I have compiled a list cf bibliographical references that are meant to offer an introduction to, and in some cases further reading on, topics that might be of interest to you. The topics are not only taken from the preceding text but were in part arrived at by questioning beginning psychotherapists as to what issues might be of interest to them for further studies. I have endeavored to offer three references per topic. You will find further bibliographic suggestions in the bibliographical portion of the volumes or articles suggested here.

CHILDREN AND ADOLESCENTS

Bromfield, R. (1999). *Doing Child and Adolescent Psychotherapy. The Ways and Whys.* Northvale, NJ/London: Jason Aronson.

Cangelosi, D. M., and C.E. Schaefer, eds. (1996). *Play Therapy Techniques.* Northvale, NJ/London: Jason Aronson.

Gardener, R. (1993). *Psychotherapy with Children.* Northvale, NJ/ London: Jason Aronson.

Landreth G. L., G. Glover, D. Sweeney, L. Homeyer, eds. (1996). *Play Therapy. Interventions with Children's Problems.* Northvale, NJ/London: Jason Aronson.

Miller, D. (1993). *The Age between. Adolescents and Therapy.* Northvale, NJ/London: Jason Aronson.

CLINICAL REPORTS

Zuckerman, E. L. (1995). *Clinican's Thesaurus: The Guidebook for Writing Psychological Reports,* 4th Ed. New York/London: Guilford Press.

CONFIDENTIALITY

Bollas, C., and D. Sundelson (1995). *The New Informants: The Betrayal of Confidentiality in Psychoanalysis and Psychotherapy.* Northvale, NJ/London: Jason Aronson.

COUNTERTRANSFERENCE

Epstein, L., and A.H. Feiner, eds. (1993). *Countertransference. The Therapist's Contribution to the Therapeutic Situation.* Northvale, NJ/London: Jason Aronson.

Langs, R., ed. (1990). *Classics in Psychoanalytic Technique.* Northvale, NJ/London: Jason Aronson.

Slakter, E., ed. (1987). *Countertransference. A Comprehensive View of Those Reactions of the Therapist to the Patient That May Help or Hinder Treatment.* Northvale, NJ/London: Jason Aronson.

Tansey, M. J., and W. F. Burke (1989). *Understanding Countertransference. From Projective Identification to Empathy.* Hillsdale, NJ: Analytic Press.

COUPLES' THERAPY

Donovan, J. (1999). *Short-Term Couple Therapy*. Northvale, NJ/ London: Jason Aronson.

Hendrix, H. (1988): *Getting the Love You Want. A Guide for Couples*. New York: Harper Perennial.

Nelsen, J. (1998). *Couple Treatment: Assessment and Intervention*. Northvale, NJ/ London: Jason Aronson.

DIAGNOSIS

American Psychiatric Association (1994). *Diagnostic and Statistical Manual of Mental Disorders*, 4th Ed. Washington, DC: American Psychiatric Association.

Kaplan, H., and B. J. Sadock (1996). *Pocket Handbook of Clinical Psychiatry*, 2nd Ed. Baltimore, MD: Williams and Wilkins.

McWilliams, N. (1994). *Psychoanalytic Diagnosis. Understanding Personality Structure in the Clinical Process*. New York/London: Guilford Press.

FAMILY THERAPY

Bowen, M. (1978). *Family Therapy in Clinical Practice*. New York: Jason Aronson.

Scharff, J. S. and D. E. Scharff, (1991). *Object Relations Family Therapy*. Northvale, NJ/London: Jason Aronson.

Slipp, S. (1991). *The Technique and Practice of Object Relations Family Therapy*. Northvale, NJ/London: Jason Aronson.

FEE ISSUES

Herron, W. G., and S. R. Welt (1992). *Money Matters: The Fee in Psychotherapy and Psychoanalysis*. New York: Guilford Press.

Krueger, D. (1986). *The Last Taboo—Money as Symbol and Reality in Psychotherapy and Psychoanalysis*. New York: Brunner/Mazel.

Rothstein, A. (1998). *Psychoanalytic Technique and the Creation of Analytic Patients*. (Chapters 1, 2, and 3). Madison, CT: International Universities Press, Inc.

FRAME ISSUES

Horner, A. (1991). *Psychoanalytic Object Relations Therapy*. Northvale, NJ/London: Jason Aronson.

Langs, R. (1994). *The Therapeutic Interaction: Synthesis of the Multiple Components of Therapy*. Northvale, NJ/London: Jason Aronson.

_____, ed. (1990). *Classics in Psychoanalytic Technique*. Northvale, NJ/London: Jason Aronson.

INTRODUCTION TO PSYCHOANALYTIC AND PSYCHODYNAMIC TERMS AND CONCEPTS

Hedges, L. E. (1983). *Listening Perspectives in Psychotherapy*. New York/London: Jason Aronson.

Langs, R., ed. (1990). *Classics in Psychoanalytic Technique*. Northvale, NJ/London: Jason Aronson.

Moore, B. E., and B. D. Fine, eds. (1990): *Psychoanalytic Terms and Concepts*. New Haven/London: The American Psychoanalytic Association and Yale University Press.

Stark, M. (1999). *Modes of Therapeutic Action: Enhancement of Knowledge, Provision of Experience, and Engagement in Relationship*. Northvale, NJ/London: Jason Aronson.

MENTAL ILLNESS

Akhtar, Salman (1992). *Broken Structures. Severe Personality Disorders and Their Treatment.* Northvale, NJ/London: Jason Aronson.

Andreasen, N. C. (1984). *The Broken Brain: The Biological Revolution in Psychiatry.* New York: Harper Perennial.

Greenfeld, D. (1994). *The Psychotic Patient: Medication and Psychotherapy* (1st Softcover Ed.). Northvale, NJ/London: Jason Aronson.

Kluft, P., and C. G. Fine, eds. (1993). *Clinical Perspectives on Multiple Personality Disorder.* Washington D.C./London: American Psychiatric Press.

Paykel, E., ed. (1992). *Handbook of Affective Disorders.* 2nd Ed. New York/London: Guilford Press.

MODELS OF HUMAN DEVELOPMENT

Erikson, E. (1980). *Identity and the Life Cycle.* New York: W. W. Norton.

Freud, S. (1962). *Three Essays on the Theory of Sexuality.* Standard Edition. Vol. 7. New York: Basic Books. (Original work published in 1905.)

Kaplan, L. (1978). *Oneness and Separateness: From Infant to Individual.* New York: Simon and Schuster.

Mahler, M., F. Pine, and A. Bergman (1975). *The Psychological Birth of the Human Infant: Symbiosis and Individuation.* New York: Basic Books.

Stern, D. N. (1985). *The Interpersonal World of the Infant: A View from Psychoanalysis and Developmental Psychology.* New York: Basic Books.

PSYCHOPHARMACA

Gitlin, M. J. (1990). *The Psychotherapist's Guide to Psychopharmacology.* New York: Free Press.

Greenfeld, D. (1994). *The Psychotic Patient: Medication and Psychotherapy* (1st Softcover Ed.). Northvale, NJ/London: Jason Aronson.

Kaplan, H., and B.J. Sadock (1996). *Pocket Handbook of Clinical Psychiatry,* 2nd Ed. Baltimore, MD: Williams and Wilkins.

Maxman, J. S., and N. G. Ward (1995). *Psychotropic Drugs: Fast Facts.* 2nd Ed. New York/London: W. W. Norton.

SUBSTANCE ABUSE

Levin, J. D. (1999). *Primer for Treating Substance Abusers.* Northvale, NJ/London: Jason Aronson.

Wurmser, L. (1995). *The Hidden Dimension: Psychodynamics of Compulsive Drug Use.* Northvale, NJ/London: Jason Aronson.

SEXUAL ISSUES

Kaplan, H. S. (1974). *The New Sex Therapy: Active Treatment of Sexual Dysfunctions.* New York: Brunner/Mazel.

_____. (1995). *The Sexual Desire Disorders: Dysfunctional Regulation of Sexual Motivation.* New York: Brunner/Mazel.

Rosen, S. R., R.C. Leiblum, R.C. Rosen eds. (1989). *Principles and Practice of Sex Therapy: Update for the 90s.* New York/London: Guilford Press.

SUICIDE

Berman, A. L., and D. A. Jobes, (1991). *Adolescent Suicide. Assessment and Intervention.* Washington, DC: American Psychological Association.

THEORETICAL APPROACHES

General

Hedges, L. E. (1983). *Listening Perspectives in Psychotherapy.* New York/London: Jason Aronson.

How theory shapes technique: Perspectives on a clinical study (1987). *Psychoanalytic Inquiry,* 7:2.

Ego Psychology

Blanck, R. (1974). *Ego Psychology: Theory and Practice.* New York/London: Columbia University Press.

Kleinian Theory

Segal, H. (1964). *Introduction to the Work of Melanie Klein,* 2nd Ed. New York: Basic Books.

Introductions to Object Relations Theory

Horner, A. (1991). *Psychoanalytic Object Relations Therapy.* Northvale, NJ/London: Jason Aronson.

St. Clair, M. (1986). *Object Relations and Self Psychology: An Introduction. Monterey,* CA: Brooks/Cole.

Scharff, J. S. and D.E. Scharff, (1992). *Scharff Notes: A Primer of Object Relations Therapy.* Northvale, NJ/London: Jason Aronson.

Self Psychology

Kohut, H., and E. Wolf, (1978). The disorders of the self and their treatment: An outline. *International Journal of Psychoanalysis* 59:413–425.

St. Clair, M. (1986). *Object Relations and Self Psychology: An Introduction.* Monterey, CA: Brooks/Cole.

Intersubjectivity

Natterson, J. M., and R.J. Friedman (1995): *A Primer of Clinical Intersubjectivity.* Northvale, NJ/London: Jason Aronson.

Stolorow, R. D, B. Brandchaft, and G. E. Atwood (1987). *Psychoanalytic Treatment. An Intersubjective Approach.* Hillsdale, NJ: The Analytic Press.

Cognitive Behavioral

Beck, J. (1995). *Cognitive Therapy. Basics and Beyond.* New York/London: Guilford Press.

Leahy, R. (1996). *Cognitive Therapy: Basic Principles and Applications.* Northvale, NJ/London: Jason Aronson.

Safran, J. (1998). *Widening the Scope of Cognitive Therapy: The Therapeutic Relationship, Emotion, and the Process of Change.* Northvale, NJ/London: Jason Aronson.

Family Therapy

Bowen, M. (1978). *Family Therapy in Clinical Practice*. New York: Jason Aronson.

Goldenberg, I., and H. Goldenberg (1991). *Family Therapy. An Overview,* 3rd Ed. Pacific Grove, CA: Brooks/Cole.

Scharff, J. S. and D.E. Scharff, (1991). *Object Relations Family Therapy*. Northvale, NJ/London: Jason Aronson.

Slipp, S. (1991). *The Technique and Practice of Object Relations Family Therapy*. Northvale, NJ/London: Jason Aronson.

TRANSFERENCE

Gabbard, G. (1996). *Love and Hate in the Analytic Setting*. Northvale, NJ/London: Jason Aronson.

Langs, R., ed. (1990). *Classics in Psychoanalytic Technique*. Northvale, NJ/London: Jason Aronson.

Sandler, J., C. Dare, and A. Holder (1992). *The Patient and the Analyst*. Northvale, NJ/London: Jason Aronson.

TRAUMA

Allen, J. G. and W. H. Smith, eds. (1995). *Diagnosis and Treatment of Dissociative Disorders*. Northvale, NJ/London: Jason Aronson.

Lewis, Herman, J. (1992). *Trauma and Recovery*. New York: Basic Books.

Meloy, J. R. (1992). *Violent Attachments*. Northvale, NJ/London: Jason Aronson

TREATMENT PLANNING

Johnson, S. L. (1997). *Therapist's Guide to Clinical Interventions. The 1-2-3s of Treatment Planning*. San Diego/London: Academic Press.

BIBLIOGRAPHY

Akhtar, S. (1992). *Broken Structures. Severe Personality Disorders and Their Treatment.* Northvale, NJ/London: Jason Aronson.

Allen, J. G., and W. H. Smith, eds. (1995). *Diagnosis and Treatment of Dissociative Disorders.* Northvale, NJ/London: Jason Aronson.

American Psychiatric Association. *Diagnostic and Statistical Manual of Mental Disorders* (1994). 4th Ed. Washington, DC: American Psychiatric Association.

———. (1994). *Diagnostic Criteria from DSM-IV.* Washington, DC.

Andreasen, N. C. (1984). *The Broken Brain: The Biological Revolution in Psychiatry.* New York: Harper Perennial.

Beck, J. (1995). *Cognitive Therapy: Basics and Beyond.* New York/London: Guilford Press.

Berman, A. L., and D. A. Jobes (1991). *Adolescent Suicide: Assessment and Intervention.* Washington, DC: American Psychological Association.

Blanck, R. (1974). *Ego Psychology: Theory and Practice.* New York/London: Columbia University Press.

Bollas, C., and D. Sundelson (1995). *The New Informants: The Betrayal of Confidentiality in Psychoanalysis and Psychotherapy.* Northvale, NJ/London: Jason Aronson.

Bowen, M. (1978). *Family Therapy in Clinical Practice*. New York: Jason Aronson.

Bromfield, R. (1999). *Doing Child and Adolescent Psychotherapy: The Ways and Whys*. Northvale, NJ/London: Jason Aronson.

Cangelosi, D. M., and C.E. Schaefer, eds. (1996). *Play Therapy Techniques*. Northvale, NJ/London: Jason Aronson.

Donovan, J. (1999). *Short-Term Couple Therapy*. Northvale, NJ/London: Jason Aronson.

Eissler, K. R. (1974). On some theoretical and technical problems regarding the payment of fees for psychoanalytic treatment. *International Review of Psycho-Analysis* 1:73–102.

Epstein, L., and A. H. Feiner, eds. (1993). *Countertransference. The Therapist's Contribution to the Therapeutic Situation*. Northvale, NJ/London: Jason Aronson.

Erikson, E. (1980). *Identity and the Life Cycle*. New York: W. W. Norton.

Freud, A. (1936). *The Ego and the Mechanisms of Defense*. Rev. Ed. 1966. New York: International Universities Press.

Freud, S. (1962). *Three Essays on the Theory of Sexuality*. Standard Edition, Vol. 7. New York: Basic Books. (Original work published in 1905.)

Gabbard, G. (1996). *Love and Hate in the Analytic Setting*. Northvale, NJ/London: Jason Aronson.

Gardener, R. (1993). *Psychotherapy with Children*. Northvale, NJ/London: Jason Aronson.

Gitlin, M. J. (1990). *The Psychotherapist's Guide to Psychopharmacology*. New York: Free Press.

Goldenberg, I., and H. Goldenberg (1991). *Family Therapy. An Overview*. 3rd Ed. Pacific Grove, CA: Brooks/Cole.

Greenfeld, D. (1994). *The Psychotic Patient: Medication and Psychotherapy*. Northvale, NJ/London: Jason Aronson.

Hamilton, N. G. (1992). *Self and Others: Object Relations Theory in Practice*. Northvale, NJ/London: Jason Aronson.

Hedges, L. E. (1983). *Listening Perspectives in Psychotherapy*. New York/London: Jason Aronson.

Hendrix, H. (1988): *Getting the Love You Want: A Guide for Couples*. New York: Harper Perennial.

Herron, W. G., and S. R. Welt (1992). *Money Matters: The Fee in Psychotherapy and Psychoanalysis*. New York: Guilford Press.

Horner, A. (1998). *Working with the Core Relationship Problem in Psychotherapy: A Handbook for Clinicians*. San Francisco: Jossey-Bass.

————. *(1991). Psychoanalytic Object Relations Therapy*. Northvale, NJ/London: Jason Aronson.

————. *(1984). Object Relations and the Developing Ego in Therapy*. New York: Jason Aronson.

How theory shapes technique: Perspectives on a clinical study. (1987). *Psychoanalytic Inquiry*. 7:2.

Johnson, S. L. (1997). *Therapist's Guide to Clinical Interventions. The 1-2-3s of Treatment Planning*. San Diego/London: Academic Press.

Kaplan, H., and B. J. Sadock (1996). *Pocket Handbook of Clinical Psychiatry*, 2nd Ed. Baltimore, MD: Williams and Wilkins.

Kaplan, H. S. (1974). *The New Sex Therapy: Active Treatment of Sexual Dysfunctions*. New York: Brunner/Mazel.

————. (1995). *The Sexual Desire Disorders: Dysfunctional Regulation of Sexual Motivation*. New York: Brunner/Mazel.

Kaplan, L. (1978). *Oneness and Separateness: From Infant to Individual*. New York: Simon and Schuster.

Kaufman, E. (1994). *Psychotherapy of Addicted Persons*. New York: Guilford Press.

Kernberg, O. (1984). *Severe Personality Disorders. Psychotherapeutic Strategies*. New Haven/London: Yale University Press.

Kernberg, O., M. Selzer, H. Koenigsberg, A. Carr, and A. Appelbaum (1989). *Psychodynamic Psychotherapy of Borderline Patients*. New York: Basic Books.

Kluft, P., and C. G. Fine, eds. (1993). *Clinical Perspectives on Multiple Personality Disorder.* Washington, DC/London: American Psychiatric Press.

Kohut, H., and E. Wolf (1978). The disorders of the self and their treatment: An outline. *International Journal of Psychoanalysis.* 59:413–425.

Krueger, D. (1986). *The Last Taboo—Money as Symbol and Reality in Psychotherapy and Psychoanalysis.* New York: Brunner/Mazel.

Landreth, G. L., G. Glover, D. Sweeney, and L. Homeyer, eds. (1996). *Play Therapy: Interventions with Children's Problems.* Northvale, NJ/London: Jason Aronson.

Langs, R. (1994). *The Therapeutic Interaction: Synthesis of the Multiple Components of Therapy.* Northvale, NJ/London: Jason Aronson.

_____. ed. (1990). *Classics in Psychoanalytic Technique.* Northvale, NJ/London: Jason Aronson.

———. (1985). *Workbooks for Psychotherapists, Vols. 1 and 2.* Emerson, NJ: Newconcept Press.

Leahy, R. (1996). *Cognitive Therapy: Basic Principles and Applications.* Northvale, NJ/London: Jason Aronson.

Levin, J. D. (1999). *Primer for Treating Substance Abusers.* Northvale, NJ/London: Jason Aronson.

Lewis Herman, J. (1992). *Trauma and Recovery.* New York: Basic Books.

Mahler, M., F. Pine, and A. Bergman (1975). *The Psychological Birth of the Human Infant: Symbiosis and Individuation.* New York: Basic Books.

Maxman, J. S., and N. G. Ward (1995). *Psychotropic Drugs: Fast Facts.* 2nd Ed. New York/London: W. W. Norton.

McClure, B. A., and R. W. Hodge (1987). Measuring countertransference in therapeutic relationships. *Psychotherapy: Theory, Research and Practice.* 24:3: 325–335.

McWilliams, N. (1994). *Psychoanalytic Diagnosis: Understanding*

Personality Structure in the Clinical Process. New York/London: Guilford Press.

Meloy, J. R. (1992). *Violent Attachments.* Northvale, NJ/London: Jason Aronson.

Miller, D. (1993). *The Age between. Adolescents and Therapy.* Northvale, NJ/London: Jason Aronson.

Moore, B. E., and B. D. Fine, eds. (1990): *Psychoanalytic Terms and Concepts.* New Haven/London: American Psychoanalytic Association and Yale University Press.

Natterson, J. (1991). *Beyond Countertransference: The Therapist's Subjectivity in the Therapeutic Process.* Northvale, NJ/London: Jason Aronson.

Natterson, J., and R. Friedman (1995): *A Primer of Clinical Intersubjectivity.* Northvale, NJ/London: Jason Aronson.

Paykel, E., ed. (1992). *Handbook of Affective Disorders.* 2nd Ed. New York/London: Guilford Press.

Robbins, J. B., and M. P. Jolkovski (1987). Managing countertransference feelings: An interactional model using awareness of feeling and theoretical framework. *Journal of Counseling Psychology*, 34:3:276–282.

Rosen, S. R., R. C. Leiblum, and R. C. Rosen, eds. (1989). *Principles and Practice of Sex Therapy: Update for the 90s.* New York/London: Guilford Press.

Rothstein, A. (1998). *Psychoanalytic Technique and the Creation of Analytic Patients.* Madison, CT: International Universities Press.

Safran, J. (1998). *Widening the Scope of Cognitive Therapy: The Therapeutic Relationship, Emotion, and the Process of Change.* Northvale, NJ/London: Jason Aronson.

Sandler, J., C. Dare, and A. Holder (1992). *The Patient and the Analyst.* Northvale, NJ/London: Jason Aronson.

Scharff, J. S. and D. E. Scharff (1991). *Object Relations Family Therapy.* Northvale, NJ/London: Jason Aronson.

———. (1992). *Scharff Notes: A Primer of Object Relations Therapy.* Northvale, NJ/London: Jason Aronson.

Segal, H. (1964): *Introduction to the Work of Melanie Klein.* 2nd Ed. New York: Basic Books.

Slakter, E., ed. (1987). *Countertransference. A Comprehensive View of Those Reactions of the Therapist to the Patient That May Help or Hinder Treatment.* Northvale, NJ/London: Jason Aronson.

Slipp, S. (1991). *The Technique and Practice of Object Relations Family Therapy.* Northvale, NJ/London: Jason Aronson.

Stark, M. (1999). *Modes of Therapeutic Action: Enhancement of Knowledge, Provision of Experience, and Engagement in Relationship.* Northvale, NJ/London: Jason Aronson.

St. Clair, M. (1986). *Object Relations and Self Psychology: An Introduction.* Monterey, CA: Brooks/Cole.

Stern, D. N. (1985). *The Interpersonal World of the Infant: A View from Psychoanalysis and Developmental Psychology.* New York: Basic Books.

Stolorow, R. D., B. Brandchaft, and G. E. Atwood (1987). *Psychoanalytic Treatment: An Intersubjective Approach.* Hillsdale, NJ: The Analytic Press.

Tansey, M. J., and W. F. Burke (1989). *Understanding Countertransference: From Projective Identification to Empathy.* Hillsdale, NJ: Analytic Press.

Wurmser, L. (1974). Psychoanalytic considerations of the etiology of compulsive drug use. *Journal of the American Psychoanalytic Association* 22:4: 820–843.

———. (1987). Flight from conscience: Experience with the psychoanalytic treatment of compulsive drug abusers. *Journal of Substance Abuse Treatment* 4: 169–179.

———. (1995). *The Hidden Dimension: Psychodynamics of Compulsive Drug Use.* Northvale, NJ/London: Jason Aronson.

Zweben, J. E. (1989). Recovery-oriented psychotherapy: Patient resistances and therapist dilemmas. *Journal of Substance Abuse Treatment*, 123–132.

Zuckerman, E. L. (1995). *Clinician's Thesaurus: The Guidebook for Writing Psychological Reports*. 4th Ed. New York/London: Guilford Press.

INDEX

ABOUT THE AUTHOR

Maxa Ott is a licensed Marriage and Family Therapist. In addition to her clinical degree she holds a M.A. in Linguistics and History from the Friedrich-Alexander University of Erlangen-Nuernberg, Germany. She is currently a Clinical Associate at the Southern California Psychoanalytic Institute in Beverly Hills, California. Ms. Ott is in private practice in Pasadena, California, where she is also a guest lecturer to graduate students in the Marriage and Family Therapy program of her alma mater, Pacific Oaks College. She has worked with beginning therapists as their teacher, supervisor, therapist, and colleague.